Everything You Know
about **Evangelicals**
Is **Wrong**
(Well, Almost Everything)

Everything You Know about **Evangelicals** Is **Wrong**

(Well, Almost Everything)

An Insider's Look at Myths & Realities

Steve Wilkens & Don Thorsen

BakerBooks

a division of Baker Publishing Group
Grand Rapids, Michigan

© 2010 by Steve Wilkens and Don Thorsen

Published by Baker Books
a division of Baker Publishing Group
P.O. Box 6287, Grand Rapids, MI 49516-6287
www.bakerbooks.com

Printed in the United States of America

Library of Congress Cataloging-in-Publication Data
Wilkens, Steve, 1955–
    Everything you know about evangelicals is wrong (well, almost everything) : an insider's look at myths and realities / Steve Wilkens and Don Thorsen.
        p.   cm.
    Includes bibliographical references.
    ISBN 978-0-8010-7097-6 (pbk.)
    1. Evangelicalism. I. Thorsen, Donald A. D. II. Title.
BR1640.W53 2010
280′.4—dc22   2010014150

10   11   12   13   14   15   16   7   6   5   4   3   2   1

To our colleagues in the School of Theology at Azusa Pacific University,
who embody all that is good about evangelical Christianity.

Contents

Acknowledgments

As we look back over the process of completing this project, it is abundantly clear that we owe a debt of gratitude to a number of people. Many colleagues and friends have been helpful sounding boards and thoughtful critics. At the risk of overlooking others who have provided important assistance, we want to acknowledge the contributions of Paul Alexander, Craig Boyd, John Culp, Don Dayton, Blake Firstman, Craig Keen, Kevin Mannoia, Teri Merrick, Lynn Losie, Josh Morris, Bob Mullins, Tim Peck, Keith Reeves, Kay Smith, Karen Winslow, and David Woodruff. A special note of appreciation is due Halee Scott, who went far above and beyond even high expectations in providing research assistance for this project. Finally, we want to thank Bob Hosack, who patiently served as our editor at Baker.

Of course, no major writing endeavor stays at the office, so we wish to thank our families for their patience in those times when our work has intruded on their lives. We are not sure that they will ever be able to understand fully how essential they are to shaping who we are, what we say, and what we do. We love and value them very much: Deb, Zoe, and Zack Wilkens; and Liesl, Heidi, and Dana Thorsen.

Azusa Pacific University has been extremely generous in providing resources to both authors in the form of a Faculty Research Grant, Accomplished Scholars Awards, and Writers' Retreats. In addition, Don enjoyed a sabbatical in which he was able to complete a major portion of his work on this book. This institutional support is deeply appreciated.

To acknowledge directly all who have shaped this book is impossible because their contributions have come over our lifetimes in forms that exemplify evangelicalism at its best—laypeople who have given their time and talents as Sunday School teachers, camp counselors, and advisers; pastors who have faithfully carried out their vocation as ministers of the gospel; friends and family members who have mirrored the face of Jesus in correction, unconditional love, and everything between; teachers, professors, and academic colleagues who have offered their wisdom and demonstrated how to enter into worship through the life of the mind. In their diverse callings, they have put their hands, feet, and minds behind the Great Commission. We are the grateful beneficiaries of their efforts.

While much in this book reflects criticism of certain tendencies within evangelicalism, it is criticism that grows out of a deep love and appreciation for this Christian tradition that has nurtured us and to which we remain deeply committed. Our prayer is that this book will be received as such.

1

Introduction

History, Agenda, and Caricatures

Evangelicalism is, as William Abraham so aptly put it, a contested concept, and everyone seems to have joined the contest to define it.[1] Self-described evangelical Christians have engaged in attempts to define themselves for years and, as we will see below, these endeavors have yielded mixed answers. However, this process is no longer simply an intramural discussion. The growing visibility of evangelical Christians over the past couple of decades, culminating in their impact in recent elections, has caught the eye of those outside. Thus, even secular sources that are normally oblivious to the impact of religion in one of the world's most religious nations are weighing in with their own definitions of the essence of evangelicalism.

This book is about the quest to find an adequate and accurate definition of evangelicalism. As part of this endeavor, we will certainly offer our own portrait. In getting to this point, however, we will examine several characteristics commonly linked to evangelicalism, and reject them as essential attributes. These characteristics, represented by our chapter titles, are indeed present within the movement. Thus, we do not intend to say that no Calvinists, premillennialists, Republicans, or inerrantists are evangelical. In some cases, individuals with these loyalties are in the majority. Unfortunately, it is also true that other adjectives such as racist, stupid, or mean also apply to evangelicals, but we hope not to the majority. Thus, rather than denying that the attributes embedded in the chapter titles apply to *evangelicals*, as individual believers, we want to say that these labels do not accurately capture the essence of a movement called *evangelicalism* and therefore do not belong in the definition.

In entering the fray generated by attempts to define evangelicalism, we have four audiences in view, each with a unique and often conflicting impression of the movement. The first consists of those who define evangelicalism from the outside. Secular non-evangelicals most frequently view the movement primarily from the perspective of its perceived social or political alignments. Christian non-evangelicals often share these sociopolitical perceptions but frequently combine them with theological concerns and differences as well.

The second audience consists of evangelicals who identify themselves as such and sprinkle the word throughout their websites and literature. However, when pressed to define what meaning the word conveys, they will frequently admit that they do not have a ready definition. This group says that defining evangelicalism is a bit like Justice Potter Stewart's observation about pornography: "You cannot say exactly what it is, but you know it when you see it." In other words, this group accepts the fact that evangelicalism is hard to pin down precisely, but it also wants to claim that the term has a reality to it. This reality is generally framed in terms of a commitment to Scripture's authority, the uniqueness of Jesus' divine/human nature and his atoning work and the cross, and a mandate to proclaim the gospel.

Like the second contingent, a third audience also identifies itself as evangelical. This group also says that this meaning can or should be clearly defined by adherence to certain carefully articulated doctrinal positions, social/political concerns, or lifestyle statements. This group's insistence on such specific boundaries will inevitably exclude some. Among those excluded will be members of the second and third groups who propose alternative boundaries as fundamental to an evangelical identity, and members of the first group, who are quite willing to be excluded.

However, we often find that those excluded by doctrines, social values, or ethical positions provided by members of our third intended audience are tempted to adopt a fourth approach. This group, which seems to be growing rapidly, has deep questions about whether the word itself remains useful. Given the dizzying array of definitions for evangelicalism, the battles that erupt around it, and the divisions created, many in this fourth contingent wonder whether it is advisable to forfeit the contest over evangelicalism's meaning and give up the term altogether.

Our response to each of these four groups will differ because each one has a different history that shapes its perspective toward evangelicalism and a different agenda in relationship to it. Thus each of these four prospective audiences tends toward what we take to be different caricatures of the movement. *The common element in our replies to each group will be an attempt to find a foundation in the empirical realities of evangelicalism's history, its present composition, and its trajectories toward the future.* Thus, a preliminary jumping-off point for our responses will be to take a very quick look at evangelicalism's history and draw attention to where it is and where it is going. We will then offer a broad outline of what we take to be evangelicalism's agenda in relationship to the agendas of the four audiences identified above. From there, we will make a few tentative remarks about the caricatures of evangelicalism that have emerged in recent years.

Given what seems to be a deep impasse in finding a common definition of evangelicalism, one easily sympathizes with the impulse of the fourth group we identified. If so much confusion about opposing characterizations congeals around the term, why not count our money or cut our losses (depending on one's perspective) and walk away from the game? In reality, however, evangelicalism has a history, and we cannot simply walk away from history. It follows us, with or without our consent, and continues to define us, whether or not we can define it. While it has not always commanded the headlines it draws today, evangelicalism has been a formative force in this country's institutions, attitudes, and ideas. It has had a powerful pull on the denominations and religious organizations that are part of the United States' landscape, and in turn, evangelicalism has reshaped, reenergized, and redirected many of the denominations and parachurch organizations that have been a part of it. The irony, then, is that those who advocate abandoning the word "evangelical" are among those whose identities have been profoundly shaped by the movement. It owns us, even if we are not sure we want to own it. Although many of our chapters below will dip into various aspects of evangelicalism's history, we want to lay out an impossibly broad framework in support of evangelicalism's historical and ongoing diversity. This breadth, we believe, illuminates the problem confronting those who attempt to confine or define the movement in the categories examined between the first and last chapters of this text.

Evangelicalism and Its History

If someone would begin a story about a Presbyterian theologian/philosopher, an Anglican open-air evangelist with strong Calvinistic proclivities, and a couple of Methodist preachers and hymn writers, then you might suspect it introduces a joke that involves this group strolling into a bar together. However, it is precisely this lineup of disparate characters—Jonathan Edwards, George Whitefield, and John and Charles Wesley—that the noted historian of evangelicalism, Mark Noll, identifies as the primary movers in modern evangelicalism.[2] These pioneers differed on just about everything. The Wesleys were high-church Anglicans, Whitefield was of mixed theological breed, and Edwards was the prototypical Presbyterian. The Wesleys had strong royalist sympathies and found the American Revolution a travesty. Edwards, although he died almost twenty years before that war, was the first president of a college that was, in many ways, the cradle of the American Revolution. When Edwards wrote, tightly argued theological and philosophical treatises emanated from his pen. John Wesley expressed his theological views primarily through written sermons, letters, and (with his brother Charles) hymns. Whitefield and Edwards were strongly Calvinistic, while the Wesley brothers promoted Arminianism with a heavy dose of Catholic and Orthodox perfectionism thrown in, both of which put considerable strain on their relationship with Whitefield.

The origin of evangelicalism, of course, does not necessarily begin with Edwards, Whitefield, and the Wesleys. They drew on Protestant roots that go back, at least, to the Reformation, and which include such evangelically formative Christians as Martin Luther, John Calvin, and other Reformers. Indeed, why go back only to the Reformation? Is evangelicalism merely a manifestation of Protestantism, or might it include adherents (past and present) of Catholic and Orthodox churches? Some would want to argue that there exists, in theory if nowhere else, an unbroken thread of evangelical Christians, going back to Jesus' disciples who first proclaimed the gospel (Greek *euangelion*, "good news") of Jesus Christ. Such historical views will be considered throughout this book; our goal is to discuss evangelicalism broadly rather than narrowly. However, in discussing modern evangelicalism, there occur high points in elaborating its history and agendas. Edwards, Whitefield, and the Wesleys provide such a high point, and it is their diversity along with their evangelical family resemblance that make them so instructive with regard to understanding modern evangelicalism.

The areas of dissonance for Edwards, Whitefield, and the Wesleys, to which many others could be added, did not find any resolution as evangelicalism grew. Instead, the movement became even more diverse, absorbing Lutheran pietists, anti–state-church Baptists, non-sacramentalist Quakers, pacifistic Anabaptists, tongues-speaking Pentecostals, Restorationist Stone-Campbellites, and a host of other groups. None of this seems a likely recipe for a movement that established a foundation for significant cooperative works! Nevertheless, despite the differences, individuals from these groups reached across denominational, theological, and social boundaries to start orphanages, rescue missions, missionary organizations, and other institutions. They built and ran schools and colleges across the country, including the first college in the world that enrolled African-Americans and women as full students alongside white males. Evangelicals of different theological persuasions joined forces to champion causes such as abolition, women's suffrage, and the temperance movement. They created the American Bible Society, the Sunday School Movement, the YMCA/YWCA, and the Billy Graham Evangelistic Association. Evangelicals of diverse traditions went to camp meetings together, planned revivals together, and sang each other's hymns.

It would certainly distort the picture to suggest that relationships between these disparate groups were devoid of friction. The irony of this cooperation is that it occurred at the same time many of these evangelical groups were going through wrenching denominational splits. The rancor was not simply focused on doctrinal differences, although there was plenty of this.

Every major denominational church body in this country, with the exception of Roman Catholicism and Episcopalianism, split into factions over slavery. Most of them did not reunify until the last half of the twentieth century, and a couple of them are still divided. This led to political divisions that resulted in evangelicalism being split for decades between the Democratic South and the Northern and New England Republicans. (My, how things change!) Card-carrying evangelicals throughout the history of the country have been on the opposite sides of major social and political issues from the Revolutionary War to the Scopes Monkey Trial.

In short, then, one obvious reason for the contested identity of evangelicalism is that it has a messy history, the sort of messiness that makes it impossible for any one doctrinal distinctive, theological tradition, or social orientation to stake exclusive claims to naming rights. Tucked into the folds of the brief historical sketch are at least three additional factors that lend support to our contention that evangelicalism has been a "big tent." First, in addition to the impressive diversity found in the history of this motley conglomeration called evangelicalism, one is struck by what we do not find for most of its story. Inerrancy does not arise as a major tension point between evangelicals until the middle of the twentieth century. Second, premillenialism had a minuscule following prior to the twentieth century. Evangelicalism had been in full swing for quite some time before the dispensationalist variation of this doctrine came into existence. Third, in terms of general popularity, Calvinism was on the ropes during much of the nineteenth century. However, our point is not that there is anything wrong with any of these views. Our argument is that none of these positions has been definitive of the movement. Evangelicalism did just fine before these positions emerged or when they were distinctly minority positions. The tides of favor have ebbed and flowed for various views and theological groups within the evangelical family. If we do not keep close tabs on this history, however, we can mistakenly conclude that certain ideas in ascendancy are constants of the evangelical identity. In several cases below, we will see how some of these mistaken conclusions have morphed into caricatures of evangelicalism.

A second feature of evangelicalism's history is that it reminds us of elements that are far too often missing today. The major impulse for the abolition of slavery in both the United States and Great Britain came from evangelicals. The tip of the spear for women's equality and educational opportunities has the same origin, and it should be noted that the mainline denominations that view themselves as front-runners in the ordination of women got around to this only many decades after it was common practice among Holiness and Pentecostal groups. In the nineteenth century, social service organizations of all kinds—rescue missions, hospitals, literacy programs, nursing organizations, and numerous other groups that ministered to those on society's fringes—were dominated by evangelicals moved by their faith.[3] This is a real irony, because for much of their history, the criticism of evangelicals has been that they have been *too accepting* of people of different races, *too egalitarian* in the matter of women's rights, and *too compassionate* toward the poor and those who live on the margins of society. Some of that criticism, by the way, came from fellow evangelicals. (I did mention that we were a rather diverse lot, didn't I?)

Our third observation has to do with a chapter in this book that has to this point escaped mention—the idea that evangelicalism can be stereotyped as rich and American. As the paragraph above notes, not only has evangelicalism's focus been directed at society's underclass, but a disproportionate number of evangelicals were, and still are, from that social stratum. Moreover, it is incorrect to view evangelicalism as an American phenomenon, specifically a phenomenon of the United States of America. Its presence in our culture is, rather, testimony to the enduring missionary impulse of a movement that predates the founding of the United States. Evangelicalism was in large part imported from Great Britain, but it also received immigrant missionaries from quite a number of European countries. To be sure, evangelicalism found a congenial environment in the New World, and soon this country, originally a missionary-receiving nation, became the world's most prolific missionary-sending country. These outreach efforts have been so successful that two-thirds of the world's evangelicals now live outside the Western Hemisphere, primarily in Africa, Asia, and Latin America! Evangelicalism is not exclusively a story centered on the United States. It is a global narrative, and trends strongly indicate that it will be increasingly so. The future history of evangelicalism will be a worldwide story, and the United States is and will be only one chapter in the broader text. In essence, then, two things are clear. First, evangelicalism is not a movement characterized by wealth, nor is it primarily a United States phenomenon. Second, when evangelicalism is viewed from a global perspective, many caricatures of this group, beyond the idea that it consists primarily of rich Americans, shatter into shards. For example, global evangelicalism certainly is not a purely Republican movement. Global evangelicalism, which may already include more Africans and Asians than Caucasians (with Hispanic numbers rising rapidly), can hardly be characterized as racially monolithic or ethnically exclusive. (Even in the United States, the percentage of the African-American population identified as evangelical is higher than the percentage among Caucasians. Hispanic-Americans will soon have a greater proportion of adherents than either group, if demographic trends continue.) A very small percentage of non-Western evangelicals are Calvinists, or even know what that means. Issues such as evolution rarely show up on the radar of Two-Thirds World evangelicals. In sum, then, many of the caricatures of evangelicalism noted in this book tell us more about our parochialism in the United States than about evangelicalism itself.

If nothing else, this brief historical glance at the jumble known as evangelicalism should conjure up a great deal of sympathy toward anyone who attempts to offer a definition of the movement. Our history reminds us that the struggle to define evangelicalism is nothing new, something we might be more aware of if evangelicals paid more attention to history. The term has always been contested, the boundaries fluid, and often the main characters in the story have been at one another's throats. This naturally gives rise to an impulse to tidy things up by closely defining the term. The danger that attaches itself to cleaning up the meaning of a word is that we frequently inject our own agendas into the definition. We now turn to this matter.

Agendas and Hyphenated Identities

One key motivation behind engaging the concept of evangelicalism is that it is an agenda-shaping term. While "agenda" often carries negative connotations, we use it here in its neutral sense: an agenda is a list of things we intend to do in pursuit of goals we find valuable. If the pursuit of goals is an important part of our lives (and we assume it is), then those ends will be promoted or hindered by the way "evangelical" is defined and who gets to define it. If some evangelicals become disenchanted by the efforts of others to constrict the boundaries and opt out of the discussion, then their agendas will be co-opted by those who do the job in their absence.

We will return to a discussion of what we think is lost when evangelicalism's agenda is co-opted by those with more narrow agendas. Before we get there, however, we want to say that it is altogether proper and necessary that Christians have both theological and sociopolitical agendas that are more sharply defined than the broader evangelical agenda. Theologically, the willingness of many to think of themselves in a hyphenated way—as Reformed-evangelical, Charismatic-evangelical, Holiness-evangelical, Baptist-evangelical, Catholic-evangelical, and so on—reveals something important. Despite the fact that the "evangelical" side of each equation indicates a sense of commonality with Christians outside one's specific theological tradition, the left side of each hyphenated pair clearly indicates that an individual finds a great deal of value within a particular theological tradition. In reality, it cannot be otherwise.

With apologies to churches that identify themselves only as evangelical, this designation—because of its ambiguity—gives little guidance about a multitude of issues they must face. For example, a church should not and cannot expect its evangelical identity to tell it whether, how, whom, or when to baptize, nor will it provide a straight answer about the salvific effects, or lack thereof, in baptism. Churches have to make a decision on this issue, but evangelicals are all over the theological map on the nature and meaning of baptism. Their guidance is going to have to come from somewhere else. Evangelical churches will respond that Scripture guides their doctrine, but that still leaves a lot up in the air. All evangelical churches claim biblical support for their baptismal theology, whether they are dunkers or sprinklers, infant baptizers or adult baptizers. Evangelical Anglicans worldwide draw a very close link between baptism and salvation; Evangelical Friends (Quakers) and those in the Salvation Army reject the practice altogether. Both sides ground their positions in Scripture. Differences do arise in how we interpret Scripture, and those differences are generally transmitted through some sort of theological or denominational tradition.

Baptism is only one of the more obvious examples we could cite as evidence that the evangelical tradition is too vague to offer direction for doctrine or practice. Whether a church will ordain a female, choose its own pastor, use creeds in worship, speak in tongues, practice confirmation, or serve beer at the church picnic cannot be answered by appeal to an evangelical identity. You are much more likely to predict what someone believes about the Lord's Supper by knowing whether they are Presbyterian, Four-Square Pentecostal, American Baptist, Disciples of Christ, or Episcopalian than you are by knowing whether they are fundamentalist, evangelical, or liberal. One important value of these different theological belief systems, then, is that they provide a framework and rudder for a church's theology and practice in a way that generic evangelicalism cannot. The specific doctrines and practices of various denominations establish the specific means by which congregations pursue their agendas.

This same process of hyphenation applies to our social and political loyalties. Hyphenations such as Republican-evangelicals, creationist-evangelicals, and anti–gay-rights-evangelicals dot the demographic landscape. As a result, action items on certain evangelical agendas include the promotion of a particular candidate for government office, carrying the banner against teaching evolution in public schools, or championing the cause against health benefits for same-sex domestic partners. If you are a convinced advocate for any of these causes, we have no beef with that. Make your case, raise money, and win as many converts as you can by honest engagements and persuasion. We do not even have a problem with those who come to these positions as a result of their theological convictions. That is what theological convictions are for. If people do not call upon their Christian identity to shape an agenda, it does not count for much. Our point is that we should not confuse the social agendas of particular evangelicals with *evangelicalism's* agenda.

The paragraphs above focus on the left side of the hyphen, which highlights our distinctive theological and social commitments and goals. To put it another way, the left side of the hyphen points toward our quest for orthodoxy (right doctrine) and orthopraxy (right practice). Since our attempts to adopt the correct Christian beliefs and practices are directed by our theological traditions and not by evangelicalism, many ask why we need the right side of these hyphenated pairs—evangelicalism—at all. If evangelicalism spans such a hodgepodge of doctrinal positions and practices, many believe it represents an unacceptable descent toward the lowest common denominator.

The problem with this position is that while orthodoxy and orthopraxy are ideals of evangelicalism, no particular doctrinal formulation or set of social positions has ever been enshrined as an essential of evangelicalism. To be sure, many students of evangelicalism have compiled lists of basic doctrinal ties or emphases that bind evangelicals together. There are two noticeable features of all these lists, however. The first is that they are *basic* doctrines, generally centering on the primacy of Scripture, the centrality of the cross, the full humanity and divinity of Jesus, and the mandate to proclaim the good news to all the earth. These basic beliefs, as we have stated above, are inadequate for setting the agenda for a full-orbed Christian life. The second observation is that our catalog of "what evangelicalism is not" is hardly radical. With only a few exceptions, those who study evangelicalism exclude them as definitive for the movement.

Orthodoxy, Orthopraxy, and Orthopathy

While evangelicalism does possess certain core doctrinal emphases, it is only when they are placed alongside something else that we catch a glimpse of evangelicalism's essence. This "something else" might be called orthopathy (right feeling or pathos), orthoaffectus (right affection or disposition), or orthokardia (right-heartedness, or correct heart). This impulse sometimes has been referred to as pietism. The Pietist Movement in seventeenth-century continental Europe emphasized the experiential dimension of Protestantism, which in turn influenced British and American Christianity. Regardless of the designation, we see it from the beginning of evangelicalism. Despite the vast theological gulf between them, orthopathy is front and center in Jonathan Edwards's focus on "religious affections" as well as in John Wesley's appeal to "heart religion." This impulse, which draws heavily from the pietism that followed closely on the Reformation's heels, is the thread that can be traced from the beginnings of evangelicalism, through the Second Great Awakening and the revivalist/social reformist evangelicalism of the nineteenth century, and into the "Neo-Evangelicalism" of the middle twentieth century, and is present in the global explosion of Two-Thirds World evangelicalism in the early twenty-first century.

The difficulty in talking about orthopathy is that many jump to the conclusion that we are talking about mushy emotionalism superimposed on our spirituality, and evangelicalism is admittedly susceptible to this.

Orthopathy is a tricky term to define, and the reason for this stems from something that distinguishes it from the other two "orthos." Orthodoxy and orthopraxy require a certain distancing and neutrality. They require that we stand back and reflect on our beliefs and actions to determine whether they conform to some standard of truth that is external to us. We want to discern whether our doctrines and activities are *correct* in view of this standard. Orthopathy, however, seeks the *right* rather than the *correct*. *Rightness*, in our use, is not the sort of thing that can be discerned through detached reflection or action. Orthopathy, or pietism, refers to a relational rightness; it is something dynamic and personal. Thus at its best, evangelicals have thought of orthopathy as the righteous internal orientation in our relationship to a responsive and personal God. Because it cannot be infallibly detected by conformity to objective standards in the way that orthodoxy or orthopraxy can, it does not yield easily to measurement. But you know it when you see it.

The interplay of orthodoxy, orthopraxy, and orthopathy in evangelicalism can be illustrated by its relationship to fundamentalism and liberalism. Evangelicals often find a great deal of common ground both doctrinally and practically with fundamentalists in their own traditions. The dividing point between the two groups is not, therefore, orthodoxy or orthopraxy, but differences in the attitude toward orthopathy. On the other hand, liberals and evangelicals often have broad swaths of agreement on orthopathy, but differ significantly on questions of orthodoxy and orthopraxy. Evangelicalism, as we conceive it, does not pit the head, hands, and heart against each other, but endeavors to bring them into a proper balance. Without striving for doctrinal or practical correctness, faith wanders astray. However, absent the proper orientation of the heart, orthodoxy turns cold and sterile while orthopraxy becomes legalism and empty ritual.

If this is anywhere close to true, evangelicalism can be considered a descent toward the lowest common denominator *only if* it is assumed that one's internal, passionate faith commitment falls lower on the scale of importance than proper doctrine or practice. Our interest in writing this book springs from the conviction that just the opposite is the case. A right-hearted desire to have one's life redeemed and mobilized toward ministry to the world has been an essential aspect of evangelicalism throughout its history, even if manifested imperfectly and often unconsciously. We cannot explain evangelicalism by appeal to doctrinal agreement or sociopolitical uniformity, and certainly not by ecclesiastical unity. Disagreement in these spheres is precisely what must be overcome in order for evangelicalism to exist. The means by which these differences have been mitigated, we believe, is the unity offered in a pietist impulse that expects that lives changed by the good news will give external as well as internal expression of this transformation.

To say that orthopathy is essential to evangelicalism's agenda is not to say that this characteristic cannot or should not be integrated to one's specific theological tradition. Nevertheless, even when this occurs, it does not eliminate the desirability of maintaining our hyphenated loyalties. First, by acknowledging that Christians of other theological stripes share similar evangelical impulses, we are reminded of the dangers of insularity and a prideful arrogance that tends toward making our theological distinctives absolute. Moreover, our evangelical identity can remind us that the winds of theological favor undergo significant shifts. For example, if you had lived in the first half of the nineteenth century, you had to search far and wide to find an evangelical premillennialist. Today they run in herds, to the extent that many identify premillennialism with evangelicalism. The point is that those who now find premillennialism deeply convincing and enriching to their faith should be thankful that a small remnant of evangelicals kept that view alive when it was viewed with deep suspicion by the vast majority of their evangelical relatives (and called a heresy by a significant segment of them). The theological diversity of the evangelical family serves as a necessary sounding board against which we can continually test our own tradition's agendas and avoid the arrogance of doctrinal absolutism.

A second reason for maintaining hyphenated identities as Pentecostal-evangelicals, Methodist-evangelicals, Democratic-evangelicals, African-American–evangelicals, or any other dual citizenship we may claim is that, despite the differences highlighted by the first member of each pair, the "evangelical" counterbalance has provided some sense of unity. While most evangelicals will acknowledge that sincere and thoughtful Christians can disagree about many things in Scripture, one biblical teaching that seems crystal clear is that division within Christ's body, the church, is nothing short of sinful. Our evangelical identities, albeit in an imperfect way, have provided a vital link across social and denominational lines.

The cooperative ventures of evangelicals have (often unwittingly) provided an ecumenical vision that is easily overlooked. While mainline Christianity thinks of ecumenicity primarily in terms of denominational unification, evangelicals have created a plethora of institutions and organizations outside denominational boundaries. Moreover, many have been remarkably "bottom-up," with the impetus coming mainly from engaged laity rather than church officials. These organizations range across a broad spectrum of religious activities—missions, education, evangelism, politics, social justice, discipleship, just to name a few. This more pragmatic approach to ecumenism (evangelicals are, ironically, more comfortable with being called pragmatic than ecumenical) means that one's denominational affiliation or social stances rarely stand as an obstacle for participation in evangelical organizations. In a sense, evangelicalism's pragmatic desire to accomplish its agenda of evangelizing and discipleship has often been more of a spur to ecumenicity than any theological impulse. While Protestant evangelicals are prone to forget that division is sinful and that they have been the worst offenders when it comes to denominational schism, they have also offered some of the best examples of what can be done when we step across theological boundaries to work together.

Caricatures

As with all forms of humor, caricature can be a very honest form of communication. Sometimes caricatures convey brutal honesties, and these realities come back to bite us if we ignore them. Poll results that gauged public opinion about certain groups in American society illustrate the impact of caricatures on evangelicalism and may offer hints on how we might move forward. This survey, taken by the Barna Group a few years back, discovered that when non-Christians were split off from the broader sample, their responses ranked "evangelical Christians" tenth out of eleven groups in terms of positive impressions. Evangelicals were viewed more favorably than prostitutes, but less favorably than real estate agents, movie and TV performers, lawyers, and lesbians! To be fair, the groups listed above were still within the margin of error for evangelical Christians, but this should not obscure an important fact: among those outside the Christian fold, evangelicals do not have a very positive public profile. The label "evangelical" clearly does not evoke images of "good news" to the very people evangelicals most want to hear the gospel of Jesus Christ. To put it in marketing terms, the evangelical brand name is pretty much on a par with Yugo and Enron.

In case you are inclined to dismiss this as a generalized attitude of non-Christians toward Christians, this survey also had a category for "born-again Christians." They came in third highest in positive impression. Thus, it seems reasonable to conclude that disapproval of evangelicalism centers on concerns we deal with in this book—notions that evangelicalism is essentially racist, homophobic, mean-spirited, dogmatic, hostile to science, and a host of other characteristics that the majority of non-Christians find repulsive. We hope that evangelicals will object to this characterization and call it, as we have, a caricature. But this is precisely where the honesty of caricatures shines through. Like all caricatures, the mental picture lodged in the minds of most non-Christians is not pulled from thin air. Instead, caricatures exaggerate what is there to some degree. They gain no traction without some connection to reality.

The problem is that evangelicalism is not fighting a poor public image on just one front. As we mentioned at the beginning of this chapter, many who embody evangelical beliefs and impulses just do not want to own the label either. Again, we have to ask why, and we do not have to dig very deep to discover why. They will tell you that if the price of admission to the evangelical party is affirmation of some particular view on scriptural authority, eschatology, or divine sovereignty, or a single political affiliation, they prefer to stay home.

If individuals place themselves outside the borders of evangelicalism because they cannot affirm that which is essential to it, that is one thing. It is an entirely different matter, however, when the obstacles to inclusion are caricatures rather than realities. The latter is nothing short of tragic in our view. Therefore, even though many will be disappointed if we cannot provide a photo-perfect portrait of what evangelicalism is, our endeavor to say what evangelicalism is not has merit. If evangelicalism is not, in its essence, mean, sexist, Republican, or any of the other attributes we address, then we have a better chance of removing barriers between nonbelievers and evangelicals and, more importantly, between nonbelievers and the good news of Jesus Christ. If one can be a real, honest-to-goodness evangelical without becoming a pre-millennialist or an inerrantist, then we think that all will be deeply enriched if reluctant evangelicals willingly show up at the party.

The good news is that we can go a long way toward clearing up some of the misleading caricatures of evangelicalism by relying on one of the essential characteristics of the movement—orthopathy. Let us be honest: those who equate evangelicalism with meanness, racial exclusion, monolithic political loyalties, or dogmatism usually do not form these impressions because of failures in orthodoxy or orthopraxy. Instead, these caricatures arise because of orthopathic breakdown. Negative images of evangelicalism often emerge precisely because we allow differences to become divisive and we depersonalize (even demonize) those who disagree with us. Again, we do not want to imply that evangelicalism is something as insipid and amorphous as mushy religious sentiment chained to kindheartedness and mindless universal acceptance. Evangelicalism does say no to any attempt to minimize the unique authority of Scripture, relegate Jesus exclusively to the category of inspiring symbol or metaphor, or undermine Christianity's evangelistic mandate. When evangelicals must draw the line, however, orthopathy should guide how we do it. In sum, one of the most effective ways for evangelicals to overcome wrongheaded and damaging cartoon images of the movement is to start acting like evangelicals.

While we believe that evangelicals could do a lot for their cause by cleaning up their own house, an alliance such as evangelicalism will forever be highly susceptible to caricature because of its very nature. It has no formal membership process, standardized belief statement, centralized organizational headquarters, or official spokesperson. As a result, any pronouncement by a particular evangelical individual or group can be perceived (or explicitly claimed) as indicative of the entire movement. This is why we endeavor to maintain a clear distinction between *evangelicalism* and *evangelicals*. When the two are confused and statements of individual evangelicals are taken as definitive of the entire movement's agenda, caricatures come into existence. We could avoid much of this confusion if evangelicalism would morph into something that had closely defined theological borders, official spokespeople, and a single organizational center. However, such attempts would fall into the category of successful surgery that kills the patient. On balance, the fuzzy boundaries of evangelicalism have been a positive element that has facilitated its power and effectiveness rather than hindering it. Thus, while some may fret about the imprecision of the term, this imprecision has opened up room for the movement's vitality and spirit.

What Should We Expect?

It should be obvious by now that we find a great deal of value in evangelicalism. If it is, in fact, something worth preserving and promoting, what should we expect from it? If one approaches this question only from the perspective of doctrinal uniformity or a clear-cut social or political agenda, then the answer is "not much." Evangelicalism cannot tell you what to believe about significant theological issues such as predestination or atonement theory, whether apostolic succession legitimizes the church, or whether the gift of divine healing is operative today. It cannot tell us whether we should support advocates of intelligent design for the local school board, nor does it offer clear direction whether we should vote Green, Democrat, Republican, or Libertarian. Some would have us believe that evangelicalism gives unambiguous signals on these and similar questions, but its history, its current manifestations, and its future trajectories tell us otherwise. The imprecision and lack of theological definition offered by evangelicalism indicate why our expectations should be set low in these areas, and this helps us understand why some find the entire evangelical project dispensable.

Our reasons for advocating evangelicalism's preservation, however, are not grounded in any guidance it offers in theological or practical correctness, although it would not be evangelicalism if it was inconsistent with the essentials of historical Christian doctrine. Instead, we value the movement because it offers empirical evidence of something that looks impossible in theory. If orthodoxy and orthopraxy are our only filters, it seems hopeless that non-sacramentalists such as the Salvation Army or Friends could span the gap that doctrinally separates them from evangelical Episcopalians. Many forms of inerrancy do not accommodate themselves easily to other views of scriptural authority within evangelicalism. Reformed perspectives on the spiritual gifts are anything but compatible with Pentecostalism's views of glossolalia or healing. Given the chasm that separates them, it is hard to know why wealthy conservative Baptists in the United States host impoverished female Chinese pastors in their homes and establish deep spiritual connections. In theory, these differences should polarize us, and sadly, they often do.

Nevertheless, it is sheer craziness to say that Christians with these differences, and a multitude of others, cannot bridge such chasms to work and worship together in significant ways. In evangelicalism today, we find Pentecostals at dispensationalist colleges. A rainbow of denominations shows up at Billy Graham crusades and have used *The Purpose Driven Life* in their Sunday school classes and home Bible studies. Through high school and college parachurch ministries, at Women of Faith conferences, in rescue missions and revival meetings, and across continents in missionary endeavors, millions have experienced the saving work of Jesus Christ through the efforts of evangelicals. All this is at the heart and soul of evangelicalism, and it happens without requiring that one be an inerrantist, Calvinist, premillennialist, Republican, or a well-to-do citizen of the United States. While evangelicalism does not ignore the fact that Christians will take different sides on postmodernism or traditionalism, creationism or theistic evolution, acceptance of homosexuals in worship or exclusion, ordination of women or submission, or Democrat or Republican, the evangelical spirit does not allow these differences to become absolutes.

The higher the stakes in any human endeavor, the more polarizing that endeavor is likely to be. One's religious commitment is most certainly a high-stakes endeavor, and history is littered with the tragic results of religious warfare that results from this polarization. Such warfare is inevitable when we absolutize our quest for conformity with an insular orthodoxy or orthopraxy. Evangelicalism has made its mark across history and around the globe because, in its better moments, it has recognized that its identity and agenda cannot be reduced to either of these. Thus, when we impose any of the doctrines, social positions, or attitudes treated in the chapters that follow as litmus tests for inclusion in the evangelical family, we do not project an accurate portrait of evangelicalism. Instead, we create caricatures that rob evangelicalism of its essence. Evangelicalism's concern for right-heartedness says, as Wesley put it, " 'If thine heart is as my heart,' if thou lovest God and all mankind, I ask no more: 'Give me thine hand.' "[4]

When evangelicals throughout history have reached across theological and social boundaries to grasp the hands of other warmhearted Christians, they have participated in a slowly unfolding miracle. Legions of laity have been mobilized for ministries of all types by an inner transformation that cannot easily be quantified or defined, but its results are increasingly difficult to overlook. Our expectations for evangelicalism's future are no less than what we have seen in the past, and with God's grace we pray that the fruit will exceed all precedents. But we fear that evangelicalism's future is endangered by various attempts, conscious or unconscious, to impose alien definitions on it.

2

Evangelicals Are Not All
Mean, Stupid, and Dogmatic

Two men, headed in opposite directions, meet in the middle of a narrow foot-bridge forty feet above a raging river. The southbound man said to the other, "Before I can let you pass, I must know if you are a believer."

The other man responded, "Yes indeed, and a Baptist believer at that."

The southbound man said. "So am I, but what sort of Baptist are you?"

The northbound traveler replied, "I am a Landstake Baptist."

At this, the other fellow replied, "What a happy coincidence. I am a Land-stake Baptist as well."

"But," the northbound hiker asked, "are you an eastern or western juris-diction Landstaker?"

"Eastern," was the answer.

"As am I. Are you, like me, a follower of the 1874 Covenant, or do you subscribe to the 1903 Covenant?"

"1874," the southbounder stated. "How about you? Pre-mill or post-mill?"

The fellow Baptist responded, "Pre-mill."

The southbound man then asked, "Pre-trib or mid-trib?"

"Mid-trib."

With this, the southbound traveler swung his walking stick at the head of the other man, sending him hurtling toward the river below. As he was falling, the pre-trib, pre-mill, 1874 eastern covenant Landstake Baptist yelled after him, "Die, heretic scum!"

For a joke to work, it must have, among other things, a ring of truth to it. The truth is that we have all seen cases in which people have lost their sense of proportion and, like the southbound stick-swinger, acted in ways that can only be characterized as mean, stupid, and dogmatic. (We are counting on your agreement that the stick-swinger's action was out of proportion to the theological issue at stake.) Unfortunately, this joke may have a bit too much truth for those who have been "knocked off a bridge" by evangelicals who believed they were doing God's work. Some of us are, without a doubt, mean, stupid, or dogmatic. Certain evangelicals even manage to hit the trifecta and possess all three of these characteristics. There is, unfortunately, ample reason to include a chapter like this in the book.

We could simply deflect this criticism by saying that evangelicalism, which encompasses tens of millions in this country alone, is bound to include some disagreeable characters. After all, any large demographic includes members who are angry, ignorant, and ideologically narrow. However, the issue goes deeper for evangelicals. While qualities such as meanness, stupidity, or a doctrinaire attitude are not inherently incompatible to the nature of groups classified according to race, political leaning, occupation, or preferred hobby, this is not the case for evangelicalism. It is hypocritical for evangelicals to act in these ways. If we are divisive over doctrine, intellectually careless, or of nasty temperament, we cannot simply say, "So what?" It is a big deal.

If this is true, evangelicalism has a "big deal" on our hands because many outsiders perceive that evangelicalism itself fosters meanness, ignorance, and dogmatism. One of our tasks is to ask whether this perception matches reality. Since perceptions and reality are often two different things, we want to do our best to get at some facts. That will account for a blizzard of statistics in some parts of this chapter. Our preliminary conclusion, which will probably not surprise a lot of people since the authors are evangelicals, is that objective measures seem to indicate that, on the whole, we are generally nice and we embrace and encourage education and learning. It is more difficult to find objective measures of dogmatism, but by some metrics, one can argue that evangelicals have greater openness to differing doctrines than many other religious traditions or secular groups.

It would be nice if that was the whole story, but we also need to come clean. It would be hard to find a single evangelical, no matter how firmly entrenched in the system, who could not recount many instances in which he or she has been the victim of mean, stupid, and dogmatic Christians. This is not incidental contact. These painful events were not mean, stupid, or dogmatic actions done by people who just happened to be evangelicals. Instead, the grief was caused by motives thought by the perpetrators to be demanded by their faith. Tragically, many non-evangelicals harbor negative views of the church and of evangelicalism because they have experienced similar things. Therefore, evangelicals need some honest self-examination that allows us to see why *we* might be the most daunting barrier between hurt people and salvation.

All Religion Is Mean, Stupid, and Dogmatic

While we will sharpen the focus specifically to evangelicalism later in this chapter, the idea that evangelicals have tendencies to be mean, stupid, and dogmatic should be set in a broader context. Over the last few years, a number of books from a group often referred to as the "new atheists" have garnered a lot of attention by claiming that religion in general is the chief threat to freedom, intellectual rigor and honesty, and a humane attitude toward others. The sampling of quotes below from some of the more prominent of the new atheists illustrates this:

- "Religious faith represents so uncompromising a misuse of the power of our minds that it forms a kind of perverse, cultural singularity—a vanishing point beyond which rational discourse proves impossible."[1]
- "Faith is an evil precisely because it requires no justification and brooks no argument. Teaching children that unquestioned faith is a virtue primes them—given certain other ingredients that are not hard to come by—to grow up into potentially lethal weapons for future jihads or crusades."[2]
- "It can be stated as a truth that religion does not, and in the long run cannot, be content with its own marvelous claims and sublime assurances. It *must* seek to interfere with the lives of nonbelievers, or heretics, or adherents of other faiths. It may speak about the bliss of the next world, but it wants power in this one. This is to be expected. It is, after all, wholly man-made. And it does not have the confidence in its own various preachings even to allow coexistence between different faiths."[3]
- "I still have a high regard for the basic decency of most human beings. Many people are good. But they are not good because of religion. They are good despite religion."[4]
- "There is, in fact, no worldview more reprehensible in its arrogance than that of a religious believer."[5]

One minor detail the new atheists are not very vocal about is that their diagnosis that religion *per se* is dangerous casts a very wide net. In fact, it implicates about 95 percent of the United States population, and a similar percentage of the global population, in meanness, stupidity, and dogmatism. That is, after all, the percentage of those who believe in the divine in some form or another. While the new atheists do not cut much slack even for those who are moderate or casual in their religious adherence,[6] their examples indicate that those who take their religion very seriously represent the greatest immediate threat to global survival and well-being. By most metrics, evangelicals fit the description of individuals who are serious about their faith, so we are apparently among the most dangerous and stupid of the lot.

The books of the new atheists are replete with anecdotes of the mayhem and ignorance fostered by religions. We need to pay close attention, because truth resides in these anecdotes. Much that is horrendous and ignorant, across history and around the world, has been done with the active support of religion in general and Christianity specifically. People of faith have a lot to account for and repent of. Evangelicals cannot claim clean hands, and we want to be brutally straightforward in this chapter about the ways we are implicated in destruction and stupidity.

To a person, the new atheists extol the possibilities available to society if we swear off religion and rebuild on careful research. In the process, though, their writings overlook two fundamental axioms of social research. The first is that "correlation does not imply causation." It is child's play to correlate religion with any event you want because, in historical terms, almost 100 percent of this planet's population has belonged to some religion. If you start from the assumption that religion is dangerous and intellectually challenged, then you can cherry-pick any horrific or dopey event and link it to a faith tradition because whoever initiated it professed some sort of religion. Change the interpretive grid, and we could also say that government, money, or sex is responsible for history's awful activities since they are each similarly omnipresent features of human society. If a historian or social scientist concluded that the only salient event in all of human history's terrors was religion, he would be laughed out of his guild. This is not to imply that religion is never a factor in these events, or even that it rarely has been a primary factor. However, the simplistic conclusions of the new atheists would never withstand a serious analysis of past and present evils.

The second social research maxim that applies to the new atheists' arguments is "the plural of anecdote is not data." These authors compile an impressive list of anecdotes, both historical and personal, to bolster their claim that "religion ruins everything" (as the subtitle of Hitchens's book declares). However, stacking up anecdotes of atrocities falls far short of supporting the claim that religion is at the root of every vile, destructive, and dim-witted activity in history. Combining anecdotes with the unquestioned assumption that correlation indicates causation further weakens their argument. Perhaps it would be helpful to examine studies that take seriously the rules of social research to ask whether, collectively, evangelicals are mean, stupid, and dogmatic.

Are Evangelicals Mean?

It is difficult to know how to measure something like meanness and its contraries, but starting at home seems to make sense. When we begin here, evangelicals do not appear to be particularly mean. Active conservative Protestant fathers spent an average of 3.8 hours per week more than religiously unaffiliated fathers as "participant, advisor, coach, or leader in school activities, community youth groups such as scouting programs, sports activities, and religious youth groups."[7] They are much more likely to hug and verbally praise their children and less likely to yell at them than nonreligious fathers.[8] Although active conservative Protestant men are more than twice as likely than those with no religious affiliation to say that husbands should be breadwinners and wives the homemakers,[9] this does not seem to result in a sense of domination or oppression. In fact, wives of evangelical men perceive that they are more appreciated;[10] they spend more time socializing with their spouses[11] and are happier with the amount of affection and understanding received from their husbands than wives of any other demographic.[12]

On the motherhood side of the home front, a longitudinal study that followed children over a twenty-three-year period found a measurable positive correlation between strong religiosity and satisfaction in the mother-child relationship. The more involved the mother was in religious activities, the more both mother and child (both male and female) reported a positive and nurturing relationship. Moreover, satisfaction with this relationship diminished if, over the course of the twenty-three-year study, the mother's religious involvement likewise diminished. If, on the other hand, the mother becomes more deeply religious over the years, the mother-child bond also became more personally satisfying to both.[13] Mothers are 21 percent more likely to attend church frequently than women without children.[14] If the caricature of evangelicals is correct, a lot of mean people are dedicating themselves to motherhood.

In more general investigations into niceness, a blind test showed those who prayed frequently were judged by interviewers to be friendlier than those who never or only infrequently prayed. Contrary to the idea that religion makes people mean, those who pray frequently were significantly less likely than those who do not pray to be resentful about not getting their way or to dislike anyone intensely. They were also more likely to lend money to a friend in need or help a stranger with bus fare.[15] If we assume that happy people are less likely to be mean and nasty, frequent church-attenders come out ahead here as well. Some 64 percent of them say they are very happy with their lives, compared with 38 percent among those who rarely or never attend religious services.[16]

Giving would seem to be an obvious measure of niceness. It turns out that those who devote a "great deal of effort" to their spiritual lives are almost twice as likely to give to charity as those devoting "no effort" (88 percent vs. 46 percent).[17] The charity of the religious person does not stop at the offering plate. Churchgoers are nine points more likely than secularists to give to nonreligious charities.[18] If we consider another form of giving—volunteer work—we find that consistent churchgoers are 25 points more likely than those who seldom or never attend to volunteer for secular causes *in addition to* their often-extensive volunteer activity in religious ventures.[19]

You do not need a scientific study to know that large numbers of hospitals, orphanages, rescue missions, prison ministries, schools, clean-water projects, drug rehabilitation programs, and numerous other efforts to reduce human suffering have resulted from the charitable and volunteer efforts of Christians. These have sprung up not just in the United States but all over the world, often far from public notice. They certainly seem beyond the notice of the new atheists. Until we start to see orphanages in Botswana and rescue missions in downtown Philadelphia funded by the American Atheist organization, their discussion of how mean evangelicals are seems premature.

Are Evangelicals Stupid?

Evangelical churchgoers are slightly less likely than the average American to have a college degree (13 percent vs. 16 percent). However, lower financial resources among evangelicals, rather than a culture that discourages the intellect, is probably the main factor.[20] Moreover, if taking one's faith seriously creates an ethos of stupidity, it does not seem to be hereditary. In fact, both men and women who had a parent who attended church two or three times a month had college graduation rates that were double those with nonattending parents. Moreover, the difference in graduation rates was even higher for women than for men, a striking result given the widespread stereotype that religion stifles opportunities for females.[21] By this measure, it looks like evangelicals put strong emphasis on higher education for their children.

Of course, one's level of educational attainment is not the only measure of smartness. The new atheists classify belief in God as superstitious and suppose that such credulity makes one susceptible to belief in all sorts of other goofy things. We will suppose that belief in the existence of ghosts, Atlantis, Bigfoot, the Loch Ness Monster, space aliens, the ability of the living to communicate with the dead, or the validity of predictions based on dreams, astrology, or tarot-card readings fit this description.[22] The problem is that no positive correlation exists between belief in God and the nine beliefs listed immediately above. In fact, it is just the opposite. Only 8 percent of those who attend church more than once a week scored high on credence in the nine occult and paranormal beliefs, compared with 31 percent who never attend church. To put it in different terms, the enlightened atheists whom Dawkins, Harris, and Hitchens trust to drag the world back to rationality are almost four times more likely than evangelicals to believe in the existence of ghosts, the predictive power of tarot-card readings, and similar ideas.

While these atheists insist that education will show us a more rational way, the effects of education barely moved the needle on occult and paranormal belief. Twenty-eight percent of those with a high school education or less gave high credence to these ideas, compared with 23 percent of those with postgraduate degrees.[23] Thus, if one desires to rid our species of irrational beliefs, the data indicate we would have more success if we sent people to church instead of graduate school.

To hear the new atheists talk about it, evangelicals sound like knuckle-dragging cretins. Maybe they are looking at different data to determine whether evangelicals are stupid, but they do not seem to get around to citing evidence other than our higher-than-average tendency to reject both evolution and a very long history for our universe. We deal with these in chapter 4, so we will postpone that discussion until then. Nevertheless, if evangelicals have a monopoly on stupidity, it is not discernable in statistics about educational achievement or credulity to superstition.

Are Evangelicals Dogmatic?

Almost every evangelical denomination and organization has a statement of faith. Within these statements, however, one finds little evidence that they are overly concerned about parsing doctrine down to its most minute details. For example, set the National Association of Evangelicals' statement of faith alongside the Apostles' Creed or Nicene Creed, statements viewed by the majority of the world's Christian population as authoritative summaries of their beliefs. You will notice that the format and wording is different, but the content of all three is strikingly similar.[24] Therefore, when we compare Christendom's most used statements of beliefs and creeds with evangelical faith statements, we have to conclude that if evangelicals are dogmatic, all Christians are dogmatic.

Adding a layer of irony to the idea that evangelicals are uniquely dogmatic is the observation that statements of faith for evangelical groups tend to stay in the background. You will find them easily in printed materials or websites that explain "what we believe," but it is a rare occasion when an evangelical group will pull out its statement of faith and recite its beliefs together. In contrast, the majority of the world's Christians—Catholics, Orthodox Christians, and most mainline Protestant denominations—recite their creedal beliefs every time they gather for worship. By this standard, it looks like non-evangelical groups are much more concerned about doctrine than evangelicals.

The reality is that evangelicalism could not exist if we were as feisty and dogmatic about doctrine and ecclesial practice as many suppose. Evangelicalism, by definition, is a coalition that draws from a variety of church families. Look into almost any evangelical organization and you will find people from a broad hodgepodge of denominational (and nondenominational) churches. Examine evangelicalism's history and you will find that its prominent leaders come from an incredible array of theological traditions. The reality is that evangelicals have founded interdenominational student ministries, missionary societies, social justice ministries, educational institutions from preschool through the graduate level, and parachurch organizations at an unprecedented rate. The alliances evangelicals have forged show a willingness to cross doctrinal boundaries to a degree uncharacteristic of any other period in Christian history.

Evangelicalism does not simply exemplify broad diversity in doctrine and practice. It puts its disagreements on open display. Look at the catalog of any leading evangelical publisher and you are likely to find a significant number of titles that begin with the words "Four (or some similar number) Views." These books examine competing theological positions within evangelicalism on every major doctrine from creation to eschatology. Our quick count turned up about sixty of these, and we are pretty sure we missed quite a few.[25] As a point of comparison, make your own list of books outside evangelicalism where political, denominational, atheist, or social advocacy groups explicitly place their internal disagreements head-to-head in the same volume. The irony, then, is that at least on one level, evangelicals are more transparent about doctrinal disagreements than many groups that accuse them of dogmatism.

If evangelicals as an aggregate are supposed to be doctrinally narrow, the indicators above reveal that we are just not doing a very good job at it. A 2004 poll found that Pope John Paul II had a higher favorability rating *among evangelicals* than Jerry Falwell or Pat Robertson, two media favorites generally tapped as spokespersons for evangelicalism.[26] In many senses, evangelicals may be the least doctrinaire, most ecumenical of all Christian movements. (Ironically, "ecumenical" is a word many evangelicals detest. It is not uncommon for evangelicals to form an ecumenical coalition to express their distaste of ecumenism.) However, that is not the whole story. There is still a sense in which our reputation for doctrinal squabbling and divisiveness is well deserved. The same is true for meanness and stupidity. This brings us to the more painful part of the chapter.

Sometimes Evangelicals Really Are Mean, Stupid, and Dogmatic

If you have hung out in evangelical circles long enough, you have stories, sometimes lots of them, about low-down, idiotic, and unbelievably hurtful things done in the name of Jesus. One's spirituality is questioned because of a political affiliation, preference for a certain type of music in worship, or unwillingness to subscribe to an obscure theological point. Heresy hunters are attentive to vocabulary that may indicate "softness" on some matter of faith. Someone takes up the cause of warning all around him of the apocalypse that will ensue from the latest Antichrist, and a congregation is split, a job is lost, or a friendship is irrevocably severed. Sadly, you probably know several people who have endured these sorts of rancorous debates and have left your church, any church, or Christianity altogether.

This is just a small sample of the carnage that plagues many within evangelical churches, but the impact is felt by those outside our congregations as well. It is a well-known sociological fact that most people make their deepest religious commitments early in adult life. Therefore, evangelicals have good reasons to be interested in what younger adults think about us. So how does evangelicalism play for this group that we would like to bring into our churches? The picture is not pretty. For "outsiders," people between sixteen and twenty-nine who are not part of a religious group, slightly more than a third have a "bad impression" of Christianity in general (38 percent) and born-again Christians (35 percent). However, this negative perception goes up considerably for evangelicals (48 percent).[27]

If we want to understand why so many younger people have unflattering impressions of evangelicals, it will help to listen to what they have to say. The book *unChristian* compiled extensive data from surveys and identified six common themes that characterized the views of young "outsiders." Their verdict was that we are hypocrites, too focused on getting converts, anti-homosexual, sheltered, too political, and judgmental.[28] Data like this tend to evoke three types of responses from evangelicals. One response that mirrors the earlier part of this chapter says, "Hey, the stats show that we evangelicals really are not all that bad after all." This contains truth, but not the whole truth. A second response takes the "persecuted minority" defense: this is the result of opponents who want to make evangelicals look bad.[29] Again, this is not completely off target, but we should admit that we are giving evangelical-ism's opponents plenty of ammunition. Finally, many evangelicals see such feedback as a mandate to mount a better public relations campaign. We just need to sell "our brand" more effectively. The assumption is that the only thing we need to change is our marketing strategy.

While all three responses have some validity, there is a deeper truth: we evangelicals are failing, sometimes miserably, in areas central to the faith we confess. Two of the six areas listed above ("too political" and "antihomo-sexual") are dealt with in greater detail in chapters 8 and 9, so we will focus attention on the other four categories—hypocrisy, too focused on getting converts, sheltered, and judgmental—in reverse order.

Some Evangelicals Are Judgmental

If we did not believe that evangelicals have some judgmental tendencies, this book would be much shorter. The reality is, many have filters (e.g., Republi-can, premillennial, anti-evolutionist) that determine, in their minds anyway, where we should draw the line that separates the evangelical sheep from the goats. Sadly, the filters identified by our chapter titles are not an exhaustive list. There are numerous "hot-button" words that will ignite certain evangelicals. If you want to check this out, casually throw out words such as "emergent," "healing," "Catholic," "feminist," "school prayer," "Harry Potter," or "open theism" in a conversation. For some people, what you believe about these mat-ters, or any number of other hot-button items, is the litmus test by which your commitment to the evangelical cause, or even the Christian faith, is judged. After this, it makes absolutely no difference where you stand on anything else.

A lot of evangelicals have a sacred cow, and some have quite a herd. Kick one of those cows and all hell breaks loose.

We want to be clear that our critique of judgmentalism does not mean we are advocating doctrinal indifference. That would truly be a very odd stance for two authors with PhDs in theology. In fact, we believe that judgmentalism is often the result of not thinking about theology carefully enough to put doctrine into a proper perspective. One fundamental step in this process is to distinguish between dogma and doctrine.

Much of our reputation as judgmental arises from the fact that we become *dogmatic* about *doctrine*. "Dogma," the term from which "dogmatic" comes, is actually a good word, although it has been so misused that it may be beyond redemption for most people. "Dogma" traditionally refers to the nonnegotiables of Christianity, beliefs and values that are essential to Christianity itself. In contrast, "doctrine" refers to specific interpretations of dogma. For example, Christianity is not Christianity without its affirmation that God provides a means to overcome sin and death. That is dogma, and we ought to hold to it tenaciously. In contrast, how and when this conquest of sin and death occurs are matters of doctrine where thoughtful and sincere Christians hold differing views. Thus, Christians throughout history have disagreed about which view of the atonement or understanding of Jesus' return best represents Scripture's teaching on this dogma.

Our personal doctrinal positions or ecclesiastical traditions include certain beliefs and practices that are important to us, and we want them to be important to others as well. There is nothing wrong with this so far. However, it would be helpful to remember that, as important as these matters may be to you or your denomination, the beliefs that distinguish one theological tradition from another do not rise to the level of dogma. Thus, if others disagree with your understanding of infant baptism or speaking in tongues, it may mean they would not make very good Presbyterians, Mennonites, Charismatics, Baptists, or Quakers. However, it does not mean they are not good Christians or evangelicals. No matter how convinced we might be of a particular doctrine's fidelity to Scripture's witness, we need to remember that the church has demonstrated it can be the church without resolution of all our doctrinal disagreements. If we elevate our particular doctrines to the level of dogma, we lose our perspective and are primarily invested in preserving not Christianity, but our specific versions of it. The result is often a dogmatism that becomes judgmental and mean-spirited, and it fails to reflect the sort of thoughtfulness that should characterize the Christian life. Lack of perspective about doctrine generates the unholy trio of meanness, stupidity, and dogmatism.

We suggest three antidotes to doctrinal obsession and judgmentalism. First, study church history. You might discover that certain pet doctrines you hold dear have not been an important factor at other ages of Christianity's existence. In other words, your favorite belief is not dogma. You may also find out that some practices or doctrines you strongly disagree with were held by the majority of Christians throughout history or were advocated by one of your theological heroes. Finally, and unfortunately, you will find all too many examples of ugly situations in which doctrinal particularity and selectivity have led to mean, stupid, and dogmatic behaviors that severely damaged the reputation of Christianity. If we learn from history, we do not have to repeat it.

Second, identify someone outside your theological tradition who takes their faith seriously and ask about how they fell in love with Jesus. Find out how they experience God's forgiveness, how the Holy Spirit gives them hope for full redemption, or how their church and its practices nurture their faith. Don't talk. Listen. If, after this, you cannot accept them as a sister or brother in the faith because of doctrinal differences, then it would be helpful to remember that the unity of God's people is not simply a doctrine. It is dogma.

Finally, if you really want to be an evangelical, do what evangelicals claim to do best. Instead of looking for someone to argue doctrine with, reach out to someone who needs the good news. If you need some introductions, I have several "evangelism projects" in my life. I would love to be the one who hears their first prayers of repentance, but if you get through to them first, then I do not care whether you are Roman Catholic, Episcopalian, Fundamentalist, Pentecostal, or Salvation Army. I will party with the angels in heaven about the homecoming. When they receive baptism, I am not going to be overly concerned about whether they are sprinkled, poured, dipped, or dunked three times in an inflatable pool filled with red Kool-Aid to symbolize the blood of Jesus. I'll show up for it.

Evangelicals are not distinct from other Christians on the matter of dogma. With a few exceptions, all Christians are unified on this. What distinguishes evangelicalism from other forms of Christianity is that it is, quite self-consciously, an ongoing renewal movement that emphasizes the belief that mere doctrinal correctness is not the primary aim of the Christian life. Instead, the goal is to have a life that is transformed and energized by a living relationship with the God whom Christian dogma affirms, regardless of our particular doctrinal commitments. The spirit of evangelicalism runs contrary to doctrinal preoccupation. When we forget this, doctrine takes on inordinate importance and quickly degenerates into judgmentalism. As a result, evangelicals have often become mean, stupid, and doctrinaire. If evangelicals remember who we are, we can avoid these pitfalls.

Some Evangelicals Are Sheltered

Many evangelicals view the current age as crazy and dangerous. Kids have immediate access to all sorts of stuff on the Internet, drugs are easily obtainable in any high school, crime surrounds us, television and the movies do not exactly offer wholesome viewing. Cohabitation and producing children outside marriage is common, and Christianity seems to be increasingly nudged to the margins of society. The list could go on, but you see where we are going. Given the trends, it is not hard to understand the impulse to hunker down in a Christian bunker. It is a dangerous world, and the natural thing to do in the face of danger is to seek shelter.

Shelters are interesting structures. Their effectiveness in keeping certain dangers from getting in is directly proportional to their effectiveness at keeping those inside from getting out. Lately, we sheltered evangelicals have not been getting out much, and others are starting to notice. Outsiders have the distinct impression that evangelicals are holed up in our Christian ghettos where we do not have to think too much about today's world. To put it differently, the belief that we are sheltered is a variation on the idea that evangelicals are stupid. In this case, stupidity is not a symptom of educational deficiencies or low IQ, but an ignorance, a willful ignorance, about the realities of our world.

We think that this criticism carries significant weight. As university professors who deal with "dangerous subjects" (theology, philosophy, ethics), we encounter students daily who have been told that Christians should not think about certain ideas. They "know," for example, that they should oppose gay marriage, but often cannot frame a rationale for it beyond "the Bible says Adam and Eve, not Adam and Steve." They are often sure that stem cell research is pure evil, but cannot even define what is meant by stem cell research. Open theism is heretical as far as they are concerned, but they have not concerned themselves enough to read anything written by any of the advocates and do not even know their names. They simply parrot the criticisms of others (who also may not have read the material). To compound matters, this willful ignorance of important issues often flies behind a smokescreen of misplaced piety. If we have a couple of Bible verses to bolster our positions, then we are justified in cutting off any other investigation or discussion of the issue. And then we wonder why so many non-Christians equate evangelicalism with head-in-the-sand ignorance.

It is our experience that fear and anger are the twin impulses that so frequently drive evangelicals into the sheltered "safety" of our holy huddles. To be sure, fear and anger are appropriate responses to real dangers, and our world is full of real dangers. Our culture is cluttered with the destructive results of ideals and activities that flout the ideals of the kingdom of God. However, if fear and anger are the only responses, then they close us off in a fortress mentality. Consider the sorts of prepositions that typically follow words such as "fear" or "anger." We are fearful "about" or angry "toward." These impulses do not simply distance us from the dangers, but they also keep us from the people who fall victim to them. The objects of our anxiety and antagonism become outsiders to be avoided, even enemies, and we become obsessed with our own safety rather than the hurt of another. If evangelicals are called to be people who reach out, then anger and fear are counterproductive if they are our final word.

We would suggest that our fear and anger should drive us toward two other impulses that draw us out of our shelters and into service to others. Love and grief both recognize the destructive aspects of sin while helping us maintain openness to others. When someone we love becomes entangled in destructive patterns of life, we may be angry about the consequences and fearful of where they will lead, but we also grieve for and suffer with them, precisely because we know life could be different, and better. Because we love them, we want their lives to be different and better. In contrast with the distancing prepositions we place behind anger or fear, the prepositions that follow "grief" are much different. We grieve *with* or *for* those about whom we care deeply.

A few years back, our university had a time when students, faculty, and staff all came together, joined hands in a circle around the campus, and prayed. We prayed facing inward toward the campus. Although this was corrected in subsequent years, it did not initially occur to those who organized the event that an evangelical university should instinctually face outward toward a confused and hurting world, not inward toward our shelter. The world is indeed a crazy and dangerous place, and it could just be that the proper evangelical response is just as crazy and dangerous. Instead of running for cover, maybe we could put ourselves right in the middle of it all. We could become tutors in failing schools, adopt babies, and become foster parents. Perhaps we could work with recent prison parolees or in drug and alcohol treatment centers. Maybe we could do something as simple as walk across the street and put our arms around a young woman who just had an abortion or offer care for a gay couple's pets while they are on vacation. If you really want to get wild, find a burning social issue and educate yourself deeply on it. Listen respectfully to those who hold contrary views. Of course, some evangelicals are doing such things, but the "outsiders" are right. Many, perhaps most of us, remain in our safe havens. To the extent we do, we betray our identity as evangelicals.

Some Evangelicals Are Too Focused on Getting Converts

Most attempts to define evangelicalism include the movement's focus on evangelism and conversion. We strongly affirm this emphasis, and do not think seeking the conversion of others is a fault. In sharing our faith, we realize that some people will be offended no matter how sensitive we are. However, *how* we think of and do evangelism often creates more animosity than necessary. A personal experience will help illustrate how we might think more carefully about our evangelism.

Some years back, I (Steve) visited a church for the first time, and a couple days later three church members showed up at my door. After I invited them in, they asked a couple of questions about my family and my job. But it did not take them too long to get to the question they really wanted to ask. "If you were to die tonight, are you 100 percent certain that you would go to heaven?"

I am not real proud of the fact that I lied to them. I said, "Yes." I doubt that it absolves me, but there were mitigating circumstances. My preferred response would have affirmed that while I have committed my life to God in faith, faith and "100 percent certainty" did not seem to be the same thing. However, I knew that this answer would have two results. First, because my wife was gone for the evening and I was riding herd on kids ages four and seven who were already up past bedtime (a situation about which my visitors seemed oblivious), my honest response probably would have resulted in conversation that extended their television time into Jay Leno's monologue. Moreover, from past experiences, the mere fact that I teach philosophy makes my faith automatically suspect for many evangelicals, and anything other than a "yes" to "the question" would likely make it impossible to shake that suspicion for as long as I remained at the church.

While this is only a single snapshot of one "convert making" scenario built on one method, it is reasonably similar to other evangelistic approaches I have encountered. Moreover, it contains several elements that I think many people find objectionable about evangelicals. First, the few introductory questions they asked did not convey a sincere desire to learn about my family and me. This was confirmed a couple years later when someone explained that these are called "bridging questions." They were only a means to get to the questions mentioned above and a follow-up question about how I would respond to God's question about why I should be allowed entrance into heaven. Although I was sympathetic with their desire to do evangelism, I found it mildly offensive that the only thing about me that seemed to matter to them was whether I would go to heaven if I was run over by a semi later that evening. I can only imagine how insulting this would seem to people less disposed toward Christianity. No matter how good our evangelistic motives, if others do not believe that Christians really care about them, it will be difficult to explain why they should care about Christianity.

Second, one of the "bridging questions" brought out the fact that I taught in the theology school of an evangelical university a couple miles from the church. Since many of our faculty, staff, and students attend this church, the evangelism team was surely aware that we all sign a statement of faith (every year). Apparently that did not matter. The only way to be sure that I was on the team was if I answered *their* two questions in *their* way. You see, in this evangelistic method, the "bridging questions" function as a means to get to what they call the "diagnostic questions." They were there to diagnose me. In short, they were the experts who had an agenda and already knew the answers. Even the "diagnosis" of a partner Christian institution about the validity of my Christianity carried no weight with them.

It has been my experience that most people will talk honestly about almost anything if you talk *with* them. On the other hand, if you talk *at* someone and communicate a certainty that only your diagnosis could possibly be right, then it is downright disrespectful. Nothing shuts down a conversation faster.

I did not get the impression that these folks respected me enough to want an authentic conversation.

Finally, the singularity of "the questions" portrayed a pretty limited definition of evangelism. If salvation can be boiled down to a "yes" answer to two questions about the afterlife, then it communicates to outsiders that Christianity has little relevance to this life. To put it in different terms, our evangelistic methods often confuse justification with salvation. We do not want to minimize the importance of justification, which specifically deals with God's declaration of a sinful person as "just." However, the Bible is clear that salvation is a holistic process of remaking us to be more godlike in every dimension of life. It is about money, sex, social relations, intellect, how we view people who disagree with us, and every other facet of life. When we communicate to others that salvation can be reduced to checking the "yes" box on a couple of questions, it leaves the impression that Christianity is pretty trivial. In addition, the expectation that deep faith questions must have simple yes or no answers does little to combat the impression that faith is blind and, quite frankly, not very bright.

All Evangelicals Are Hypocrites.
Some Are Hypocritical in All the Wrong Ways.

One problem with placing so much emphasis on justification in our efforts toward conversion is that we often forget another aspect of salvation—sanctification. If we confess that Jesus is Lord but do not live like Jesus, we are indeed hypocrites. In this sense, Christians are inevitably hypocrites. Our endeavor to become what God calls us to be is always unfinished business in this life. The very public failures of high-profile leaders have been damaging, to say the least. However, these are only the tip of an iceberg. The shortcomings of everyday Christians often leave non-Christians wondering what sense they can make of our claims of transformed lives.

An honest response to the accusation that evangelicals are hypocritical is that we are guilty as charged. It is inevitable. While we need to hold ourselves and others accountable for this, we should not stop there. There is more to this charge of hypocrisy. People are generally charitable enough to cut some slack to those who fail to achieve high ideals, and Christianity most certainly calls us to high ideals. Given this, it may be that much of the reason Christians are branded as hypocrites does not derive from the fact *that* we are hypocritical, but *the ways in which* we are hypocritical. As odd as it sounds, if we are inevitably hypocritical, then we might spend some time thinking about the right and wrong ways to go about it.

One "wrong way" to be a hypocrite is to be selective about what we count as sin. Evangelicals have a well-deserved reputation for coming down hard on those who "drink, smoke, and chew and run around with women who do." However, you frequently get a pass if you hold grudges, make racist statements, or unfairly characterize (i.e., lie about) those who do not share your views, as long as you show up at church on Sunday and follow certain carefully selected behavioral rules. I often hear it said that Christians should refrain from activities such as dancing, watching movies, or consuming alcohol because they "damage our witness." Ironically, few outside Christianity care at all about these things, except to the extent that this reinforces their belief that evangelicals are sheltered and out of touch. In reality, our witness is most severely damaged when we act in an unloving and mean-spirited manner or when we seem inclined to believe the worst about others. It may be that many non-Christians have a better grasp on what constitutes sin than some evangelicals. While we are preoccupied with avoiding a few observable behaviors, they are watching us to determine whether we embody qualities such as kindness, love, and gentleness—dispositions at the heart of a Christian life.

A second "wrong way" to be hypocritical is to be dishonest about it. A comedienne whose name I have long forgotten used to say, "You know the [insert your own denominational name here] are doing what everyone else is. You just can't catch them at it." As we said above, there is far too much truth in the first line for Christians of all flavors. In addition, we compound the problem by creating a culture of dishonesty around our sins. We hide our real lives because we know our activities fall short of the ideal. In many cases, it is not our failures that cause us to be labeled as hypocrites, but our lack of transparency about it. Outsiders are willing to overlook a lot of flaws, but they have little tolerance for inauthenticity and dishonesty.

A final wrong way to be hypocritical is to be graceless and legalistic about it. Philip Yancey recounts the words of a friend who is a recovering alcoholic: "When I'm late to church, people turn around and stare at me with frowns of disapproval. I get the clear message that I'm not as responsible as they are. When I'm late to AA, the meeting comes to a halt, and everyone jumps up to hug and welcome me. They realize that my lateness may be a sign that I almost didn't make it."[30] If anyone should know that God's grace is the only thing standing between them and all of life's irresponsibilities and ugliness, then it should be evangelicals. It is nothing less than tragic that those who struggle with certain forms of sin are met with our arrogance rather than gracious humility. Countless evangelical congregations have "grace" somewhere in the church's name. If we decide to not change the sign in front of our church, then we should do a better job of treating others with a grace that reflects God's mercy toward us. Otherwise, the charge that evangelicals are hypocritical is deserved.

Conclusion

A friend used to quip, only half jokingly, that the church he grew up in would have no reason to exist if homosexuals, alcoholics, evolutionists, and adulterers would all just go away. His point was that his congregation was happy to define itself by what it opposed rather than what it was for. Unfortunately, his church is not the only example of this inclination. Many evangelical leaders know that identifying a common enemy is often the most effective strategy for mobilizing people. As a consequence, it is not just evangelicals who are clear about what we oppose. The word is out. Everyone knows who our enemies are, what annoys us, and what we want to eliminate from our society.[31] The question is this: does anyone know what evangelicals are *for*?

As we pointed out earlier in the book, "evangelical" comes from the word from which we get "gospel" (good news). Surely the "good news" we proclaim is more than just a laundry list of evil ideas and social trends we oppose. If our lives are transformed by Christ, then to what should we be transformed? It is not a total answer, but a good start would be to reexamine the fruit of the Spirit. In case you do not remember them, Paul gives us a list of some important ones in Galatians 5:22–23: "But the fruit of the Spirit is love, joy, peace, longsuffering, gentleness, goodness, faith, meekness, temperance: against such there is no law" (KJV).

We note this as a good beginning point for defining evangelicalism for a couple of reasons. First, when characteristics such as love, peacefulness, and goodness grow in us, other characteristics—meanness, thoughtlessness, and dogmatism—diminish. It is not very easy to be dogmatic or mean at the same time that we are being gentle and loving, which should tell us something about the spiritual status of dogmatism or meanness. The second reason is that the fruit of the Spirit exerts centripetal energies. We are instinctively drawn *toward* those who are joyful and longsuffering (patient). By contrast, most of us do not find dogmatism or willful ignorance compelling attributes. Instead, they exert centrifugal forces that push others away; to put it more bluntly, they are repulsive qualities. It is impossible for us to frame any justification for preserving evangelicalism if it is built upon that which is centrifugal and repulsive. However, if evangelicalism is grounded in the sort of fruit about which Paul speaks, then it will give the world a glimpse of all that is good, beautiful, and compelling about the Christian life.

Our suggestion that developing the fruit of the Spirit is an important antidote to meanness, foolhardiness, and doctrinal narrowness comes with an added bonus. We noted above that evangelicals often disagree on doctrine. However, we have yet to see a "Four Views" type of book that outlines differing evangelical positions on the fruit of the Spirit. We do not think this is because the issue is insignificant. Instead, we suspect that such a book has not appeared because evangelicals simply do not disagree about the virtues that should characterize the Christian life. In fact, we have argued that, when we are at our best, evangelicals have coalesced around a renewal that encourages this sort of fruit.

As a dad, I am thrilled that my two kids have been surrounded by "fruit of the Spirit" sorts of evangelicals who have loved, supported, challenged, and nurtured them. The good qualities we mentioned about evangelicals toward the beginning of the chapter have been manifest in the lives of these Christians. Nevertheless, I have concluded that one of the most important things I can do for my children during church is to hold their hands or put my arm around them. I will keep this up as long as their early adolescent sensibilities will tolerate such public displays of parental affection because I know that, sooner or later, someone in the church will likely hurt them deeply by some stupid, mean, or dogmatic action. My hope is that my attempts to mediate the love of Christ through my physical expressions will be sufficient to override the pain so many inflict under the banner of Christianity.

Throughout this book, we have tried to communicate that evangelicals can and do make different theological and social commitments. Beliefs about inerrancy, the schedule for Jesus' return, evolution, or political affiliations do not go to the heart of evangelicalism. That is not the case with qualities such as maliciousness, stupidity, or a doctrinaire attitude. They are not a variant on the gospel we are to proclaim. They stand in opposition to the essence of our message. The good news is that we see glimmers of the sort of life that evangelicals are called to, manifested as graciousness, kindness, and thoughtful engagement with the world. The bad news is that these characteristics are not the first thing the new atheists and many others think of when the word "evangelical" comes to mind. Adding to the bad news is that some evangelicals use their faith as a justification for acting in ways that are mean, stupid, and dogmatic. That all too often we live in such a way that causes others to equate evangelicalism with these attributes is a tragedy that ought to compel repentance and penance.

3

Evangelicals Are Not All
Waiting for the Rapture

I (Don) was a junior high school kid when the Six-Day War occurred in 1967, and Israelis captured Jerusalem from the control of Arab neighbors Jordan, Egypt, and Syria. Almost immediately, end-of-the-world doomsayers started coming to my church. If they had been there before, I do not remember them. But they came in droves after the Six-Day War, also known as the Arab-Israeli War, packing huge posters that lined the walls of our church and sprawled from the inside of the sanctuary to the narthex. The pictures were graphic, illustrating literalistic depictions of the Book of Revelation and prophesying that Jesus would return any day to secretly rapture believers and kick off seven years of unthinkably horrific tribulations! Some said that Jesus would return by 1974, since that would approximate one generation (thirty years) after Israel became a nation in 1948. Others cautioned against setting dates, since additional preconditions needed to occur; for example, the rebuilding of the Jewish temple in Jerusalem, proclamation of the gospel to all nations, and so on. Still, there was a heightened sense that Jesus' *parousia* (or second coming) would soon occur!

Expectation of Jesus' return was heightened by songs by Christians, such as Larry Norman, who in 1969 dramatically sang, "I Wish We'd All Been Ready." For those who miss out on a secret rapture, expected by many who anticipated Jesus' second coming, the song ends powerfully with, "You've been left behind." Those words were given new life by the enormously popular *Left Behind* series of novels by Tim LaHaye and Jerry Jenkins, which started in the 1990s and continues today. I also remember being traumatized by the scary 1972 movie *A Thief in the Night*. That movie graphically described what would happen when the rapture occurred. Its formula of speculation and fear whetted the appetites of millions, inside and outside churches, who craved the fantastic and seductive notion that they could predict the future!

In 1970, Hal Lindsey wrote *The Late Great Planet Earth*, which forecast the imminent end of the world.[1] It was the best-selling nonfiction book, other than the Bible, during the 1970s. Since that time, many evangelical Christians expectantly examine national and international tragedies as portents of the end times. With a sense of *Schadenfreude* (German, "enjoyment obtained from the troubles of others"), some welcomed "wars and rumors of wars . . . famines and earthquakes"—all signs of the coming "of the end of the age" (Matt. 24:3, 6, 7). The concept of "end times" (or "the last things") comes from the Greek word *eschaton*, from which we get the theological term eschatology—the study of the end times. Since the mid-nineteenth century, evangelical Christianity has been influenced by dramatic conjectures about the end times promoted by premillennial eschatology. This was popularized by Lindsey, the earlier Scofield Reference Bible, and the *Left Behind* series of books and movies, which expected a rapture that will secretly remove Christians from the suffering of end-time wars, famines, earthquakes, and other cataclysmic manifestations of tribulation and divine wrath before the public return of Jesus, who initiates his thousand-year reign (or millennium) on earth (see Revelation 20).

This rapture-oriented theology swept through the ranks of evangelical Christians, starting in the latter half of the nineteenth century. It was reinforced by the growing sense in the early twentieth century that Christianity was being nudged to society's margins. As a result, earlier optimism that the world would be increasingly redeemed was replaced by a sense of despair (and more than a little anger) about the trajectories of history and the belief that it was headed hell-bent for an apocalyptic end. As we move toward the present, the hype that surrounded end-times hoopla was encouraged by the secular media as well as Christians, churches, and denominations. Predicting the future sells! News outlets love to focus on doomsayers, and moviemakers discovered that movies about the end of the world, the Antichrist, demons, and celestial battles made a lot of money, especially since it seems evident they wasted little cash on hiring real actors.

Be that as it may, not all evangelical Christians bought into end-times expectations and speculation. It was not a part of their historical theological beliefs, and the values and practices prompted by a rapture-watch were not considered biblical, wise, or just. Of course, these evangelical Christians did not always feel free to voice their questions and concerns, lest they be labeled doubters of Jesus' second coming, or naysayers against prophecy—prime candidates for those who would be "left behind"!

Expecting Jesus, But Not Necessarily When, Where, and How

While many evangelical Christians do not believe in premillennial eschatology, most of them agree that we should expect the physical return of Jesus. After all, Jesus clearly told his disciples that he would come again (Matt. 16:27; 24:30; 25:31; Mark 13:26; 14:62; Luke 12:40; 21:27; John 14:3). This promised return was attested to by angels (Acts 1:11) as well as the apostles (Acts 3:20–21; 1 Cor. 11:26; Phil. 3:20; 1 Thess. 1:10; 3:13; 4:16; 2 Thess. 1:7–10). It would be the second coming of the Messiah!

However, non-premillennialists shy away from specifying when, where, and how it will occur. Jesus was not forthcoming on the particulars, although he made a number of suggestive comments. He was mostly concerned about exhorting his followers to be ready at all times—to live as if he might return any day: "Keep awake therefore, for you know neither the day nor the hour" (Matt. 25:13).

Even though premillennialism is not the unanimous choice, many are surprised to discover that there is more than one view of eschatology, especially among other evangelicals. One big reason for this is that premillennialists spend a lot more time talking about eschatology than those who hold different positions. This is natural because many of them believe that our generation will be the last. The urgency imposed by this expectation gives their eschatological views a more prominent place in their teaching. As a result, the assumption that premillennialism is the default view is perpetuated by pastors, churches, denominations, Christian books, radio and television talk show hosts, and others, who give only one interpretation of the Bible and what they believe it says about the end times. They do so out of earnest conviction, but they also may do it out of ignorance of the alternatives or the presumption that these alternatives are dangerous and should not be aired.

In reality, a number of eschatological views were held by Christians long before the relatively modern phenomenon of rapture-oriented theology. Historically speaking, prior to the nineteenth century virtually no Christians believed in a secret rapture that would occur in addition to and distinct from Jesus' second coming. Other views were dominant. Today it can be easily argued that the majority of Christians worldwide still do not believe in a rapture, since most Christians are a part of Catholic and Orthodox churches, which do not affirm premillennial eschatology. It is probably also true that most Protestants do not believe in a rapture, since Anglicans, mainline churches, and other Protestant traditions around the world affirm alternative eschatological views. Even among evangelical Christians, it can be argued that premillennial and particularly pretribulational eschatology that emphasizes a secret rapture is not as prevalent as the popular literature and TV evangelists might indicate. Although it is difficult to assess numbers, many evangelicals opt for alternative views of eschatology and increasingly point out difficulties with rapture-oriented theologies.

While the past century has been the first in which a sizable number of Christians have adopted premillennial-pretribulational eschatology, it certainly has not been the only century in which Christians have thought about the subject. This chapter will provide a glance at a broad spectrum of Christian eschatological views. In addition, we want to examine how these eschatological ideas might shape the way we live. Evangelicals are not always aware of the practical implications (practice) of our theological beliefs (theory), nor how the day-to-day practice of our lives may conflict with our purported beliefs.

If we desire to have integrity between our beliefs and our actions, we need to examine how our eschatology shapes the way we live. Do evangelical Christians live and plan their lives as if Jesus will come today or tomorrow? Should they? If so, are we aware of how zeal for the end times may distort Christian values and practices in ways that are actually contrary to Scripture? Are we aware of the potential implications of our views on the international stage? These and other questions need to be answered with some historical perspective, so we now turn to a discussion of the varieties of Christian views of eschatology.

Premillennialism, Amillennialism, and Postmillennialism

The most notable forerunners and early leaders of evangelicalism—Luther, Calvin, Wesley, Whitefield, Edwards—said nothing explicitly about premillennialism, much less a rapture. They would likely be rather puzzled by these because such beliefs are relative newcomers to the history of Christian beliefs about the end times. Historically, most Christians—including evangelical Christians—affirmed a view called amillennialism. Although the prefix (a-) implies that they do not believe in a millennium, advocates argue that the millennium in Revelation 20 is a symbolic reference to the age of the church (thus, many advocates prefer "realized millennialism" rather than amillennialism). This interpretation is based on the binding of Satan in Revelation 20:1–2, which ushers in the millennium. Amillennialists view this as a parallel to Jesus' words about the binding of Beelzebub and the coming of the kingdom of God in Matthew 12:27–29. In this passage, Jesus speaks of Beelzebub's/Satan's binding as a done deal, an event initiated in his Spirit-empowered ministry, not something that will occur centuries into the future. Thus, amillennialists believe that we also experience the kingdom of God in the present under the guidance of the Holy Spirit, and look forward to Jesus' second coming, the resurrection of the dead, and eternal life. However, they do not speculate about the timing and exact nature of these future events because Scripture provides insufficient data for conjecture.

Augustine is often cited as the most important early advocate of amillennial eschatology and, like most subsequent Christians, he considered premillennialism to be unreasonably speculative. The year after Augustine's death, the Council of Ephesus in AD 431 condemned belief in a literal, future millennial kingdom of God on earth as superstitious and heresy.[2] From the time of Augustine forward, the overwhelming majority of Christians throughout church history have echoed this rejection and affirmed amillennialism. The dominance of amillennial eschatology continued through the establishment of the Catholic and Orthodox churches, the Protestant Reformation, and evangelical revivals of the seventeenth and eighteenth centuries. Martin Luther, Thomas Aquinas, John Calvin, Anthony Hoekema, and J. I. Packer are some of the more well-known advocates of amillennialism.

Premillennialists have a different interpretation of church history. They argue that premillennialism was the dominant view of Christians prior to the time of

Constantine and the legalization of Christianity in the Roman Empire in the fourth century. Prior to that time, premillennialism was thought to dominate, since Christians talked about the visible, physical return of Jesus and of the reign of God, represented by references to the millennial kingdom. Examples of ancient Christian authors to whom premillennialists appeal include Justin Martyr, Irenaeus, Methodius, Lactantius, Tertullian, and Hippolytus of Rome. Given this information, premillennialists consider Augustine and others like him guilty of distorting biblical Christianity and suppressing widely held truth among ancient Christians and churches. This suppression represented one more example of the "Babylonian Captivity" from which Christians and churches suffered due to the enculturation of Christianity after the time of Constantine. Under growing influence of the Roman papacy, Christianity was thought to be progressively torn from its biblical moorings.

Of course, premillennialists are not the only ones to expect a visible, physical return of Jesus and of the reign of God. Although Christians may not believe that the Bible provides meticulous details about the end times, that does not mean that they symbolically interpret everything. On the contrary, most Christians in church history expected the return of Jesus, reign of God, resurrection of the dead, and eternal life. The fact that not everyone agreed with regard to the details about Jesus's second coming meant that they disagreed about everything!

Moreover, Augustine was not the only one to promote a more amillennial-oriented view of eschatology. Other ancient Christian authors with similar views include Origen, Dionysius of Alexandria, and Eusebius. There was no conspiracy to undermine biblical teaching.[3] In time, however, certain interpretations of the Bible superseded others, just as the ancient Christian councils advocated for the truth of other theological teachings such as the incarnation and Trinity. Christians expected the return of Jesus and the reign of God, but they discouraged date setting and other speculations about the millennium and end times.

Occasionally, other millennial views appeared. Postmillennial views found advocates among the Anglican and Puritan traditions soon after the English Reformation and are held today among some evangelical Christians. Postmillennialists agree with amillennialists with regard to how they interpret apocalyptic literature, especially the Book of Revelation. Scripture affirms that Jesus is coming again, but it does not specify when and how he will return. In the meantime, postmillennialists believe that—by the grace of God—Christians are to spread the gospel, be salt and light in the world, and generally promote the kingdom of God on earth. Because of their confidence in the presence and power of God's Holy Spirit, they are optimistic with regard to the degree to which they may Christianize the world. Postmillennialists believe that God has called Christians to establish God's millennial kingdom here and now. After God's reign is established on earth (Revelation 20), then Jesus will come again (Revelation 21–22). The most prominent evangelical advocates of postmillennialism are the Princeton theologians Charles Hodge and B. B. Warfield, and Loraine Boettner.[4]

The variant of premillennialism often associated with evangelicalism today goes by a label that is a real mouthful—dispensational, pretribulational premillennialism. This view seems to have arisen first among Plymouth Brethren in Britain during the early nineteenth century. Their ideas found few followers until the British evangelist John Darby emerged as a promoter of this theology during the latter half of the nineteenth century. A critical step in the growth of this view was the publication of the Scofield Reference Bible, which incorporated dispensationalism and this version of premillennial eschatology into its study notes. The Scofield Reference Bible became very popular among conservative Christians and thus a formative influence in shaping the eschatological views of many evangelical Christians.

The dispensational piece of this theology refers to the belief that the Bible divides history into a series of periods, or dispensations (classical dispensationalism envisioned seven one-thousand-year dispensations). Each of these eras is thought to be marked by the unique way God works within history. The millennium referred to in Revelation 20 is considered to be the seventh and last of these one-thousand-year periods. However, before this dispensation begins, the secret rapture will occur (hence, pretribulational), followed by seven years of the Great Tribulation, culminating with the return of Jesus and the establishment of the millennial kingdom (hence, premillennial).[5] Given the strongly chronological orientation of dispensational theology in general, painstaking detail was given to a literalistic interpretation of the Book of Revelation and other apocalyptic literature, speculating about the who, what, when, where, and how of the last days leading up to Jesus's return. Biblical passages were synchronized with current events and contemporary individuals and were reproduced in charts, posters, and eventually PowerPoint presentations.

While the pretribulational form of premillennialism is familiar to many evangelicals, we should recognize that premillennialism is not a single view but one that takes on a variety of permutations. Before the rise of pretribulationism, post-tribulational premillennialism emerged among the Millerites and subsequent Adventists in the early nineteenth century. They believed that a supernatural gathering of believers would occur after times of tribulation (post-tribulationism), when Jesus visibly returned to establish God's millennial kingdom. William Miller (who predicted that Jesus would return in approximately 1843) argued that 1 Thessalonians 4:15–17 portrays a public return of Jesus rather than a secret rapture. So, believers should not think they will avoid tribulation; instead, they should steel themselves in order to endure it, lest "the love of many will grow cold" (Matt. 24:12). After the tribulation, believers will be raptured into the air; Jesus will meet and return with them to earth in order to establish his millennial kingdom on earth. Because these so-called post-tribulational views were established prior to those of pretribulationism, the former is sometimes described as classic premillennialism. Pretribulationism was considered by classic premillennialists to be a more speculative and less biblical variation of premillennialism because it argued for two returns of Jesus, one secret (the rapture) and the other public (the parousia).

Further variations occurred among premillennialists in the twentieth century. For example, Harold Ockenga, founding president of the National Association of

Evangelicals, advocated a midtribulational view of premillennialism. According to the premillennialist interpretation, a period of tribulation—the so-called Great Tribulation—will last approximately seven years. Post-tribulationists believe, on the one hand, that a public gathering of believers will occur at the end of the tribulation; and on the other hand, pretribulationists believe that a secret rapture will occur at the beginning of the tribulation. In contrast with both, midtribulationists distinguish between the first and second halves of the tribulation. The first half of the tribulation (three and a half years) is thought to involve pain and suffering of cataclysmic proportions, based on what the evil people do to one another. However, the latter half of the tribulation (three and a half years) is thought to involve God's wrath on their evil. Although God permits believers to experience the evil of others, God will not make them suffer from divine punishment on the remainder of unbelievers. Thus God will rapture believers midway through the tribulation. At the end of the tribulation, Jesus will return in glory and institute his one-thousand-year reign on earth.

Why Believe in a Secret Rapture?

Pretribulationists and midtribulationists find support for the rapture primarily from 1 Thessalonians 4:17, which says, "Then we who are alive, who are left, will be caught up in the clouds together with them to meet the Lord in the air; and so we will be with the Lord forever." The words "caught up" (or "taken away") derive from the Greek word *harpazo*, and more specifically from the Roman Catholic's Vulgate translation of the Bible, which used the Latin word *raptus*, from which the eschatological concept of the rapture was coined. Those who argue for a rapture interpret the statement that Jesus will meet believers "in the air" to mean that he does not come all the way to earth. Thus, the event referred to in 1 Thessalonians is distinct from the second coming, which will be public ("in glory").

The time of tribulation derives from scriptural references to Daniel's prophecy about "seventy weeks" and how there will be, more or less, seven years of tribulation (Daniel 9, 12; cf. Revelation 11). For pretribulationists, the tribulation will occur immediately after the rapture and before the second coming of Jesus. During the tribulation, the Antichrist will rule the earth, wreaking havoc and persecution upon people. Those "left behind" may or may not be saved, depending on the particular version of pretribulationism. Likewise, depending on the version of pretribulationism, Jews will all be saved—based on God's promises to Abraham—or they will be left behind along with everyone else (Rom. 11:25–29).

How Do We Interpret the Bible?

From our brief survey above, it is evident that eschatological views among Christians diverge significantly, and all these variations are alive and well, in varying degrees, among evangelicals. So how do evangelicals, committed to the authority of Scripture, come out in such different places on this issue? The divergence between the various eschatological views comes down, largely, to disagreements about how we interpret apocalyptic literature. Apocalyptic literature pertains to passages in Scripture that have to do with the genre of (biblical) writings often associated with the end times. The Book of Revelation represents the most prominent example, but the genre also includes dream-visions in the Book of Daniel and New Testament statements by Jesus and the apostles about the end times. At the center of our disagreements about interpreting apocalyptic language is one basic problem: we have no modern analogues to this genre, so it is not immediately clear how we should read it. Given this obstacle, we will identify four areas where disagreements pop up.

The first area of disagreement is a "when" problem. The term "apocalyptic" comes from a Greek word that means "to reveal, uncover." The underlying idea is that apocalyptic literature reveals something that was not apparent earlier. However, Christians disagree about *when* this revelation occurs. Does apocalyptic literature uncover something previously hidden about God's plans to the original audience who read and heard these words, or does the meaning of the words remain hidden until sometime in the future? Amillennialists and postmillennialists argue the former—God reveals something to those who first heard these words. In general, what apocalyptic language communicates is that, despite the appearance that good has been overcome by evil, God is working behind the scenes to bring salvation. These interpreters note that apocalyptic language occurs in writings in which the immediate audience is confronted with extremely trying circumstances. For example, the author of Revelation tells us that he is in exile on the island of Patmos and is addressing churches facing severe persecution. Similarly, the original audience for the Book of Daniel faced exile and occupation. In the midst of their suffering, God's presence was not readily evident. What is revealed, then, is that despite the apparent hopelessness of the situation, God will be faithful and will ultimately prevail. In short, post- and amillennialists view apocalyptic materials as pastoral in nature, providing confidence in God's victory through the darkest of times for both the immediate audience and all who follow.

In contrast, premillennialists argue that the message of apocalyptic literature was hidden to the original readers. To be sure, it communicates hope that God will be victorious over the forces of evil. However, the full meaning comes into focus only generations later as historical events unfold toward their apocalyptic climax. This approach understands apocalyptic literature as predictive. It offers a preview of eschatological events for faithful readers who correctly discern "the signs of the times" and interpret Scripture accordingly. Thus, one fundamental difference in reading this material centers on whether we look at apocalyptic literature as intended primarily for an immediate audience in biblical times, or whether the audience that will most completely understand these passages is centuries removed from their writing.

The second question, one closely related to the point above, is how we interpret the symbolism of apocalyptic language. Premillennialism sometimes represents its view as the more literal reading of Scripture. This is true in some cases, such as their belief in a literal one-thousand-year millennium, which amillennialism and most postmillennialists take as symbolic. However, the difference is more complex than simply literal versus symbolic interpretation. Because premillennialists view apocalyptic materials as predictive, the actors and places mentioned in these texts are often viewed symbolically (e.g., the Dragon of Revelation 12 and Gog and Magog of Ezek. 38:2; Rev. 20:8). Indeed, approaches that claim to favor literal interpretation often relish in speculating about imagery in the Book of Revelation: Who is the Antichrist? (Henry Kissinger was the frontrunner when I was growing up, but Barack Obama seems to be the leading candidate today.) What constitutes the mark of the beast and what do the numbers 666 represent? (Bar-codes, computer chips, GPS?) What modern-day nations represent the armies mentioned in Revelation? Since Gog and Magog do not currently have membership in the United Nations General Assembly, what countries do they symbolize? What modern weaponry represents the fantastic creatures? and so on.

In contrast, amillennialism and postmillennialism, which are often accused of not interpreting biblical materials literally, usually draw a close connection between the symbolic language of Scripture and the immediate audience's situation. Thus, for example, some argue that the Antichrist of Revelation was a veiled reference (but one that would have been recognized by Christians of that time) to Caesar, who persecuted the church at the end of the first century. Similarly, post- and amillennialists would remind us that there is ample evidence that the church, from the time of Augustine, understood the millennium as a symbol of God's present reign amid the turmoil of the age. They argue that these words were similarly understood by those who first read Revelation during the suffering and persecution they faced at the end of the first century.

A third disagreement in the interpretation concerns how we use the various snippets of apocalyptic literature within Scripture. For example, premillennialism goes to 1 Thessalonians for the rapture, Daniel for data about the tribulation, and Revelation for the millennium. In this perspective, coordinating the eschatological chronology becomes a bit like assembling a jigsaw puzzle. While the meaning of these Scripture portions has been concealed for centuries, historical events gradually provide the clues that allow us to see how they all fit together. Amillennialists and postmillennialists reject this form of interpretation, arguing that nothing in these texts suggests they were intended to be lifted out of context and synchronized with passages elsewhere in Scripture. Instead, they remind us that texts such as Daniel and 1 Thessalonians were not combined into the book we know as the Bible until well after their composition. Thus, they argue that when we pull bits and pieces from these texts, it violates their integrity and causes us to obscure their message to their first audiences.

A final question is about how we interpret the urgency so often embedded in apocalyptic materials. Apocalypticism, as we noted above, deals with a revealing of that which was hidden, in this case the visible manifestation of God's reign. In many apocalyptic passages, there is a sense of immediacy in statements about the coming of God's kingdom. For example, Jesus said the following about "the end of the age" (Matt. 24:3):

> So also, when you see all these things, you know that he is near, at the very gates. Truly I tell you, this generation will not pass away until all these things have taken place. Heaven and earth will pass away, but my words will not pass away.
>
> Matthew 24:33–35

Similarly, apostolic writings emphasized the imminent return of Jesus. James said: "You also must be patient. Strengthen your hearts, for the coming of the Lord is near. Beloved, do not grumble against one another, so that you may not be judged. See, the Judge is standing at the doors!" (James 5:8–9). In the Book of Revelation, John prophetically records words of Jesus: " 'See, I am coming soon! Blessed is the one who keeps the words of the prophecy of this book.' . . . The one who testifies to these things says, 'Surely I am coming soon' " (Rev. 22:7, 20; cf. 3:11).

These passages certainly promote a sense of urgency with regard to the end times. But what is the significance of apocalypticism, if it was predicted almost two thousand years ago? To what degree should first-century urgency about the end of the world continue today? Do the words lose a sense of immediacy and literal, predictive clout, since the expectations of Jesus' second coming have remained unfulfilled for so long? Amillennialists and postmillennialists argue that the language of urgency functions as a reminder to be in a continuous state of anticipation and readiness for Christ's return. For those who embrace premillennialism, words that anticipate the imminent return of Christ are intended for the final generation of Christians. More than a few contemporary premillennialists believe that we are that final generation and should expect Jesus to return soon. Therefore, the message of apocalyptic literature for the last generation is twofold. While believers have always had a mandate for evangelism, the urgency to spread the gospel has never been greater. Similarly, the implications for the nonbeliever are dire. God has made the time of the rapture known: repent now or face the dreadful calamities of the Great Tribulation.

The previous sentence reminds us that our struggle to interpret the apocalyptic language of Scripture is not a "how many angels can dance on the head of a pin?" sort of exercise. It makes, or should make, a real difference in how we live out the Christian life, a discussion we will engage in more fully below. If apocalyptic literature is primarily predictive in nature and we overlook the signs of the times, missing the opportunity to make the winning shot as the clock runs out would be a tragedy of massive proportion. However, there is also a cost if the predictive interpretation turns out to be a misinterpretation. Those who expect Jesus to return in our lifetime are not the first to think they would be the last Christians. Certainly, apocalypticism has reoccurred throughout church history, when numerous Christians, churches, and denominations expectantly awaited (sometimes sitting on the tops of hills, after having given away all their earthly goods) Jesus and the full manifestation of God's reign, only to be disappointed . . . again. Great disappointments, so to speak, occurred in the first century as well as in the eighteenth, nineteenth, twentieth, and twenty-first centuries.

Evangelicals believe that Jesus will come again—someday. Therefore, those who predict an imminent *parousia* eventually will be correct. However, evangelicals disagree about whether those who are able to predict this event will do so from correctly reading the signs of the age, or whether it will be a matter of "even a broken clock is right twice a day." Premillennial theology says that Scripture's apocalyptic language provides clues (e.g., the reestablishment of the nation of Israel or the increase of natural calamities) for the time of Jesus's reappearance. Other Christians, while confident of God's final victory and the full realization of the kingdom, do not interpret apocalyptic literature as veiled language that, when properly decoded and synchronized, gives up a time line of the who, when, and how of history's consummation. Thus, while discussions about interpretation often cause our eyes to glaze over, we should recognize that there is much at stake in how we read these important passages of Scripture.

We have attempted to show in the preceding paragraphs why evangelicals can devote themselves to a careful reading of the Bible's apocalyptic materials and come to divergent interpretations. If we stop here, we are in danger of leaving the impression that no common ground exists in how we ought to understand and apply apocalyptic literature. However, Shirley Guthrie Jr. suggests four general principles for understanding eschatology that seem to be amenable to most evangelicals, although we will disagree about where to place the boundaries on these principles.

1. We must not want to know too much.
2. Biblical language about the future is symbolic.
3. There is no one consistent biblical picture of the future, but a development in its thought.
4. The best insight we have about what God will do is found by looking at what he has done already.[6]

First, there are important things for Christians to know about the end times. We know, for example, that God has promised that death will be defeated and that those in Christ will share in his resurrection. It is human nature to desire certainty about what is to come, but—as Jesus cautioned his disciples—no one has a lock on knowing the future! Indeed, conjecture about what God has planned can waste our time and make us negligent with regard to clear-cut things God wants us to do here and now. Moreover, we should be aware of the dangers of conjecture. Some have lost faith when their expectations of Jesus' imminent return proved to be wrong. Second, most of what the Bible has to say about the end times is symbolic. Even those who claim to interpret apocalyptic literature literally find vast amounts of symbolic meaning in who the Antichrist may be, how the mark of the beast may occur, the significance of the number 666 (and other numbers), the type of modern weaponry possibly symbolized in fantastic creatures described, countries possibly involved in the final battle at Armageddon, and so on. Use of the word "symbolic" does not mean that the Book of Revelation is untrue; on the contrary, it suggests that God's ways surpass our thoroughgoing understanding of them. Third, biblical information about the future gives a trajectory in which God is in control, and we can learn more about that control as we study Scripture. But the final picture has not been fully revealed. So, we may need to be more humble and patient as we participate in God's present work in the world (and not merely wait for the end). Finally, we may not know as much as we want to know about the future. This is not out of character with what we find throughout Scripture. Story after story record times when God's people were in seemingly impossible situations without a clue about how God would come through. Similarly, we may be confident with regard to what God has planned for the future because we know how faithfully God has provided for us in the past and present!

Theory and Practice

For all the talk that evangelical Christians have about the end times, they do not always seem aware of the social, political, and economic implications of what they believe and value. They are not all that aware of the influence of their eschatological *theory* on their day-to-day *practice*, and vice versa. Let me explain. Those who zealously talk about how soon Jesus will return often live in a manner that seems inconsistent with this expectation. They start savings accounts for their children's college education, purchase homes (although a thirty-year mortgage seems like a good idea if Jesus's return is imminent), invest for the future, plan for retirement, and so on. They build businesses, churches, universities, seminaries, and other public edifices to last a hundred years or longer. They often live as if Jesus's return will not occur until well into the future, even though what they love to hear preached, taught, and written is that they should expect the rapture before the forces of natural mortality take their course. If the way people live offers a glimpse into what they truly believe, far fewer believe in the imminent return of Jesus than what we might expect.

We suspect this inconsistency is a natural response to awareness that we impose great hardships on ourselves and those around us if our timing is wrong. However, it may be that the social application of expectation of Jesus's imminent return has been more consistent. For example, in the early centuries of the United States, Christians established universities and seminaries at an astounding pace. However, with the rapid growth of pretribulational premillennialism in the early twentieth century, fundamentalists and evangelicals started Bible colleges (but relatively few liberal arts colleges) at a similarly astounding pace. Why the difference in the type of educational institutions? In large part, it resulted from anticipation that Jesus would come any day. Time was too short to educate lawyers, scientists, business leaders, and scholars. Instead, the Bible schools pumped out pastors, missionaries, and other church workers by the thousands in a last-ditch effort to save as many souls as possible while there was still time. This decision about what type of educational institutions Christians should establish makes a lot of sense—as long as you are correct about Jesus' imminent return.

Our intent is not to criticize Bible schools. The church benefits from the training that people receive from them, as long as it matches their calling. However, this choice has come at a cost. For two generations, evangelicals deemphasized Christian liberal arts and graduate education for those who have callings outside full-time church or missions work, and our ministry to the world has suffered. Perhaps even more pernicious is the attitude some adopt toward the problems of our age because of their rapture-oriented theology. Individually, those who believe in a secret rapture may not live as if Jesus will soon come, but socially, they often live as if the world is going to hell! Although the worst of tribulation and divine wrath is yet to come, there tends to be an expectation of increased problems—famines, earthquakes, wars, rumors of war, and so on. Rather than grieve over and minister to alleviate such calamities, their occurrences are welcome! Instead of working in Christlike ways to make the world better, they often seem all too happy to see the world spiral downward. Because the rapture will exempt true believers from the worst of tribulation, pain, and suffering, why worry too much about present world problems: impoverishment, homelessness, disease, hunger, and starvation? They are inevitable. Natural disasters: floods, earthquakes, and plagues? There is no stopping them. Wars? Bring them on!

These comments may sound flippant, yet adherents to pretribulational premillennialism too often encourage an almost world-denying view of the future. This fatalistically oriented view of the end times can result in disengagement from efforts to minister to present problems, needs, and suffering because positive change is not thought possible (or wanted), given their expectation of Jesus' imminent return. Indeed, making the present world better might somehow thwart or delay the *parousia*. Thus, anticipation of Jesus' second coming may diminish Christians' present participation in the world—participation that expresses God's concern for justice, care for the poor, and other socially redemptive practices advocated in Scripture and embodied in the life and ministry of Jesus. Elevating apocalyptic expectations over the social care and justice portions of the Bible results in the kind of neglect Jesus chastised among those who, so to speak, were so heavenly minded that they are of no earthly good (Matt. 25:31–46).

If it is true that Jesus will return in the next few years, then how should we live? How should our lives take a different direction if we do not expect an imminent return? Most Christians believe there should be integrity between what we believe and how we live. So, what is the relationship between one's eschatology and day-to-day life? The answer goes far beyond personal-life decisions and their implications, and even beyond social awareness and activism, or the lack thereof. It also includes political, economic, and potentially military implications. This is certainly true for the United States, and because of its influence as an international superpower, there are profound implications for the entire world. So, what are potential implications, in practice, of Christians' view of eschatology for the world and its future?

Israel, the Mideast, and Christian Zionism

Throughout church history, Christians have had conflicting views about Jews and Judaism, alternating between romanticizing, on the one hand, and demonizing, on the other hand. During periods of romanticism, Christians thought that Jews, Judaism, and indeed the state of Israel could do no wrong. During periods of demonization, Christians thought that Jews, Judaism, and Israel could do nothing right. The latter led to unjust treatments of Jews. Injustices occurred in too many places, at too many times, and in too many ways to enumerate here. From the Crusades, to the Inquisition, and most notably to the Holocaust, Christians do not have a good record with regard to the just, righteous, and loving treatment of Jews.[7]

After the Holocaust, nations worldwide established (or reestablished) the state of Israel in 1948. Regardless of the motivations behind the United Nations' establishment of Israel, its presence has become a centerpiece in eschatological watches and speculation. Predictive approaches to eschatology, such as those found in pretribulational premillennialism, have been at the forefront in supporting Israel politically, economically, and militarily. Christians around the world, regardless of their eschatology, have been generally supportive of Israel. However, some evangelical groups have taken support to the level of "Israel, right or wrong." This is often based on an interpretation of Romans 9–11 (especially Rom. 11:26) as a guarantee of Israel's salvation as a people and corresponding national privilege.

Christian Zionism is a term that is increasingly applicable to Christian activists on behalf of Israel who support expansion of Israel's political and military power, including occupation of land from past wars and expansion in the procurement of land in the future. Historically, Zionism had to do with the establishment of the state of Israel. There are Jewish as well as Christian Zionists, and Christian Zionism—generally speaking—has to do with

Christians who support the nation of Israel. However, Christian Zionism has increasingly taken on a more specific meaning, pertaining to Christians who take Old Testament promises of land to Israel as modern-day justification for the perpetual occupation of lands captured from Arab countries in past wars, and potentially the future military conquest of other Arab lands. For example, Genesis 15:18 talks about land promised by God to Abraham and his descendants: "On that day the LORD made a covenant with Abram, saying, 'To your descendants I give this land, from the river of Egypt to the great river, the river Euphrates.'" Today this "Promised Land" grant includes land in modern-day Egypt, Jordan, Saudi Arabia, Syria, Lebanon, Turkey, Iraq, and possibly Kuwait. Furthermore, Genesis 27:29b describes how Isaac blessed Jacob, later renamed Israel, saying, "Cursed be everyone who curses you, and blessed be everyone who blesses you!" The implication, Christian Zionists say, is that Christians—or anyone, for that matter—will be blessed when they support Israel. In fact, it is their religious duty to do so. Thus, Israel should be supported in every possible way. Conversely, anyone or any nation that questions, challenges, or opposes Israel should be cursed, condemned, and defeated. This may include military defeat as well as social, cultural, and religious defeat.

The sad irony, however, is that Christian Zionists do not always support Israel out of love for the country and for Jews. Instead, Israel and its future actions are merely a prelude to the end of the world, a means to an end that does not necessarily bode well for Jews. Some believe that Jews, again because of promises to Abraham and his descendents, will automatically receive eternal life. Others think that Jews must convert to Christianity, leading to a kind of Messianic Judaism that observes a Hebraic form of Christianity. Still others think that Jews will suffer in the impending tribulation, culminating in a final battle at Armageddon. Thus, the support that Israel and Jews receive from Christian Zionists does not necessarily represent the kind of support they want. Israel, for example, receives millions of dollars in support from evangelical Christians in the United States. In an ironic twist, while Israelis receive this funding in hopes of bolstering their defenses and preserving their nation, many Christian Zionists give in the hopes that this will lead to Armageddon and destruction of this world.

Christian Zionism represents the impulse to be on God's side in our relations in this world. While the aim is good, it is certainly not unreasonable to ask whether this is the best means of taking God's side. Despite good intentions, pretribulational premillennialists enable Israel to treat Palestinians unjustly. Have Palestinians done violence to Israelis? Yes. In fact, more than a few would be happy to see Israel disappear from the face of the earth. Does that justify a free pass for Israel on violations of human rights? No. Despite good intentions, pretribulational premillennialists enable militarism in the Mideast that destabilizes the region and perpetuates violence, persecution, oppression, marginalization, and neglect, all of which are lamentable for all sides involved.

Scripture seems to make it clear that taking God's side involves working for peace and justice, from the individual to the international level. It would seem that this should always be the default position for Christians. To overlook this mandate on account of a particular interpretation of a few highly contested biblical passages threatens to put us on a dangerous path. Even if one believes that the world is going to end in a fiery ball of nuclear annihilation, it is dangerous to believe that anyone has a lock on the particular time and place of the event. It is even more dangerous to presume that our role should be to accelerate annihilation. History includes some very sad examples of those who started wars in full confidence that God would enter the fray on their side, just to discover that they only facilitated widespread slaughter.

Our bigger point is this: in large part, Christians have been far too absent in offering thoughtful reflection on international issues. One of the few places evangelicals have taken notice of world affairs has been in the struggles of the Middle East. However, even here, we often do not engage these issues for the sake of peace or to ease the suffering so many experience in this geopolitical tinderbox. Instead, to put it bluntly, many evangelicals are interested in this region only because of their narrow interest in seeing a return of Jesus during their lifetimes. Surely our proclamation of Jesus' lordship over all creation has to be bigger than this.

The good news is that we see a younger generation of evangelicals who have captured the vision of a globally engaged Christianity. They are convinced that our mission as Christians requires that we jump into the middle of the biggest and messiest problems that face humanity. Whether it involves advocacy for the urban poor, fighting human trafficking, working to reverse environmental degradation, running health clinics, or a multitude of other Christian endeavors, they are impatient with the cultural disengagement of older generations of evangelicals. Many of them, recognizing the complexity of the issues they deal with, are aware that other Christians may not agree with the means by which they express their love of Christ. However, moved by their zeal for the gospel and concern for the suffering, they would rather be doing the wrong things for the right reasons than doing nothing at all.

It seems to us that these young Christians have borrowed a page from the social engagement of their evangelical great-great-grandparents. Of course, those earlier evangelicals believed that we either participate already in God's millennial kingdom (amillennialism) or are working, with the help of God, to establish the conditions for God's reign on earth (postmillennialism). Both eschatological positions easily accommodate both an expectation of Jesus's return and a focus on here-and-now ministry. However, many of our current globally and socially active younger evangelicals are committed premillennialists. So why are they more ardent about diving into cultural and global problems? Unless we assume that they all suffer from theological schizophrenia, it seems they have concluded that premillennialism does not imply a renunciation of Christian social engagement. Perhaps they are less convinced than earlier premillennialists that we are on the verge of Jesus's return. In any case, they are not sitting in the rapture waiting room to catch the next flight off the planet. Whatever the reason for this unwillingness to turn a blind eye to suffering, injustice, corruption, starvation, and all the social evils that grieve God, we find it a refreshing change from the world-denying tendencies found in many quarters of evangelicalism today.

Conclusion

Like a lenticular print, the impression one gets of evangelical eschatology is determined by our angle of vision. The picture most commonly seen portrays evangelicalism as synonymous with pretribulational premillennialism. It is not hard to see why this is the only way many view eschatology. This is, in fact, a position held by millions of evangelicals. On a popular level, many people—Christians and non-Christians—are convinced, or at least influenced, by books, movies, and websites dedicated to the rapture and Armageddon. Moreover, there is a certain "wow factor" to a theology that envisions mysteriously missing neighbors, the anguish of those left behind, global calamities, and full-blown international warfare, all just over the horizon.

However, when the picture is turned to a slightly different angle, we find that most theologians, church leaders, churches, and denominations do not buy into this view of the end times. This is certainly true worldwide when you consider that most Christians tend toward amillennialism—which holds that Jesus will come again, but that the Bible is not literally and historically predictive of how it all will unfold. Most evangelical organizations, congregations, and denominations do not commit themselves to an institutional stand on a particular version of eschatology. For example, only about 30 percent of the member denominations in the National Association of Evangelicals affirm belief in premillennialism, much less belief in pretribulationism.[8]

In contrast, the overwhelming majority of member denominations reflect the NAE's own affirmation of Jesus's "personal return in power and glory,"[9] while minimizing details of when and how he may return. Similarly, most evangelical universities and organizations do not identify any specific eschatological model as the official theological stance of their body. Might there be those within these groups who personally expect a pretribulational, premillennial view of eschatology? Of course; it is not only possible, but probable. However, the majority of these evangelical groups prefer to allow their members latitude with regard to what is believed about the end times.

As is the case on so many doctrinal topics, there is no evangelical consensus on eschatology. We do not even agree on how much effort we should direct toward the subject. Some evangelicals are willing to leave their conclusions open-ended and are comfortable with a simple expression that God will prevail over evil and death. Others would like to nail down a specific position. For those in the latter group, there is no shortage of books and websites that advocate for one eschatological position or another. We think it would be a good idea to spend some time looking at a few, since we have only skimmed the surface of eschatological options. However, advocacy of one position to the exclusion of others has not been our goal. Instead, we have aimed to raise awareness about the variety of eschatological views held by evangelicals, examine some of the factors that lead to differences in the interpretation of Scripture's apocalyptic writings, and reflect on the implications of our eschatology on our lives and actions. We would like to conclude with some modest suggestions about where we might go from here in thinking through this important topic. Because evangelical views vary greatly on the matter, we would like to start with some proposals for amillennialists and postmillennialists, then offer some suggestions for premillennialists, and conclude with comments aimed at all evangelicals.

Several months ago I presented a paper at a conference on Christian Zionism, and I was struck by the realization that, although premillennial, pretribulational, rapture-oriented eschatology does not represent all evangelical Christians, alternative eschatological views (I'm talking to you, my amillennialist and postmillennialist friends) have not been presented with sufficient detail, persuasiveness, and hope to captivate and inspire people. You frequently complain that premillennialists are preoccupied with the last days, but you too often go to the other extreme and never speak of it at all. Amill and postmill folks are inclined to grumble about how the premill church down the street has a perpetual sermon series on Revelation. Fair enough. But when was the last time you had a single sermon from Revelation or discussed eschatology in a Sunday School class? Both amillennialism and postmillennialism have long histories and are blessed with competent and godly advocates. But the odds are very high that you do not know these positions nearly as well or advance them with as much vigor as premillennialists do. You have some work to do.

Second, even if you do not agree with the assessment that Jesus's *parousia* is right around the corner, perhaps amillennialists and postmillennialists should catch some of the evangelistic zeal that seems to be in greater supply among your premill cousins. You may not like the "this world is not my home" tendencies of those expecting to be raptured before their eight-year-old graduates from high school, but it is also possible to get a bit too comfy here and lose the urgency of our evangelicalism mandate. Jesus might not return tomorrow—but, then again, he might!

To premillennialists we would suggest that it is helpful to pay more attention to history. First, you probably noticed that two thousand years have passed since the birth of the church. While Jesus could return any time, two thousand years of history indicates that it is possible the church may be around for another two thousand years. If your theology precludes the possibility that you might well be sticking around this planet for the long haul, the impact of the gospel will be impaired. Second, evangelical history reminds us that evangelistic zeal is not dependent on belief in Jesus's immediate return. There are good reasons to spread the gospel even if Jesus's return may be on hold for a few more centuries. Moreover, when the emphasis is placed on getting saved while there is still time, we often convey the idea that Christianity is about being saved *out of the world* instead of being saved *for service to the world*. This shortchanges the gospel. Finally, Christian history reminds us that premill/pretrib theology is a relative newcomer, true even when the scope is narrowed to evangelical history. Yet we know of no one who argues that premillennialists should not be considered evangelical or allowed membership in their church. However, some premillennialists use their eschatology as a filter to determine who may join their churches, attend their universities, or be considered a "true" evangelical. We believe that some historical perspective should prompt a rethinking of these sorts of policies.

Christians of all kinds need to remember that eschatology is a broader category than simply a few years of events leading up to a millennial reign. It includes, first and foremost, the belief that "Christ has been raised from the dead, the first fruits of those who have died" (1 Cor. 15:20). Through him, we already participate in his kingdom as "citizens of heaven," although this citizenship is not fully realized until we share in Christ's resurrection. The climax of the Bible's teaching on the last things is when the powers of death are ultimately defeated (1 Cor. 15:26) and God is "all in all" (1 Cor. 15:28). Viewed in this broader context, the primary responses that Scripture's eschatological teaching should evoke are confidence, hope, and gratitude, not fear and anxiety.

We would suggest that perhaps the visual and symbolic language of apocalyptic literature might provide some cues for how we should express our hope for the future God has in store for us. Rather than focusing on decoding the Bible's language so we can identify the earthly players and plot future events on our Day-Timers, we might better express through imaginative means our hope of the unimaginable things God has prepared for those who believe. The beauty and mystery of Revelation's language may tell us that its truths should be dramatized, artistically illustrated, and set to music and poetry. Unfortunately, evangelicals have been far too uncomfortable with employing artistic means to communicate the gospel. However, C. S. Lewis represents an astounding example of one who helped people focus on what their lives may be like in the future, especially after death. In both his theologically oriented books (e.g., *Mere Christianity*, *The Problem of Pain*) and his imaginative fictional writings (e.g., *The Great Divorce*, *The Last Battle*), Lewis inspired people to think about a future end time, the joy of heaven, and the despair of hell. He remains a model for how evangelical Christians may creatively and persuasively promote hope for the future, without the need to emphasize only one view of the eschaton, of heaven and hell, and of how life may be until the full manifestation of God's reign.

Christianity has so much to offer to the world both in terms of future hope and for life here and now. The vision Scripture conveys about our future hope, in which strife, privation, disease, and death are conquered, tells us a lot about our mission in the present. If the eschaton is about God's reversal of death, illness, and suffering, it seems that our task, with the help of the Holy Spirit, is to build toward that end from our direction. Thus, when I teach students about the doctrine of salvation, I try to explain how the gospel of Jesus Christ applies to more than a future life. It is directly relevant to how God wants to work in and through people's lives now, on both the individual and the social level. This seems consistent with Jesus's view of his own public ministry, which he initiates by saying, "The Spirit of the Lord is upon me, because he has anointed me to bring good news to the poor. He has sent me to proclaim release to the captives and recovery of sight to the blind, to let the oppressed go free, to proclaim the year of the Lord's favor" (Luke 4:18–19). If God is a God of miracles, then how extensively may God want to work in the lives of people and nations today—salvifically? socially? politically? economically? environmentally?

An overwhelming majority of evangelical Christians expect the personal, physical return of Jesus Christ. One could even say that they expect his imminent return. However, historically and today, the majority of evangelical churches and denominations prefer to not speculate about when and how he will return. They do emphasize the need to be ready for Jesus's second coming, and how Christians need to have Christlike lives in anticipation of his coming reign over all creation. Certainly pretribulational and premillennial views of eschatology, characteristic of dispensationalism, have had great popular appeal, but such views do not represent the whole of evangelical Christianity. It does not even come close. It would be a gross misunderstanding of evangelicalism to equate it specifically with the eschatology of dispensational theology. More general affirmations about the personal return of Jesus are far more representative of evangelical Christianity.

How then should evangelical Christians live in light of Jesus's second coming? A bumper sticker seen recently offers this advice: "Jesus Is Coming! Look Busy." While we suspect that the intent may be more cynical than we would prefer, it contains a nugget of truth. Jesus *is* coming. Therefore, we should live expectantly, anticipating the full manifestation of God's reign. We should live as if there will be no tomorrow, but should be cautious about speculating with regard to how and when the world comes to an end. In the meantime, God's Holy Spirit works in and through the lives of believers. Thus, instead of simply looking busy, we should engage vigorously in the work of God's reign. Who knows? We may be surprised with regard to the breadth and depth of what God yet wants to accomplish in the world.

4

Evangelicals Are Not All
Anti-evolutionists

"Better late than never" is almost always a wise policy, especially if you need to apologize. However, an apology offered more than 350 years after the fact puts a significant strain on the spirit of this saying. Yet it took this long for the Roman Catholic Church to get around to officially reversing its condemnation of Galileo and his ideas about the movements of the heavens.[1] His trial occurred in 1633, and he was finally rehabilitated by the church in 1992.[2]

Galileo's "crime" is well known. He advocated the idea that our planetary system is heliocentric rather than geocentric—that our planetary system revolves around the sun, not the earth. Copernicus had come to the same conclusion almost seventy-five years earlier based on mathematical calculations. Outside of some highly educated mathematicians, few people understood Copernicus's work, and he encountered little opposition. However, when Galileo determined by means of telescopic observations that our corner of space had a heliocentric structure, he was not content to let his ideas fly under the radar. He took his findings public, and they were condemned by the church. He was forced on pain of torture to recant his findings and prohibited from writing about this theory, and he spent the rest of his life under house arrest.

Looking back on the condemnation of Galileo from our twenty-first-century vantage point, it may be puzzling why Christian leaders at that time found his ideas so dangerous. Starting from early elementary school years, we teach as fact that the planets, including our own, revolve around a star we call the sun. We have never heard of a case where a teacher or school official has received a call from an irate parent or pastor wondering why such heretical, anti-Christian ideas were being propagated in the school system. Why would they? Teaching a sun-centered planetary system is not a theologically problematic theory like, for example, evolution. Or is it?

While the specific issues differ, a close look at Galileo's condemnation reveals some interesting similarities between his case and the evolution debate of today. First, at the heart of both debates was the issue of whether the proposed theory challenged the unique place of human beings in the order of creation. If the place of human habitation is not the center of the universe but only one large rock among several revolving around the sun, then this seems to demote the human race to the periphery of creation. Similarly, if evolution means that human beings are nothing more than the highly unlikely outcome of a very long series of random mutations, how can we preserve anything that sets us apart as exceptional? Second, Galileo's opponents argued that a literal reading of Scripture was incompatible with his interpretation of the universe's construction. Since insistence on a literal reading of Scripture is front and center in many Christians' rejection of evolution, this similarity should not be overlooked. A third parallel is that the Catholic Church was not alone in its rejection of Galileo's theory. Most scientists of his day considered it far out of the mainstream of good science. Over time, however, science accepted his cosmological views as settled fact. Similarly, when Darwin's theory of evolution was presented, it took some time for natural selection to move into the scientific mainstream. Now, however, few in the physical sciences doubt it as an explanatory mechanism for biological change.

These parallels between Catholicism's condemnation of Galileo and evangelicalism's fairly broad rejection of evolution should give us pause. The vast majority of Christians in Galileo's day were anti-heliocentric. They were wrong. Really wrong. Most evangelicals would probably describe themselves as anti-evolution. Are we wrong? As we noted at the beginning of the chapter, it took Catholicism over 350 years to admit that it made a bad decision in its condemnation of Galileo and his theory. The year 2209 will mark the 350th anniversary of the publication of Darwin's *The Origin of Species*. After 350 years, will evangelicalism be so overwhelmed by the evidence supporting his theory that we will be compelled to apologize?

Our question about whether evangelicals will eventually admit error on evolution is not rhetorical. Just because Christians have been wrong about one matter of science, it does not mean those who reject evolution are mistaken this time. Moreover, while we noted that analogies do exist between the Galileo affair and the evolution dispute, analogies are not the same as equivalents. The questions differ in important ways. So the question remains open. Still we need to remember that we have been wrong, and remaining entrenched in mistaken ideas has harmed the reputation of Christianity.

We will make no attempt to answer the question of whether evangelicals should or should not reject evolution, although we will try to clear up possible misconceptions about what this means. Plenty of good books (and more than a few pretty bad ones) have been written by evangelicals whose goal is to promote a particular view on evolution. We will provide resources for investigating these options in endnotes sprinkled throughout the chapter. Our goals, however, are different.

Our first objective is to identify and clarify some key issues. To be blunt, experience has shown us that far too many evangelicals have jumped the gun by adopting positions on this debate without bothering to know the real questions or options. Since the evolution issue obviously involves science and Scripture, we need to familiarize ourselves with information from both areas—not an easy task given the mountains of data coming from each direction. We will only touch on a small amount of this and completely ignore other areas because of space limitations. All we can do here is offer a taste of the complexities.[3]

Second, we want to show that evangelicals have staked out a broad range of positions on human origins. If we make any claim at all about evolution, it is that one's evangelical *bona fides* are not determined by whether or not we reject it. We will argue that evangelicals do not necessarily need to jettison evolution (which is different from saying that we should accept it), but should be much more careful about how we speak of evolution. We will also argue that evangelicals should reject *evolutionism* (which we will define below) because it deals away essential aspects of Christianity.

Our final goal involves thinking about *how* we should handle our disagreements about creation and evolution. As we have emphasized in other chapters, evangelicalism is not just about what we believe. It is also about how we treat others. In that respect, this chapter can be viewed as a practical application of chapter 2 ("Evangelicals Are Not All Mean, Stupid, and Dogmatic"). If we are reactionary, intellectually careless, and disrespectful of those who disagree, and we compromise in how we search for truth, then we betray the ideals of our faith. Quite frankly, we think evangelicals have often been guilty of all of these in discussions about evolution.

A big reason evangelicals (and non-evangelicals) frequently have been reactionary, careless, and disrespectful in the evolution/creation debate is that emotions run deep on this question. Our emotions have a valid place in this discussion because the stakes are high. However, sometimes we get so emotionally wrapped up in the matter that we lose sight of the real issues and forget how Christians ought to conduct an honest search for the truth. This is when rancor and closed-minded dogmatism take over, and no side of the debate has a monopoly on these misguided emotional responses. We will have much to say about the latter as we go along, but first we want to lay out why the subject of evolution evokes such strong emotional responses.

What Is at Stake?

No matter whether you are a six-day creationist, an atheistic Darwinian evolutionist, or somewhere in between, we all have one thing in common. We recognize that certain positions put at risk beliefs we view as absolutely vital. In debates about evolution, everyone has "a dog in the fight," an issue that is crucial. However, it is hard to come to a thoughtful conclusion unless we are clear about what those issues are, not just for us but for those who disagree with us. For evangelicals, the main issues tend to converge at two key points.

1. **Does evolution destroy the foundation for human dignity and uniqueness?** The Bible seems quite clear that, even though human beings come from dust and are mortal, we play a unique role in God's economy. This is the presupposition for almost everything we read in Scripture. Only human beings are assigned moral responsibility for actions. God's covenant is made with *homo sapiens*. We humans are called to a discipleship that is distinctive to our species. However, most do not believe that human exceptionality is grounded solely in what Scripture says. Let's face it. The Darwinist picture of human origins does not flatter most of us. We would like to think that a family reunion of even our most distant relatives would take place somewhere other than the primate section of the zoo. Moreover, no matter how biologically or genetically similar certain mammals might be to human beings, human capacities seem too distinctive to explain by a gradual and accidental evolutionary process. While orangutans may learn complex behaviors, human activities—creating music or art, writing laws, or reflecting on the meaning of the distinctions between human and orangutan capacities—seem to be qualitatively different, not just more complex variations on animal behaviors.

2. **What does the theory of evolution mean for the authority of Scripture?** Evangelicals are united by the confession that Scripture reveals God's truth, and one of the most fundamental truths of Scripture is that God is the Creator of all that exists. That is pretty basic. If evolutionary theory requires that we take God out of the picture (and some forms of evolutionary thought do just that), we obviously have a problem. Moreover, evangelicals do not claim that Scripture is *an* authority for truth, one source among others. Instead, we view the Bible as the *final* authority. We might grant scientific thought some level of authority, but if it comes into conflict with Scripture, we do not doubt Scripture's witness. Instead, it seems that our commitment requires that we reject the claims of science.

At the other end of our spectrum, we find evolutionists who agree with Christians on one thing: where one comes out on this issue is of vital importance. However, their reasons differ. We can boil down their primary concerns to two points as well:

1. **Does religion undermine the efforts of science?** Advocates of evolution remind us that those who buy into natural selection do not arrive at this decision by looking around for a theory designed to annoy Chris-

tians. Instead, they are examining the evidence and seeking the best explanation for the data. If the vast majority of biological scientists have concluded that Darwin's theory provides the clearest picture of truth on the origin of species, then respect for truth requires that we go wherever it leads us. Moreover, visualize an evangelical driving her hybrid-electric car to receive radiation treatment. On the way, she picks up her cell phone, calls her aunt in Toledo, and bends her ear about the evils of science because her son learned about evolution in sophomore biology. In short, evolutionists argue that evangelicals are often selective about science. When it produces what we want, we love it. When it comes to evolution or the age of the cosmos, though, "science" becomes the enemy. Advocates of evolution argue that the same scientific methods that allow for transcontinental cell phone calls also support belief in evolution. You cannot simply pick and choose.

2. **By insisting on Scripture's account of creation, does religion become oppressive?** The Galileo case is only one example of the church's suppression of ideas viewed as contrary to its goals. On the surface, the church seemed more interested in its own preservation than in getting to the truth. Thus, many champions of evolution raise the question of whom we should trust. Religions have a vested interest in keeping adherents in their camp. When this is the goal, the pursuit of truth sometimes takes a backseat. Science, on the other hand, does not appear to be burdened with these sorts of concerns about self-preservation, and thus deserves a higher degree of trust in its pronouncements, especially when those matters clearly fall within its expertise. In short, the argument goes, science is content to make its case by persuasion, not by imposing its ideas through force and fear.

With these basic issues in place, we can see how emotional reactions on both sides can nudge aside a clearheaded and fair-minded examination of this issue. As evangelicals, we are invested in preserving human dignity and the supreme authority of Scripture. These are not places where we can compromise and still hold to evangelicalism. Those who champion an evolutionary model of human development recognize the important contributions of scientific discovery to our lives and also have a strong emotional commitment to the free expression of honest ideas. However, when it is presented like this, most of us immediately recognize that this offers up an either/or situation that few want to buy into. A deep-seated commitment to scriptural authority and human dignity does not imply a desire to devalue science, inhibit the free flow of ideas, or oppress those who disagree. Far from it. Similarly, while a few fringe evolutionists may believe that natural selection levels off all distinctions between humans and chimps, most evolutionists are committed to human dignity. Moreover, a good number of evolution advocates do not question scriptural authority. In short, these emotional allegiances are not unique to one end of the spectrum or another. They are often shared commitments. However, if we fail to recognize these shared commitments, our emotions can take control. When this happens, it is not uncommon (on both sides of the debate) to see misrepresentations and downright falsehoods about the ideas and motives of those who disagree.

While the question of evolution and creation seems neat and tidy at the ends of the spectrum, it gets a lot messier when we try to avoid an "either Christianity or science" position. A few years back, Gallup did some polling on attitudes about creation and evolution, and the responses reflected this messiness. First, people were asked to respond to, "Evolution, that is, the idea that human beings developed over millions of years from less advanced forms of life." Some 53 percent thought this was either definitely or probably true, compared with 44 percent who considered it probably or definitely false. Next, the same group was asked to evaluate, "Creationism, that is, the idea that God created human beings pretty much in their present form at one time within the last 10,000 years." Sixty-six percent said this was definitely or probably true, while 31 percent thought it was definitely or probably false.[4] On the surface, these numbers seem illogical. How can the majority of people espouse *both* beliefs since they are stated in ways that seem to be mutually exclusive?

Perhaps the apparent incompatibility of these responses reflects a great deal of muddleheaded thinking, but we believe something else may account for this. It could be that the majority of people found something in each view they wanted to affirm, ignoring the fact that the questions, as written, did not give much room for compatibility. For example, they may agree that Scripture correctly affirms God as the Creator, but want to reserve some place for the evolutionary account as well. To some who take strong positions on the evolutionary end of the spectrum, these two things seem incompatible. Many creationists agree with this premise. However, a number of theological options reflect what seems to be indicated in the survey above, that perhaps the accounts offered by science and evolution are not irreconcilable with God being Creator. Before we get much further in our discussion, we want to offer an overview of these perspectives, which all have at least some evangelicals aligned with them.

Speaking Clearly about Evolution

One obvious function of language is to communicate ideas and beliefs. "Look out!" is sufficiently precise to warn a friend in the path of a speeding bus. In more complicated discussions, however, general statements obscure more than they clarify. This is perhaps more the case in debates about evolution than on any other subject. We have witnessed countless examples of people talking past each other because ideas were not clearly defined and expressed. If we want to clearly communicate and understand the issues in our present topic, then we need to put some definitions on the table.

The first distinction we want to make is between "creation" and "creationism." All creationists believe that God creates, but not all who believe that God creates are creationists. "Creation" is a general term that affirms that God is the ultimate origin of all things. In this broad sense, it does not assume any particular position on the means or time line by which God gives existence to the universe. In contrast, "creationism" refers to a family of theories that argue that Scripture outlines at least a sequence, and perhaps even a chronology, for God's creative process.[5] Creationism may not say too much about the way God creates, but it excludes certain processes as viable options. Most notably, creationism excludes evolutionary accounts of how humans came into being.

We referred to creationism as a "family" of theories because it branches into two main streams. "Young earth creationism" (YEC)[6] asserts that the created order is in the neighborhood of six thousand to ten thousand years old, based on interpreting the days of creation in Genesis 1 as twenty-four-hour periods and using Old Testament genealogies as benchmarks to measure backward to the time of creation.[7] While many advocates of YEC admit that this chronology puts us at odds with scientific consensus, they argue that this more literal interpretation is demanded by our commitment to Scripture's authority.

The second form of creationism, "old earth creationism" (OEC), has several variants.[8] The "gap theory" works from a translation of Genesis 1:2 that renders this verse as, "In the beginning, the earth *became* [rather than *was*, as in the KJV and other versions] formless and void." This reading allows the possibility of a significant time gap (perhaps billions of years) between the creation and subsequent decay of the original created order (Gen. 1:1–2) and a new phase that involved a renewal of creation to bring it to its present state (starting at Gen. 1:3).[9]

Another popular version of OEC is usually referred to as "day-age" creationism.[10] This position points out that the Hebrew word translated as "day" sometimes clearly refers to an era rather than a twenty-four-hour timespan (Ps. 77:2; Eccles. 7:14; Isa. 9:4; Ezek. 16:56). When scientific arguments about the age of our planet are taken into account, "day-age" creationists argue that the "days" of Genesis 1 are best viewed as epochs. Thus, the first day (or age) of creation precedes the creation of human beings on the sixth day by a long span of time, perhaps billions of years.[11] While OEC disagrees with its YEC cousins about the age of creation, they share two fundamental characteristics. Both argue that the human race is of recent origin and reject an evolutionary account of human origins (although OEC sometimes allows for evolution in other life forms).

A third evangelical option is "theist evolution" (TE).[12] TE affirms that God is Creator of all but shies away from the "creationist" label because it implies rejection of evolution. Those who hold this position confess both that God is Creator *and* that God ordains the evolutionary process as a means by which the created order (human beings included) develops. In the background of the dividing line between creationism and TE is a theological disagreement about *how* God carries out his creative work. Creationists usually see God's creative acts as interventions that interrupt the course of nature, while TE is inclined to view God as working within and through nature's processes. As in the positions above, there are variations within the TE family, most of which focus on the degree to which human beings attained their present form by evolutionary means. Some TE advocates argue that God intervenes to bring about a quantum leap that separates human beings from their biological ancestors, often expressed as the infusion of a soul. Others see an incremental and uninterrupted evolutionary process, by means of which God guides humanity to its current state.

While some evangelicals accept evolution, evangelicalism is incompatible with *evolutionism*.[13] "Evolutionism," as we use it in this chapter, is an over-arching worldview that is not a potential complement to Christianity, but a competing worldview. It offers itself as an alternative to all other worldviews, religious or secular. Evolutionism is characterized by two main features. First, it views evolutionary theory as a complete and self-contained framework for explaining every activity, trait, and capacity of any living thing. Thus, evolutionism does not simply apply natural selection to biological changes within organisms. Everything in our world—culture, religion, sports, mate selection, gender roles, why we pick our noses at stoplights, and all matters in between—is most completely comprehended through the explanatory power of natural selection. The second feature of evolutionism is a metaphysical naturalism, the view that only material realities exist. Both factors place a distinct boundary between evolutionism and TE. TE credits God with creating and directing the evolutionary process. Evolutionism, on the other hand, argues that our origins or present attributes and activities are solely the result of blind material forces functioning according to evolutionary rules.[14]

Our final bit of vocabulary work concerns the term "evolution." While most evangelicals claim to reject evolution (in theory), the reality is that no one really does (in practice). After all, evolution, in its stripped-down definition, simply means "change over time," and we are not aware of anyone who disputes the idea that things change. Thus, if we say we reject evolution, we should specify what sort of evolution we have in mind. Biological evolution provides a bit more specificity, but even here, the basic idea should not be objectionable. For example, when we hear concerns that the avian flu virus may mutate (evolve) in such a way that it can be transmitted from human to human, we are talking about the evolution of a biological organism. While we may doubt that this specific mutation *will* happen, most do not doubt that this sort of biological evolution *can* occur. To this point, we are not at the place where evolution becomes problematic for most Christians.

While most evangelicals allow for biological evolution (although they may be skittish about the word), some draw the line between micro- and macro-evolution. Microevolution refers to biological changes within a species, as in our example above. Macroevolution, on the other hand, envisions a cumulative series of evolutionary modifications that lead to the emergence of new species. In general, both young earth and old earth creationists reject macroevolution, while theistic evolutionists tend to have little problem with macroevolution (although some qualify this with regard to human evolution).

Finally, for many people, evolution only creates tensions when we get into the mechanisms by which evolution occurs. This is where Darwin comes in. It is a common misconception that Darwin originated the concept of biological evolution. Theories about biological evolution had been around long before Darwin ever wandered into a lab. (Back then it was usually called "transmutation of species" rather than evolution.) His grandfather, Erasmus Darwin, was a biological evolutionist. Many biologically minded folks prior to Darwin's publication of *The Origin of Species* (1859) were theistic evolutionists.

The specific idea that put Darwin in the spotlight was his theory of evolution's mechanism, natural selection. In very brief form, natural selection begins with the observation that organisms must compete to survive and that organisms well suited for their environment have a better chance of staying alive. If an offspring differs in some way from its parents and that mutation is beneficial for the offspring's continued existence, the bearer of this trait is more likely to survive and pass on that trait to its offspring. Over time, perhaps hundreds of generations, the changing environment leads to an accumulation of traits that exhibit sufficient distinction from the original species so that we see the emergence of a new species. Natural selection raises the question of whether it is nothing more than a blind natural process (certainly not an option for Christians) or a mechanism that God creates and governs. Some evangelicals see the latter as a theological possibility and argue that it brings science and theology together. Others argue that it is hard to see God behind a process that yields few beneficial mutations in comparison with the overwhelming percentage of mutations that are harmful or fatal to offspring.

While the distinctions and definitions in this section do not resolve our questions about human origins, we hope they accomplish one of our goals: providing clarity to the discussion and correcting some common false assumptions. Not everyone who believes in divine creation is a creationist. You can believe in evolution (and you almost certainly do) without believing in some types of evolution. Embracing natural selection does not necessarily imply embracing metaphysical naturalism or evolution*ism*. A person can believe that our planet is billions of years old and also argue that the Genesis 1 account should be read literally. A literal reading of the Bible does not preclude the presence of nonscientific genre in the biblical texts. All of these are live options among thoughtful evangelicals, although it would be hard to know this if we only listened to the voices that frequently dominate these debates. We have not made it our job here to determine which view is most likely to be right. Our task is simply to say that if you want to stake out a position in the evolution debate in a way that honors God, it is important to understand these sorts of distinctions. Otherwise, you will generate heat rather than light.

Creation, Evolution, and Interpretation

Some Christians read Genesis 1 and conclude that it refers to a six-day series of events that occurred about seven thousand years ago. Others, reading the same Bible, argue for a much older universe. Similarly, one geneticist, noting the striking similarities between human and chimpanzee genomes, may conclude that we are simply evolved apes who figured out how to invent iPhones. Another geneticist may see the human species as a reflection of the divine image, even though she is well acquainted with the same data. Why is this? The simple answer is that data and interpretation are two different things. Data has to be interpreted to get at meaning, regardless of whether that data comes from Scripture or from science. We do not know what the Bible or biology *means* for the question of origins apart from interpretation.

Some folks get very nervous about any mention of interpretation, assuming that it is the prelude to the claim that one interpretation is equivalent to any other. If this is your suspicion, then you have misinterpreted our idea of interpretation. The concept that all construals of either Scripture or science are of equal validity is disrespectful of the fundamental idea of truth, and no one actually functions in this way. It is absurd to interpret biblical or genetic data as support for the belief that legislation proposed by Herbert Hoover is responsible for the creation of the world or the genetic similarities between humans and chimps. Some interpretations are clearly wrong.

However, in other cases, the jury is still out because the available information leaves open a number of plausible interpretations. That is where many people are with the creation/evolution debate. Creation itself had no human witnesses. We cannot interview the Holy Spirit or those humans inspired by the Spirit about the intended meaning or perfect translation of the relevant texts. Science is in much the same situation. Fossils, light from distant stars, and geological strata say something, but we struggle to hear their messages clearly. Thus, if we really want to know the truth about God and creation, we need to think about how we interpret the data, especially when that information is open to different interpretations. Interpretation is not a sign of disrespect for the concept of truth. High regard for truth requires thoughtful reflection on interpretation.

One of the basic problems of biblical interpretation is that we often interpret without being aware that we are doing so. In this brief survey of Genesis 1 and interpretation, we want to examine four assumptions that we may not immediately be aware of as we read this passage. The first assumption is that a particular view of the nature of Scripture necessarily yields a certain interpretation. Some evangelicals assume, for example, that belief in inerrancy requires a literal reading of Scripture and adherence to YEC.[15] However, both turn out to not be the case. Quite a number of inerrantists believe that our universe has had a very long history.[16] Similarly, most evangelicals will say a literal reading of some Scripture passages leads to the wrong interpretation. For example, reading all of the Bible literally would mean that trees have hands capable of clapping (Isa. 55:12) and that God has at least one hand, a right one (Ps. 63:8; Mark 14:62).

The condemnation of Galileo relied in part on interpretations of Ecclesiastes 1:5 ("The sun rises and the sun goes down, and hurries to the place where it rises") and Psalm 93:1 ("He [God] has established the world; it shall never be moved").

Read literally, one would conclude that the sun revolves around an immovable earth. It seems safe to say that these words are best read as figurative language. Our goal here is not to say that we should not read Genesis 1 literally. Instead, we are simply pointing out two things. First, we do not always read Scripture literally. Sometimes we should, but at other times a literal reading distorts the meaning. This relates to the second point. We read certain biblical materials figuratively, not because we lack a high view of Scripture, but precisely *because* we have a high view of Scripture and want to understand its message properly.

Our previous point brings us to the next assumption. When we read the Bible, we usually assume that we know what sort of material we are looking at. Thus, biblical interpreters quite correctly state that we know the Psalms are poetic literature and we should read phrases such as "God's right hand" accordingly. We recognize that the genre (literary form) of the Psalms is different from the epistles of Paul, so a respectful Bible reader allows the text to inform the way it is read.

What if, however, some ancient genres are not readily recognizable today? Imagine that a space alien started monitoring our television broadcasts to learn about events on earth. To do this, the alien taps into CNN and the *Colbert Report*. The set and format of the shows have strong similarities, so the alien might suppose they are both news venues. If these are the sole sources of information about our planet, however, our inquisitive alien would arrive at some very odd conclusions. News reporting and satire both communicate information, but if the alien did not recognize the difference in genre, interpretations of this information would be sorely distorted.

This brings us back to Genesis. The text has time-designating words such as "day," "morning," and "evening." It certainly looks like something that should be read as a historical report. However, Genesis comes from a cultural context quite foreign to our own. Thus, while our idea of poetry often includes rhyme or set syllabic patterns, Hebrew poetry frequently employs devices such as parallelism. Some biblical scholars see, for example, parallelism in the structure of the creation days, in which the first three days describe preparation of an environment (light/dark, sky/water, dry land), while the next three days show the filling of that environment with inhabitants suited for these respective realms (stars/moon, birds/fish, land animals/human beings). Thus, some conclude that, rather than reading Genesis 1 as a historical account, we should read it more like a poetic expression of theological truths.[17]

Our intent is not to offer the definitive statement about the literary genre of Genesis 1. Instead, we want to show that educated representatives on different sides of this debate do not pull their interpretations out of thin air. They can agree completely that we should respect scriptural authority and demonstrate this respect by carefully examining the Bible to determine its literary form. The disagreement is about genre, and this leads to differences in interpretation. Those who view this as a more poetic genre are less inclined to read the time markers as indicators of chronology or sequence. Those who take this as more of a historical report will interpret these words in a more chronological manner.

Third, interpreters of Scripture often disagree about what Genesis 1–2 intends to teach. Some key points in these early chapters are unambiguous. The Bible clearly intends to tell us that nature is not divine, that the universe is neither eternal nor self-sufficient, and that human beings have unique duties in the created order. The brevity of this creation material also indicates that God did not intend to provide exhaustive knowledge of the origin of the universe, our planet, its flora and fauna, or the human race. That brings us to the disputed middle area. Does Scripture propose a traceable chronology that allows us to date creation to a time in the past ten thousand years, outline a general sequence of creation's stages, or provide the mechanics by which God creates humans, or are these also outside Scripture's intent?

As noted above, Genesis 1:3–2:4a speaks of a creation sequence broken into days. However, things get a bit messier with Genesis 2:4b, which says, "In the day that the LORD God made the earth and heavens." If read literally, this appears to collapse creation into a single day, and nothing in the story indicates that the creation of the first man in 2:7 occurred on a separate day. This tension within the text raises questions for some about whether the intent is to provide a chronology. At minimum, it opens the door to differing interpretations. Again, the diversity of interpretations does not arise because one party ignores Scripture while another side in the debate respects it. Each group seeks an interpretation that best gets at the biblical purpose.

Finally, a broader question of interpretation hinges on philosophical matters. Scripture claims to communicate knowledge; so does science. What do we do when truth claims appear to conflict? Should Scripture be used to rebut scientific claims? Should science trump Scripture, even invalidate it? Are there other options? These sorts of questions lurk in the background of our discussions, and our assumptions about how Scripture and science are related will shape how we interpret the data, even when we are not conscious of what those assumptions are. Therefore, we need to examine a few models of how we integrate (or do not integrate) faith and science.

The first is what we call the conflict model. In this paradigm, we can accept the findings of science until they clash with Scripture. When conflicts occur, however, Christians are compelled to follow Scripture. Many creationists take this approach, and generally support this position in two ways. First, they observe that scientific knowledge is incomplete and fallible. It was clearly wrong about the movements of the universe in Galileo's day. More recently, it was wrong about a "steady-state" view of the universe, in which it was believed that movements of the cosmos were constant and perhaps eternal. This left little room for a creation. Now, there is broad consensus among scientists for a "big bang" cosmology and an expanding universe, clearly a major shift in scientific understanding. Some creationists do not care much for the big bang because it points to a universe much older than their chronology allows, but others see it as vindication for the Bible's claim for a created universe. Thus, advocates of the conflict model believe that when science gathers enough information and fine-tunes its consensus (if it ever does), it will confirm what the Bible has told us all along on disputed questions, including human origins.

A second common element in the conflict paradigm says that perceived tensions between Scripture and science are really conflicts between Scripture and scientific *interpretation*. The conflict view allows that science usually comes to true conclusions when the data is extensive and minimal interpretation is required. However, some questions, such as our question about origins, have large evidential gaps that require significant interpretive leaps. When scientific method requires that natural events be explained by material causes (what is called methodological naturalism), any explanation that includes God will be automatically vetoed. Thus, those who adopt a conflict model say their beef is not with science, but with the assumption, widespread in science, that nature cannot be explained by supernatural causes.

A second model for understanding the relationship between science and theology is sometimes referred to as the NOMA (nonoverlapping magisteria) paradigm.[18] NOMA argues that theology and science operate in separate domains (magisteria), each of which operates according to very different rules. Science is not designed to discern truths about nonphysical realities such as God, souls, or morality. Likewise, while theology is oriented toward questions about divine reality and human worth, it is ill-equipped for modeling a DNA double helix or calculating the speed of light. Generally, NOMA argues that where the two realms overlap, they do so in particulars that are not decisive for either domain. Thus, for example, science tells us that the mustard seed is not, after all, the smallest of all seeds. On the surface, this seems to contradict Matthew 13:31–32. However, those who adopt the NOMA model argue that no great theological truth hinges on whether Scripture is technically correct about which seed is indeed the smallest.

A third model is the interaction paradigm. This view argues that God is not just revealed in Scripture. God also is revealed through creation, although less clearly than in Scripture. To the extent that we properly understand the physical universe, we gain insight into its Creator. Thus, science interacts with theology and sometimes provides correctives to it (since theology, unlike Scripture, is fallible). For example, Galileo's heliocentric hypothesis brought about changes in theology. Prior to Galileo, theologians believed that human dignity was exhibited, in part, by our location at the center of the created order. The problem, as science discovered, is that the earth is not at some cosmic bull's-eye. This did not change the belief that the human race has a special place within creation, although some feared that would be the case. (After all, was the quality of wine that Jesus produced in Cana diminished because it had previously been water [John 2]?) This discovery did, however, change the theological reasons used to support human uniqueness.

Similarly, interactionists argue that theology should inform science. For example, scientists are prohibited from injecting active viruses or carcinogens into humans to do medical research, even if the aim is to find cures. Medical researchers certainly have the know-how to do these sorts of things, but science relies on moral values to set limits on its actions. However, these rules, and the ethical values behind them, do not come from science itself. They come from places such as theology, which provides science with foundations and limitations that should shape its methods and motives. Thus, science and theology should rely on each other for support, correction, and guidance.

It is not difficult to see that commitment to one of these paradigms will cause us to gravitate toward certain interpretations. The conflict model sets the final authority of Scripture over against the incompleteness and the naturalistic assumptions of modern science, so scientific claims are most likely to be viewed with suspicion when a perceived conflict arises. Evangelicals who accept the interactionist model do not doubt the Bible's authority. However, they recognize that our theology is fallible and believe that science can help fine-tune our interpretations. The NOMA model argues that science and theology address two very important dimensions of human existence, and that we will distort the nature of either of these areas of study if we try to make them play by the rules of the other. As we have pointed out, each of these models is found among evangelicals, and each influences the way we read Scripture and understand its relationship to science.

There is also a fourth model, one that is not an option for evangelicals because it absolutizes the evolutionary account. The fourth paradigm is simply a version of the first one, the conflict model, but with a twist. This modified conflict model is adopted by evolutionism, which argues that, in the event of conflict between science and theology, we dump the theological claim. Their argument for preferring science over theology is simple. Scientific claims can be verified or falsified. In contrast, theology does not provide a public, objective, or experimental method for testing its claims. Therefore, when the vast majority of scientists find that natural selection makes sense of the data, sound reason requires that we reject theology's claim that the human race is a special creation of God.

It is not hard to understand why some people find this modified conflict model attractive. Reasonable people recognize that science provides countless benefits. Some of us would not be alive today except for recent medical advances. Because of what science has brought us, information that might have taken months to track down and compile is available at our fingertips. We can get almost anywhere in the world in less than a day, we can communicate with almost anyone anywhere instantaneously, and our teeth are whiter. Science's tools offer tremendous explanatory power for analyzing the physical universe and widely agreed-on methods, centered on observation and experimentation for testing and verifying its claims. Nevertheless, many within the sciences, perhaps most, reject the philosophical assumptions behind the modified conflict model, despite the impressions one might get from evolutionism's advocates. It is not that these scientists reject science. Instead, they reject evolutionism's claim that science in itself is sufficient to replace theology and stand alone as a comprehensive worldview. They recognize that, for all its good, science is limited.

What Science Cannot Do

Clint Eastwood's movie characters are usually good for some pearls of wisdom. As "Dirty Harry" Callahan (*Magnum Force*), Eastwood gives us useful guidance when he says, "A man's got to know his limitations." Not bad counsel, both for individuals and practitioners of any discipline. Science has limitations.[19] If we do not recognize them, we get into trouble. First, science cannot prove such foundational ideas as the uniformity principle, the belief that the laws governing change in the universe have remained constant throughout time. This is an assumption, one that is essential to the very foundation of the sciences. To call it an assumption does not imply that we should reject the uniformity principle, but we should be aware that science has no means of proving it.

Similarly, science may be very good at explaining how certain things attained their present state, but we are not aware of any scientist who claims to know the ultimate origin of things or that science even has the tools for this task. Thus, for example, Darwin's *The Origin of Species* may or may not be an accurate explanation for how new species arise from natural selection. The "big bang" may or may not be a good theory for illuminating the very early stages of our universe. Neither, however, gets us to the ultimate origin of anything. *Even if* human ancestors were primates, we would need to know where the primates came from, and where the ancestors of the primates came from, and so on. *Even if* an incredibly hot, super-compact energy bundle exploded to start the chain of events that brought about the present configuration of our universe, science offers no explanation of why that energy was there, or why the stuff that was the source of that energy existed, and so on.

Finally, science cannot get at value and purpose. Chemistry can explain how rotting vegetation and critters become crude oil. However, whether we should place more value on a million-barrel pocket of crude oil or a million people is beyond chemistry's scope. A neurologist can provide some intriguing insights into what regions of our brains are stimulated when we have romantic feelings, but this does not explain the purpose of love. We can observe things such as size, weight, and velocity, but no microscope is powerful enough to observe goodness or purpose. We may evaluate something we have seen as good or purposeful, but these are *evaluations* of our observations, not observations *per se*. Scientists often have to make these types of evaluations, but when they do, they move outside the realm of science.

When evolutionism offers itself as a complete worldview built wholly on science, it misleads us. To answer some of the most basic questions of human life—questions about ultimate origins, ethics, and purpose—it must smuggle in ideas from outside science. Why we should pursue certain goals in life, judge a sunset beautiful, declare murder wrong, and a myriad of other ideas are not questions that can be answered by scientific tools or methods. Thus, as "Dirty Harry" might say, by attempting to transform evolution into an all-encompassing worldview, evolutionism is claiming for science certain capacities that fail to acknowledge its limits. Ironically, then, advocates of evolutionism show disrespect for the very scientific disciplines they claim to honor.

Dealing with Evolution and Other Complex Questions

We have covered a lot of ground in a short space, raising just a few of the fundamental factors that beg for consideration if we are to make an informed decision. Even with this, we have barely scratched the surface. The complexity of the issue is not just a matter of digesting large amounts of information from one direction. Instead, theology, science, and philosophy all intersect here, and this convergence requires that we carefully consider all these factors in coming to a conclusion. Moreover, we often confront this mountain of materials with little more than a couple of biology or chemistry courses under our belts and little if any working knowledge of the languages of Scripture, its historical context, the various literary genre of Scripture, and a host of other interpretive tools. Add to this the fact that few of us have carefully examined the philosophical assumptions behind our understanding of the Scripture/science nexus, and we can quickly feel overwhelmed.

Confronted by this complexity, many are satisfied to come to their conclusions by means of a surrogate. Here is how it usually works. People recognize that these are tricky issues and do not know how to start untying the knots, or they are, to be blunt, too lazy to think them through. So they find the "really smart person" (RSP) to be their surrogate. The first qualification for the RSP is that he or she is really smart about science, or at least seems to be. (It is hard for most of us to know for sure.) The second qualification is that this RSP supports whatever position the inquirer already believes. We do not need to have a clue about what the RSP's arguments really are because, after all, we are not the RSP. However, we have the warm glow of believing that our position is intellectually respectable because some RSP believes it.

The problem with attempting to resolve the evolution/creation debate by surrogate is that this game can be, and is, played from every position on the debate's spectrum. Regardless of whether the car in front of you has the Darwinist two-legged mutant fish bumper sticker or the "Truth" fish swallowing the Darwin fish bumper sticker, it is unlikely that either driver has actually read *The Origin of Species* or thought carefully about differing views on the matter. However, both could list all the RSPs who support their respective views. Letting really bright proxies fight our battles does not solve anything because we still have to make the decision about which RSP is right. Every position we have outlined above has several of them.

If relying on an RSP to resolve the evolution question is a dead end, then where do we go from here? It is not really permissible simply to punt on the debate, because it involves some of the most important questions the human race encounters—the origin of our universe, the manner in which God works, the foundation for human dignity, and the authority of Scripture, just to name a few. Even if adults can avoid the issues, our children cannot, especially if they attend public schools. Where does a good evangelical go from here? Fortunately, we have solid answers to these questions that evangelicals can agree on. What is the origin of the universe? God created it. How does God work in this process? God creates lovingly and makes gracious provision for every created thing. What is the foundation for human dignity? We are deeply and intimately loved by an all-powerful God. How should we understand the authority of Scripture? It is God's revelation and the ultimate measure of truth. There it is: our proposal about what every evangelical should believe about creation and evolution.

Many evangelicals will find our resolution to the evolution debate frustrating, not because they disagree with our positions above, but because they believe we have not gone far enough. We did not explain whether 144 hours or 13.7 billion years transpired between the creation of light and the creation of human beings. We failed to mention whether human beings started out as a pile of dirt in God's hand or evolved from apes. We do have views on these sorts of questions, but hold them lightly. While the Bible is explicit about the fact that God creates, the broad variety of positions adopted by godly and thoughtful evangelicals leads us to suspect that uniformity about the time line or mechanics of creation is not required for evangelicals. Evangelical statements of faith reflect this. While they are unanimous in affirming that God is the loving Creator of all that is, they are usually content to put the specifics in the realm of secondary issues.

Conclusion

To this point, we have said little directly about *how* evangelicals should engage in the conversation about creation. One of the most famous (or infamous) chapters of the evolution debate, the so-called Scopes Monkey Trial of 1925, provides some insight. This episode reflects two common characteristics of the broader discussion. First, most evangelicals will evaluate the Scopes verdict as a win for their team. John Scopes was convicted for teaching evolution. The verdict was much different in the arena of public opinion, however. For a variety of reasons, the Scopes case convinced many Americans that conservative Christianity was antiscience and anti-intellectual. Oddly, it was not just outsiders who drew this conclusion. Many Christians decided that the only way to remain truthful to our faith was to resist science and other intellectual pursuits. Rather than combating the image that Christians are anti-intellectual and narrow-minded, we often became the stereotype.

Since the Scopes trial, evangelicalism has had rather persistent anti-intellectual tendencies, especially when it comes to science. There are times when we wonder how many advances in knowledge the world has missed because bright young evangelicals were discouraged from intellectual pursuits. More tragically, however, we wonder how many people have failed to enjoy the benefits of God's grace because they perceive Christianity as anti-intellectual. Our anti-intellectualism and resistance to science have erected a barrier between many who love the life of the mind and Christianity.

We want to be clear about what we are saying. Our argument is emphatically not that Christians should simply capitulate to scientific consensus to win souls. Instead, our message comes directly from what we have said about creation. If God is Creator of all things, one of those things is the mind. If we fail to use it carefully and responsibly to investigate every corner of God's creation, we sin. It is as simple as that. Intellectual and scientific pursuits are not merely permissible for Christians. They are a mandate that follows from creation. Maybe in all our wrangling about the secondary issues surrounding creation, we have missed this important point, and Christianity is poorer for it.

Second, the courtroom context of the Scopes trial reflects the way we often approach the evolution issue. The stated goal of our system of justice is to arrive at truth. That is a terrific goal, but the adversarial structure of our judicial system creates some potential problems for attaining this goal. You have two sides with opposing claims, represented by advocates (lawyers) whose sole job is to defend their clients. In the end, one side wins and the other side loses.

Our task is not to debate whether our legal structure should be changed, but to illustrate something we all know. When the game is about winning and losing, the first casualties are often truth and fairness (just ask anyone who hangs around athletic fields). That seems to be a characteristic of much of the evolution debate today. We may say that we value the truth and trust that the process will bring it to light. However, more often we are like the partisan observers on both sides of the Scopes trial.[20] Their minds were made up before the trial began. Likewise, modern partisans in the evolution debate usually believe they already know the answers.

Evangelicals often view themselves as the last line of defense for the very concept of truth. Defending truth is essential to Christianity, and if we are going to do it well, then we ought to pay enough attention to the word "truth" to recognize that it is not just a noun. "Truth" also has adjectival (true) and adverbial forms (truthfully). In the courtroom, lawyers are prohibited from telling lies, but they do not have to act truthfully. It is perfectly acceptable for them to use rhetoric that misleads or obscures the truth. They can caricature an opposition witness as biased, or dismiss testimony out of hand if it does not suit their purpose of winning the case. Good courtroom strategy may require that you ignore the other side's strongest evidence. We could debate whether these tactics should be allowed in the courtroom, but they are. However, they fall far short of Christianity's requirements for a truthful process of pursuing truth.

All too often, evangelicals have treated the evolution/creation debate as a court case in which winning is the only thing that matters. We question our opponents' motives, while acting as if our motives are above reproach. We vigorously identify the knotty problems associated with the positions of others, but fail to note where our own positions leave big questions unanswered. We may have bolstered the confidence of those who are already fans of our view, but often at the expense of truth, trueness, and speaking truthfully. The evolution debate does not seem to have evolved much since the Scopes trial. If evangelicals really believe that the truth about evolution is the most important thing, then the only way we truly win is to be truthful in how we get to our conclusions, and honest and loving in how we treat those who disagree.

Perhaps you are convinced that you have satisfied the conditions for how Christians should work their way through this evolution issue. You may also be satisfied that your conclusions are crystal clear and should be obvious to anyone with a lick of sense and a desire to know God's truth. If this is the case, then you are not alone. A lot of evangelicals are there. Of course, many of them disagree with you, so that means not all of you are right about the details. It could be you are right, but even if that is the case, there is still one important truth that should compel some humility. While evangelicals battle over the proper interpretation of Genesis's early chapters, we seem united about one thing. The Bible makes it pretty clear that we (as in all of us) are finite, susceptible to pride, and fallen. You do not have to read too far beyond the Genesis creation accounts to get hammered on this point, and we cannot find a single evangelical statement of faith that does not say this explicitly. You can get a perfect score on a test for every factual question about creation's time line and still utterly flunk Christianity 101 if you are not humble and kind about how you come to your conclusions and how you use them.

The Bible begins, "In the beginning, God created the heavens and the earth" (Gen. 1:1 NIV). The immensity, complexity, interrelatedness, and beauty of this created order should evoke a sense of awe, mystery, and gratitude. Science does not minimize any of this. Whether we examine the most minute processes of creation through an electron microscope or gaze through the Hubble telescope at the vastness of millions of galaxies, each unimaginably enormous, our sense of awe and mystery is also magnified. All this raises an obvious question. What is it that compels us to worship the Creator of the universe? Is it that we have figured out the details of how and when God did it? Or does worship come because the immensity and mystery of creation reminds us of our finitude and draws us in a Godward direction? If it is the latter, then perhaps too much certainty about the specifics concerning our doctrine of creation (regardless of which version we hold) draws us away from the purpose of doctrine itself: to compel a grateful worship of God and thankfulness for creation.

5

Evangelicals Are Not All
Inerrantists

Don Bastian told me (Don) a story about conversations he had regarding the prospect of merging two evangelical Christian denominations. Bastian was bishop of the Free Methodist Church, one of the charter members of the National Association of Evangelicals. Conversations with leaders from the other denomination went on for months in order to work out details. The prospect of merging two denominations was daunting. There were many issues to discuss theologically, ministerially, and administratively.

Conversations progressed well. The two denominations had much in common. They were of comparable size, theological backgrounds, missions, and overall religious cultures. It made great sense to merge their ministries, which overlapped in various ways. Of course, there were differences between the denominations. So the leaders met to see whether consensus could be built in order to overcome what separated them.

One of the theological sticking points had to do with differences in the two denominations' articles of religion. In particular, Bastian recounts concern from leaders in the other denomination about the Free Methodist Church's statement regarding Scripture. The statement did not mention inerrancy in its description of the Bible, although the Free Methodist Church strongly affirmed its sufficiency, including the Bible's inspiration, authority, and trustworthiness. Bastian and other leaders in the Free Methodist Church mostly agreed with the other denomination's view of Scripture, but inerrancy had not been part of their historical description of it. So the leaders from the other denomination argued for the need to affirm explicitly that the Bible does not err.

Bastian was a scholar as well as a denominational leader, so he was well prepared for dialogue on the topic of Scripture. He welcomed their arguments, since he was sympathetic to their theological point of view. What galled Bastian, however, was that the main advocate of inerrancy used the Living Bible, which is a paraphrase rather than a translation of the Bible! Since the inerrancy position depends on the complete accuracy of the autographs (original texts) of Scripture, it is difficult to offer a persuasive argument for the view when you rely on a paraphrase from English versions rather than a Bible whose translation is based on the most ancient manuscripts. While the irony of this seemed to be lost to Bastian's counterpart, the dialogue between church leaders was not a laughing matter, since it potentially impacted so many people, institutions, and ministries.

The Free Methodist Church changed its article of religion regarding Scripture. Although it still did not contain the word "inerrancy," it came as close as it could without use of the explicit term. Regrettably, the merger did not go through, for a variety of reasons that make any merger difficult to complete. Interestingly, the Free Methodist Church changed its statement of Scripture again, decades later. However, the second change brought the statement more in line with what had been contained in the original articles of religion, without the admixture of compromise terminology.

This case, to the extent that concerns about inerrancy arose, is a microcosm of a decades-long debate among evangelicals, in which differences over the inspiration of Scripture have created obstacles to unity. However, much of this debate has gone on behind the scenes, and the vast majority of evangelicals have only passing knowledge of the issues. When the topic bubbles to the surface, the natural response is usually, "Of course the Bible is inerrant. God doesn't make mistakes." At the same time, most would not see any difference in the definitions of inerrant and infallible. Thus, many are confused and unnerved by this debate. What is inerrancy and why do some evangelicals view it as an essential, even *the* essential, hallmark of the movement? Why is it that other evangelicals are quite intentional in avoiding the term?

What Is Inerrancy?

Before we launch into what has become a sometimes rancorous debate among evangelicals, we should remind ourselves of where we share common ground on Scripture. While evangelical Christians differ on certain doctrinal specifics, we are united in confessing the sufficiency, trustworthiness, and divine inspiration of Scripture. There is no disagreement that it is the final authority for Christian life and that it reveals fully what is necessary for our salvation.

That much we agree on, and it covers a lot of territory. Where we disagree is on the scope of Scripture's purpose and the vocabulary that best conveys our view of Scripture's inspiration and authority. This is where the question of inerrancy arises. Inerrancy is the doctrine that the Bible does not err. It is thought to make no mistakes in any claim it makes. Inerrancy is not a new doctrine, and it can be argued historically that many Christians presupposed the inerrancy of Scripture, although they did not always use the term. Roman Catholics affirm it. However, Protestants did not promote the doctrine of inerrancy until after the rise of the historical-critical movement in the nineteenth century, which increasingly questioned the historical, scientific, and theological content of the Bible. The Princetonian School at the end of the nineteenth century presented what some evangelical Christians consider the classic statement of the doctrine, articulated by scholars such as B. B. Warfield and A. A. Hodge.

The Fundamentalist-Modernist controversy of the early twentieth century focused on the trustworthiness of Scripture and whether there were certain *fundamental* doctrines required by it. Instead of inerrancy, fundamentalist Christians sometimes emphasized the *verbal plenary inspiration* of the Bible, as found in *The Fundamentals: A Testimony to the Truth* (1910–15).[1] Verbal inspiration meant that every word was inspired by God, and thus the whole of Scripture does not err. Some Christians, churches, and denominations, especially fundamentalist and evangelically oriented ones, adopted the language of verbal plenary inspiration or inerrancy. However, not all of them did. There were various reasons for this. Some saw no substantive need to change historical statements of belief; others rejected the terminology because of exegetical and theological concerns. There was no consensus among evangelical Christians, churches, and denominations.

A watershed event for evangelically oriented Christians in the United States took place in 1942 with the establishment of the National Association of Evangelicals (NAE). The NAE came into being because a so-called silent majority of Christians identified with neither fundamentalism nor modernism, the latter sometimes identified with liberal Protestantism. Such terms are contested in their meaning, since they are defined in more than one way. However, Christians with leaders such as Harold Ockenga and Billy Graham wanted to avoid perceived excesses in fundamentalist Christianity, characterized by ecumenical organizations such as the American Council of Christian Churches, led by Carl McIntire. The ACCC was considered doctrinally narrow, anti-intellectual, polemical, and culturally disengaged. Members of the NAE also wanted to avoid perceived excesses in mainline Christianity, characterized by ecumenical organizations including the National Council of Churches, which was formed through the merger of the Federal Council of Churches and International Council of Religious Education. The NCC was considered weak in its affirmation of traditional biblical doctrines and practices. Thus, the NAE was formed as a middle way or more balanced means of understanding and advancing biblical, historical, and orthodox Christianity.

Although many churches engaged in dialogue about joining the National Association of Evangelicals, only fifteen initially founded the organization. Within a few years, however, dozens of other denominations joined, and today more than fifty constitute the NAE. It is instructive to know what they considered essential beliefs. The NAE Statement of Faith says the following about the doctrine of Scripture:

> We believe the Bible to be the inspired, the only infallible, authoritative Word of God.[2]

Notice that "inerrancy" was not considered essential to evangelical Christianity. Instead, the word "infallibile" was used. After all, "infallibility" represents centuries of use among Protestants. The Westminster Confession of Faith (1646) describes the Bible as infallible, whereas inerrancy is a relatively modern term championed at the end of the nineteenth century.[3] Use of "infallibility" represented a more traditional and consensual description of Scripture.

Inerrantists often say there is no substantive difference between the terms "infallibility" and "inerrancy." However, "infallibility" was strategically chosen by the NAE in order to encompass a broad range of evangelicals and avoid controversy over the doctrine of Scripture. The inspiration, authority, and trustworthiness of the Bible were all affirmed, but inerrancy was not considered inclusive of evangelical Christianity. This broad-based coalition of evangelical denominations made a conscious choice that inerrancy would not function as an evangelical litmus test. Less than one-third of NAE denominational members use the word "inerrancy" or one of its cognates to describe the dependability of Scripture. Most use other terms, such as infallible, trustworthy, reliable, and so on.

Importance of Inerrancy

If evangelicalism seemed to get by pretty well in earlier centuries without the word, why has there been such focus placed on "inerrancy" in recent decades? Why do so many seem to consider it the most important theological test in determining evangelical Christianity? The answer is that many have theological reasons for believing it is the best way to express the trustworthiness of Scripture. We do not want to overlook these reasons, and will deal with them later in this chapter. However, when a new term becomes widely used, there are often other forces at play, although no single explanation encapsulates the total dynamic of its rise to prominence.

First, there are historical reasons for adoption of this term. While many evangelicals do not find inerrancy to be essential to evangelicalism, the same cannot be said of fundamentalism. Christians who identify themselves as fundamentalist are unanimous that inerrancy is a nonnegotiable component of the movement. This is important because many Christian denominations with large numbers of evangelicals have deep fundamentalist roots. Many of these denominations came into existence during the fundamentalist-modernist debates, and the term "inerrancy" became a way to clearly distinguish their view from modernist positions. Because of historical precedent, many groups have been reluctant to revisit inerrancy language in their statements of faith, even if many members have strong reservations about it.[4]

In addition to historical reasons, inerrancy has functioned as a boundary marker for segments of evangelicalism. The first scholarly society of evangelical Christians to be established was the Evangelical Theological Society (ETS) in 1949. It had only one prerequisite for membership: the doctrine of inerrancy. There were many reasons, of course, for emphasizing inerrancy. Obviously, the founders believed inerrancy was a necessary component of evangelicalism. However, since it came into being several years after the NAE, which quite intentionally avoided the use of inerrancy, ETS's identification of inerrancy as its sole requirement for membership signaled a border dispute about what distinguishes evangelicals from nonevangelicals. Inerrancy became a wedge that excluded a large number of people who considered themselves evangelical. The narrow theological focus on one doctrine powerfully influenced who could join; what ideas could be presented at annual meetings; and consequently what papers, journals, and books would be published among evangelically oriented publishers.[5] Control over publications powerfully influenced evangelical Christianity in the United States, because a relatively small number of people decided what would and would not be published. Such publications inordinately influenced what was read in popular Christian bookstores as well as institutions of higher education. A term that had not been on the radar for most of evangelicalism's history was now used by some to define the movement's boundaries.[6]

Third, some theological frameworks, particularly the eschatologically oriented traditions of evangelical Christianity, are so closely related to the doctrine of inerrancy that they rise and fall together. Dispensationalism, for example, promotes a premillennial and pretribulational view of the end times, which warns people about a secret rapture of Christians before a cataclysmic period of tribulation. (More is said about eschatology in Chapter 3.) Advocates of dispensationalism also tend to affirm the doctrine of inerrancy and literalistic interpretations of the Bible, especially apocalyptic literature found in the Book of Revelation. So, eager belief in the imminent return of Jesus, predictions about contemporary geopolitical conflicts, and the prospect of the world coming to an end both rely on and reinforce belief in an inerrant Bible.

Which Inerrancy?

"Inerrancy" is a single word, which leads us to believe it has a single definition. This is not the case, however. Several definitions have arisen that complicate the debate. Most important doctrines receive a great deal of critical discussion, and it is predictable that various understandings arise. People outside of academic institutions, however, do not always know about the differences. We will identify three different ways that inerrancy is described, but even this is not an exhaustive list.

The most common understanding (and the one we have referred to as inerrancy thus far in the chapter) is called *absolute inerrancy*, or full, complete inerrancy. Absolute inerrancy is the belief that Scripture is truthful in all that it affirms; it does not err in any way. A classic statement of this view appears in *The Chicago Statement on Biblical Inerrancy*. Dozens of evangelical scholars and ministers met in Chicago in 1977 and created a brief, albeit wide-ranging, statement of the doctrine of inerrancy. The document includes a variety of statements of what inerrancy both affirms and denies. Below is a sample of *The Chicago Statement*:

Article X.

WE AFFIRM that inspiration, strictly speaking, applies only to the autographic text of Scripture, which in the providence of God can be ascertained from available manuscripts with great accuracy. We further affirm that copies and translations of Scripture are the Word of God to the extent that they faithfully represent the original.

WE DENY that any essential element of the Christian faith is affected by the absence of the autographs. We further deny that this absence renders the assertion of Biblical inerrancy invalid or irrelevant.

Article XI.

WE AFFIRM that Scripture, having been given by divine inspiration, is infallible, so that, far from misleading us, it is true and reliable in all the matters it addresses.

WE DENY that it is possible for the Bible to be at the same time infallible and errant in its assertions. Infallibility and inerrancy may be distinguished, but not separated.

Article XII.

WE AFFIRM that Scripture in its entirety is inerrant, being free from all falsehood, fraud, or deceit.

WE DENY that Biblical infallibility and inerrancy are limited to spiritual, religious, or redemptive themes, exclusive of assertions in the fields

of history and science. We further deny that scientific hypotheses
about earth history may properly be used to overturn the teaching of
Scripture on creation and the flood.   *what does scripture?*
teach

Article XIII.

WE AFFIRM the propriety of using inerrancy as a theological term with
reference to the complete truthfulness of Scripture.

WE DENY that it is proper to evaluate Scripture according to standards
of truth and error that are alien to its usage or purpose. We further
deny that inerrancy is negated by Biblical phenomena such as a lack
of modern technical precision, irregularities of grammar or spelling,
observational descriptions of nature, the reporting of falsehoods, the
use of hyperbole and round numbers, the topical arrangement of
material, variant selections of material in parallel accounts, or the
use of free citations.[7]

When people think of inerrancy, they probably think most often of absolute
inerrancy. After all, errorlessness conjures up the idea of absolute errorlessness. Besides, if God is thought to be perfect, then the Bible would logically
be considered perfect. Notable signers of *The Chicago Statement on Biblical
Inerrancy* include Norman Geisler, Carl Henry, Harold Lindsell, Roger Nicole,
J. I. Packer, Francis Schaeffer, and R. C. Sproul.

A second understanding of the doctrine is called *limited inerrancy*. Whenever something is considered limited, then it could be considered limited in
countless ways. With regard to Scripture, limited inerrancy argues that the
Bible's witness is inerrant in theological matters. In areas such as history or
science, Scripture may contain inaccuracies, which does not imply that the
Bible is always in error with regard to historical events and scientific phenomena. On the contrary, it is mostly considered trustworthy, truthful, and
authoritative with regard to such matters. However, Scripture is thought to be
inerrant, properly speaking, when it deals with theological truth. Historical
and scientific information needs to be studied critically, and corrected in light
of other sources of knowledge. However, errors that may occur are considered
inconsequential in relationship to the theological and spiritual truths contained
in Scripture and do not discount the trustworthiness of its theological and
spiritual truths. Advocates of this position include evangelical Christians such
as Daniel Fuller, Stephen Davis, and William LaSor.

A third understanding of the doctrine is called *inerrancy of purpose*. This
view claims that Scripture does not err for the purposes for which God intended
it. This position says that the judgments about the veracity of Scripture need
to take into account what Scripture intends to accomplish. For example, we
would not question the trustworthiness of a love poem if it speaks of the rising
of the sun, even though, technically speaking, the sun does not rise. Offer-

ing a scientifically accurate record of astronomical movements falls outside the purpose of love poems. Similarly, inerrancy of purpose argues that if the Bible is primarily intended to reveal to people God's plan of salvation and the attendant way of life, then God's Holy Spirit will not fail to use it for these purposes. In fulfilling these purposes, the Bible may contain inconsistencies and errors on matters that fall outside the concerns of salvation and Christian life, but they will not thwart the unerring purposes for which God intended it. The best-known instance of this view is found in the writings of Clark Pinnock, in his book *The Scripture Principle* (1992). Pinnock employs form and historical criticism, yet he considers the Bible entirely trustworthy for the purposes for which God intended it. Others who support views similar to inerrancy of purpose include Jack Rogers and James Orr.

So, when people say that they believe in inerrancy, you may want to find out what they mean by the term. It is used in different ways! Further complicating the issue is that the descriptors are not constant. While some who hold the last two positions describe themselves as inerrantists, probably most who embrace these views prefer the term "infallibility" as a means of distinguishing their position from absolute inerrancy. From here, it gets even more complex. First, absolute inerrancy is not as absolute as the name implies, because it, as with the other two versions, acknowledges that there are portions of the Bible that, given certain definitions of "error," would clearly be in error. At the same time, all three of the positions above can argue that there are no errors in the Bible. They are, after all, three different versions of *inerrancy*.

What Constitutes an Error?

The idea that inaccuracies are not necessarily errors or that a person can claim the Bible includes errors and still call oneself an inerrantist sounds like theological doublespeak. However, most of us unconsciously distinguish between inaccuracies and errors if, by error, we mean something that would throw into doubt the veracity and trustworthiness of the source. For example, the Bible describes the sky as a dome covering the earth (Gen. 1:20; Job 37:18), a statement that even absolute inerrantists agree is not factually accurate (or else NASA would be bouncing some very expensive equipment off a large roof). Even though they want to maintain Scripture's inerrancy on matters of science, inerrantists exempt imprecisions created by such things as "observational descriptions of nature."[8]

Why is it that most Christians, even when committed to the absolute inerrancy of Scripture, are not thrown into a crisis of faith about Scripture's reliability by an inaccuracy such as the one above? For one thing, most people intuitively recognize that we should not "evaluate Scripture according to standards of truth and error that are alien to its usage or purpose," as the *Chicago Statement* puts it. Indeed, all three views are inerrantist views; they maintain that the Bible contains no errors with regard to its usage or purpose. So why are there three different positions? Because the real disagreement is not about whether Scripture contains errors, but about the extent of Scripture's purpose.

Because decisions about how we understand the inspiration of Scripture hang on our understanding of Scripture's purpose, the obvious question is, "What is Scripture's intended purpose, and thus its proper usage?" We can agree that certain uses go beyond God's purpose. For example, it does not seem to be intended as a repair manual for Fiats, although the Bible, of necessity, would be read more frequently if this were the case. However, other areas are murkier, especially scriptural claims that touch on history and science. Are these within the scope of God's purposes? Absolute inerrancy says they are, and Scripture's statements about matters of science and history are without error (see *Chicago Statement*, Article XII, above). The other two views argue that science and history fall outside the sphere of God's intention and thus might contain inaccuracies.[9]

These discussions are not purely hypothetical. They arise because portions of Scripture itself include claims that appear to be historically or scientifically inaccurate or contradictory. Many Christians are reluctant to examine these tensions because they feel (or fear) that there is no end to the number of challenges people may bring against the Bible, once they no longer give it the benefit of the doubt with regard to its truthfulness. Indeed, dealing with such matters is often uncomfortable. The reality is, however, that most people who read the Bible in more than a casual way find claims that are difficult to square with claims in other locations of Scripture. So what do we do when we come across these troubling problems or apparent errors? Even though initial impulse may be to ignore them, evangelicals, who claim Scripture as their final authority, cannot take this route. Instead, if we are deeply devoted to Scripture, and not just devoted to some preconceived notion about it, we need to give careful and honest attention to the problematic passages and make some determination about how best to understand or resolve them.

Consider the following:

- Were people the culmination of God's order of creation (Gen. 1:27), or did God create at least Adam before other creatures (Gen. 2:7)?
- Did David kill Goliath (1 Sam. 17:50–51), or did Elhanan kill him (2 Sam. 21:19)?
- Did Saul commit suicide (1 Sam. 31:4), or was he killed by an Amalekite (2 Sam. 1:10)?
- Was the priest from whom David received bread on the Sabbath Abiathar (Mark 2:25–26) or Ahimelech (1 Sam. 21:2–3)?
- Did God incite David to take a census (2 Sam. 24:1), or was it Satan (1 Chron. 21:1)?

- In Jesus's genealogy, were there forty-two generations (Matt. 1:1–17) or seventy-seven generations (Luke 3:23–38)?
- After Jesus's birth, did his parents flee to Egypt (Matt. 2:14), or did they return to Nazareth (Luke 2:39)?
- Was Jesus correct in saying that the mustard seed is the smallest of all the seeds (Mark 4:31)?
- After Jesus's resurrection, was there at the empty tomb one young man (Mark 16:5), two men (Luke 24:4), one angel (Matt. 28:5), or two angels (John 20:12)?
- Did Jude know that his quotation from Enoch was from the apocryphal book of 1 Enoch 1:9?

How advocates of infallibility and inerrancy handle these tensions illuminates how the positions differ.[10] Inerrantists attempt to resolve these tensions in a number of ways. For example, was Ahimelech or Abiathar the priest who provided bread to David? Some inerrantists argue that the correct name is present in the autographs (original texts) and that a scribal error crept into later texts; others argue that these are variants of the same name; others argue that, while it is a discrepancy, mistakes from free citation of Scripture do not constitute an error. Similarly, the problem of the number (one or two) and species (human or angel) of those found at Jesus's empty tomb are resolved by "harmonizing" the Gospel accounts and arguing that these are records of different visitations or that the man or men were angels, but not recognized as such. Inerrantists have argued that there is no contradiction between 2 Samuel 24:1 and 1 Chronicles 21:1 because God uses Satan to persuade David to take a census. Second Samuel just cuts out the middleman. Inerrancy must rely on these sorts of explanatory steps to deal with what might be called a "slippery slope" problem. Absolute inerrancy, as the name implies, is an all-or-nothing position. If the Bible includes even a single error, the whole is imperfect. Thus, it is imperative for inerrantists to argue that no errors occur in Scripture. However, they are confident that, for each apparent miscue in Scripture, an explanation exists that will confirm the error-free character of Scripture (even if the explanation is not yet knowable, due to God's timing in making it known).

The infallibility positions take a different approach to scriptural conflicts. For example, advocates might say that, even though Jesus's statement about the mustard seed is scientifically mistaken (there are smaller seeds), it is inconsequential to the theological point he makes about the kingdom of God. The Bible might inaccurately report who killed Saul or who and how many were at Jesus's empty tomb. However, these would not be considered errors that cast doubt on Scripture's trustworthiness because such details have no direct bearing on doctrine or Christian life. Indeed, defenders of this position argue that it is precisely the presence of historical or scientific inaccuracies that lead them to infallibility. Scripture itself seems to indicate that getting all these facts lined up is outside the salvific purposes of Scripture. Thus, rather than attempting to relieve the tensions by extra-biblical theories or hypothetical events to harmonize Scripture, or appealing to biblical texts we do not have (the autographs), those in the infallibility camp say that we should base our doctrine of inspiration on Scripture itself.

Infallibility's critics are quick to point out that they have a "slippery slope" problem of their own.[11] If they admit to certain types of errors in the Bible, then how do they determine what parts are true and what parts are false? How can they be sure that any parts of Scripture are true? Moreover, while defenders of infallibility positions almost always argue that Scripture does not err on matters of faith and practice, it is not always clear whether or when inaccuracies on historical or scientific details can be isolated from doctrine and practice. Surely theological truth presupposes the veracity of certain historical events. For example, we could hardly maintain that the words attributed to Jesus are theologically trustworthy if there was no historical Jesus. So where do we draw the line on allowing for these types of errors? Once Pandora's Box—so to speak—has been opened, how can the Bible continue to have credibility in an increasingly skeptical world?

Inerrancy and Infallibility

The Chicago Statement on Biblical Inerrancy says there is no substantive difference between the terms "inerrancy" and "infallibility." Historically, however, this has not been the case. We have already seen that certain evangelical organizations and denominations have intentionally selected one or the other to describe their understanding of inspiration. We have also briefly surveyed different versions of inerrancy/infallibility and touched on how they deal with certain types of apparent conflicts in Scripture. However, there are a few additional facets of these respective concepts of inspiration that we need to recognize. Howard Marshall, for example, compares and contrasts the two terms:

> Here we have encountered two points of view. One group of scholars defends inerrancy. They argue that inspiration implies inerrancy, and that the inerrancy of the Bible is a fact either accommodated within the definitions of inerrancy or assumed to be merely apparent errors. The other group of scholars defends the entire trustworthiness of the Bible for the purpose for which God inspired it; inspiration means that God made the Bible what he wanted it to be for his purposes. This school of thought holds that a greater degree of imprecision may be compatible with God's purposes. It will be apparent that the former group holds that the Bible was the result of a process giving the same results as divine dictation, while the latter group leaves the precise mode of inspiration somewhat uncertain.[12]

Marshall's summary of the inerrantist position reveals two key elements. First, since God inspires Scripture and is perfect, it follows logically that the Scripture inspired by a perfect God would itself be perfect. Errors or inaccuracies of any type fall short of perfection, thus God-inspired Scripture will have no errors. The second piece of the inerrantist view is found in the idea that "the Bible was the result of a process giving the same results as divine dictation." This picks up inerrancy's embrace of verbal inspiration. Verbal inspiration does not mean that the Holy Spirit overrides the mind of the human author and simply dictates the words that end up in the Bible. Instead, the Holy Spirit inspires the human author in such a manner that Scripture contains the exact words God desires to be included. Thus, as a corollary to God's perfection, inerrantists argue that the God who inspires does so completely, right down to the very words within God's Word.

Marshall prefers to use infallibility, since it allows for what he considers a more open and honest assessment of Scripture. While he does not think that infallibility takes anything away from the inspiration, authority, and trustworthiness of the Bible, he does acknowledge that it is a somewhat "messier" view of inspiration. Although Scripture perfectly fulfills its spiritual aims, historical or scientific mistakes are present within it. The benefit, in Marshall's view, is that infallibility encourages evangelical Christians to study Scripture based on what is found in it rather than what interpreters hope to find. Sometimes presuppositions cloud people's perceptions of what they can and cannot find in the words of the Bible. In other words, Marshall's approach might be described as more inductive in nature. Rather than basing our understanding of Scripture on a particular set of assumptions about the implications of God's perfection, we instead should take our cues from Scripture itself. If a careful reading of the Bible seems to indicate that an inerrant account of historical or scientific matters lies outside God's purpose, we should limit the scope of inerrancy.

While Marshall's criticism of absolute inerrancy is concerned about imposing assumptions on what counts as truth, other critics argue that, rather than preserving our confidence in the Bible, absolute inerrancy actually endangers evangelical Christian beliefs, values, and practices. For example, William Abraham says:

> I myself would argue that inerrancy is both inadequate and dangerous as a predicate of scripture. It stems historically from a doctrine of dictation, which evangelicals themselves have rejected. It creates enormous difficulties no one has satisfactorily resolved. It inhibits an honest reading of the text, as it is, blemishes and all. It fosters an obsession with epistemological questions that overshadows the substance of the gospel. It creates expectations in young converts that can never be fulfilled and then proceeds to provide circuitous harmonizations and theories to relieve the ensuing disappointment. It is not based on scripture itself, it is ultimately irreconcilable with the actual scripture as normative for Christian faith and practice.[13]

This aversion to the term "inerrancy" illustrates why not all evangelical Christians use it to describe their view of the Bible. It further illustrates why critical junctures in the recent development of evangelical Christian identity chose to affirm infallibility, not as a synonym of inerrancy, but as an intentional contrast with it.

Abraham's concerns about the dangers of inerrancy point to an irony in the inerrancy/infallibility debate. Both sides come to their conclusions in large part out of concerns about dangers they perceive in the opposing views. Inerrantists do not in any way want to consider the Bible other than perfect, reflective of their belief in God's perfection. Thus, they fear that believers lose confidence in Scripture's reliability with anything less than a totally inerrant Bible. Those who affirm infallibility fear that inerrancy endangers faith because, if one finds the harmonizations of scriptural tensions unreliable, then they will also find Scripture unreliable.

Behind this disagreement we find an important common thread: both parties are concerned about fostering love and respect for Scripture. Since all evangelicals share this goal, it seems logical to spend some time talking about the Scripture we love and respect. Certainly part of this process is studying the actual contents of the Bible. However, another aspect of understanding Scripture involves awareness of how it came to be as it is and how the church throughout the ages has read and interpreted it. To some, it is as if the divine revelation found in Scripture dropped out of heaven, being dictated by God! (This is essentially what Muslims believe about the Koran, and Mormons believe about the Book of Mormon.) However, the Bible has a history, and histories are important for understanding books.

A Brief History of the Bible

The Bible is thousands of years old, and the various texts within it were probably written by dozens and dozens of authors over the span of about one thousand years, give or take a few centuries. Parts of it were written in Hebrew, and other parts in Aramaic or Greek. Some books of the Bible were probably written by a single author, while others may have been written by numerous authors. There is also evidence that editors played a role in compiling and modifying its content before it gained its present form.

Since there were not always people present who recorded the words said by others, oral traditions first arose in order to remember past events and conversations. Of course, the memory capability of ancient people is thought to be better than people's memories today. However, long periods of time undoubtedly passed before some stories were written, usually on skins or parchment. Once stories were written, they had to be copied by hand if the information was to be preserved and shared with others. During this time, writings may have undergone various transformations. There was a growing sense that certain writings were more sacred and authoritative than others, but there was not yet a concept of standardized Scripture.

The Old Testament contains extensive information prior to the first century, and the New Testament contains information about Jesus Christ and his disciples during the first century. Interestingly, there are as many questions about the historicity and reliability of the New Testament as there are about the Old Testament. For example, take the words of Jesus. Most of what he said, according to scholars, was probably spoken in Aramaic, which was an ancient Near Eastern language. However, the New Testament was written in Greek, which means the words of Jesus had to be translated before they were written in the New Testament. So, when people read the words of Jesus today in the Gospel accounts of his life, they should know the words had to be translated at least twice before they could be read in English. This brings a whole new meaning to a "red-letter edition" of the Bible (with the words of Jesus printed in red ink)!

Once written, it took time before collections of writings were accepted into the canon, that is, established as the official standard of sacred writings—"the Scriptures" (e.g., Matt. 22:29; 1 Cor. 15:3). The Old Testament, which is called the Hebrew Scriptures, was not fully arranged into a canon until after the time of Jesus. So, when Jesus and his disciples referred to the Scriptures, it was not yet a standardized list of writings.

A list of New Testament writings does not appear in church history until the end of the fourth century, nearly four hundred years after the time of Jesus, although most of the major books in our New Testament had been considered authoritative in church use from the second century forward. When a canon of the New Testament was finally confirmed, there occurred great debate over which writings should and which writings should not be included. Dozens of writings were not included in the canon (although many of these were still viewed as edifying texts), and some that were included required extensive debate and argumentation. The Synods in Hippo (AD 394) and Carthage (AD 397) first identified the canon of Scripture that Christians have used since then. The Old Testament consists of thirty-nine books, and the New Testament consists of twenty-seven books.

There still were no printing presses, of course. So copies of the Bible were transcribed by hand, often by monks in monasteries in the first millennium after Jesus. Ancient manuscripts of Scripture are available today, containing fragments thought to date back as far as Emperor Constantine in the fourth century. Thousands of fragments of the Bible exist; however, not all of them match each other. It is important to recognize that the vast majority of these variants are theologically inconsequential, involving simple copying errors, such as skipping or repeating a line while copying or misreading a letter in the source text (spelling mistakes are nothing new). Moreover, there are criteria used by scholars to prioritize manuscripts, generally favoring the reliability of older ones. Textual criticism (sometimes known as "lower criticism") seeks to establish the most reliable manuscripts for the sake of providing Scripture for people today. But there is no agreement, for example, with regard to which ancient manuscripts should serve as the cornerstone of Scripture. Fans of the King James Version (and New

King James Version) argue that the *Textus Receptus* (Latin, "Received Text") represents the best ancient manuscript from which to translate the New Testament. But most subsequent translations use other manuscripts, thought to be older and thus more reliable, such as the Codex Alexandrinus, Codex Sinaiticus, and Codex Vaticanus. Notations in contemporary Bibles often make references to which passages are (or are not) included in the most ancient manuscripts (e.g., Mark 16:9–20; John 7:53–8:11). Readers of the Bible are sometimes perplexed by why there might be variations in ancient texts. Usually they read on, rather than take time to understand how and why such discrepancies occur.

Authority and Inspiration of the Bible

Although the Scriptures, presumably the Old Testament, are mentioned authoritatively in the New Testament, Christians have not always considered them their primary religious authority. Jesus gave authority to his disciples, especially Peter, and they were first to have authority over churches (e.g., Matt. 16:16–18; 18:18). They had apostolic authority, which was given to them by Jesus (e.g., Matt. 28:18–20; Luke 10:19). Later, the Council at Jerusalem, under the apparent leadership of James rather than Peter, made authoritative decisions with regard to how Gentile converts should live (Acts 15:1–21). So authority in the first-century churches was exercised mostly by the disciples and other leaders in consultation with the disciples.

When Christianity was legalized in the Roman Empire under Emperor Constantine, there arose an informal alliance between the emperor and the leaders in churches around the Christian world. Constantine called a council where the first creed was developed after leaders from the known churches assembled in Nicea (AD 325). A draft of the creed was sent out to churches throughout the ancient world, before leaders met again, in Constantinople (AD 391). There the Nicene-Constantinopolitan Creed—usually known as the Nicene Creed—was confirmed, stating publicly for the first time an ecumenical (universal) summary of Christian beliefs.

The focus of the Nicene Creed was primarily on God the Father, Son, and Holy Spirit. The only reference to Scripture was the statement that the Holy Spirit inspired it:

> We believe . . . in the Holy Spirit, the Lord and life-giver, who proceeds from the Father, who is worshipped and glorified together with the Father and the Son, who spoke through the prophets.[14]

No doubt this alludes to such passages as 2 Peter 1:20–21:

> First of all you must understand this, that no prophecy of scripture is a matter of one's own interpretation, because no prophecy ever came by human will, but men and women moved by the Holy Spirit spoke from God.

The Bible was affirmed as God-given, but there was not a formal canon at the time the Nicene Creed was approved. The creed, like the historical apostolic authority, preceded the formal Christian establishment of both the Old and New Testaments. Indeed, the "one holy catholic and apostolic Church" described in the Nicene Creed represented the primary religious authority of the ancient church.[15] The church believed Scripture to be inspired, but the final determination of the canon had not yet occurred.

The most commonly known reference about Scripture is found in 2 Timothy 3:16–17:

> All scripture is inspired by God and is useful for teaching, for reproof, for correction, and for training in righteousness, so that everyone who belongs to God may be proficient, equipped for every good work.

The word "inspiration" literally means "God-breathed," that is, God breathed the words of the Bible. Thus, these verses represented powerful arguments for the growing recognition, canonization, and authority of Scripture in churches. It affirms the church's belief that the Holy Spirit has been engaged in the entire process, from the original writing of the texts through the canonization process.

Scripture was still difficult to understand, for reasons already enumerated. Church leaders, ministers, and scholars needed to study it, interpret it, and make a case for beliefs, values, and practices that became official church doctrine. Dogma, after all, merely represents official doctrines of a particular church or group of churches. Although the Bible was considered authoritative, the authority of churches and their leaders were considered primary, both chronologically and logically. Their authority was chronologically primary because Jesus first gave authority to Peter and the disciples, and because it was the church and church councils that decided the canon of Scripture rather than the other way around. Church authority was also considered primary, logically speaking, because there were differences with regard to how the Bible should be interpreted. What good is an inspired, authoritative, and trustworthy Bible if it must still be interpreted by people, limited by human and social finitude, not to mention the effects of sin! Consequently, authority was initially thought to reside in churches, their leadership, councils, and—eventually—traditions, which were viewed as part of the ongoing work of the Holy Spirit.

Protestant Reformation and the Bible

During the sixteenth-century Protestant Reformation, a profound shift took place in how evangelically oriented Christians understood the Bible. Of course, there was no explicit identification of Christians as being evangelical. But Martin Luther renewed theological interest in proclaiming the *euangelion*— the Greek word for "evangel, gospel, good news."

Luther emphasized the principle of *sola Scriptura* (Latin, "Scripture alone"). He faced the daunting task of challenging approximately fifteen hundred years of Western church authority. The Roman Catholic Church considered the pope, magisterium, councils, and other church traditions the primary authorities in establishing religious beliefs, values, and practices. However, Luther argued that such authority had become corrupt, distorting biblical truths. In order to restore fidelity to Scripture and challenge the Roman Catholic Church, Luther thought he had no other recourse than to appeal to the authority of Scripture alone. Indeed, *sola Scriptura* became one of the founding principles of the Protestant Reformation, affirmed by other Reformers such as Ulrich Zwingli and John Calvin.

Of course, Reformers such as Luther and Calvin interacted with more than Scripture. They had been educated in the humanist-oriented academic institutions of the Renaissance, reflective of Christian humanism and not secular humanism. So they were aware of classic knowledge as well as contemporary advances in education. In talking about the Bible, both Luther and Calvin drew from patristic authors, such as Augustine, as well as Renaissance and humanist authors. They discussed the relationship between Scripture and reason, philosophy, and other scholarly disciplines. However, their focus was primarily on the Bible, advocating it as the final authority.

Over the centuries, Protestants have continued to emphasize the primacy of scriptural authority. It remains an identifying principle that distinguishes Protestantism from Roman Catholicism. Evangelically oriented Christians have prominently affirmed the importance of the Bible for their beliefs, values, and practices. Thus, they have been adamant and consistent in promoting the uniqueness of its religious authority.

Scripture, Tradition, Reason, and Experience

Protestantism developed in more than one part of the world. In England, a British Reformation occurred, although for quite different reasons than in Continental Europe. As the Church of England (Anglican) developed, Christians thought of themselves as a *via media* (Latin, "middle way") between the Continental Reforms of Luther and Calvin and the Roman Catholic Church. In terms of religious authority, Anglicans thought that reason, along with Scripture and church tradition, functioned authoritatively in making decisions about religious beliefs, values, and practices. The Bible, however, was considered the final authority. In this sense, Anglicans saw no conflict between their theology and the emphasis on *sola Scriptura*. The authority of Scripture is unique since it is inspired by God's Holy Spirit. However, Christians are also instructed by the traditions of the historical church. So reason functions as the "middle way" of deciding between the authority of the Bible and the authority of church tradition.

As Protestantism developed, various manifestations of it occurred throughout more of the world. Pietism, for example, first emerged in German Lutheranism during the seventeenth century. Other Pietist manifestations occurred in Methodism in Great Britain and the First Great Awakening in the American Colonies. Pietism, which many consider the most immediate forerunner of the evangelical movement, places emphasis on the heartfelt religious experience to which believers testify and which Scripture affirms. Manifestations of the Pietist impulse in Christianity included revivalism, small accountability groups, and the emergence of Protestant missions. Revivalism, in particular, emphasized the experiential dimensions of conversion as well as discipleship.

John Wesley, founder of the Methodist movement, recognized that experience, under the witness and influence of the Holy Spirit, functions as a religious authority. Although the authority of Scripture remained primary, he believed in the secondary, albeit genuine, authority of church tradition, reason, and experience. This view of religious authority has become known as the *Wesleyan quadrilateral*.[16] More and more, Christians recognized the diversity of authorities involved in theological, ecclesiastical, and ministerial decision making. Without diminishing the primacy of scriptural authority, the dynamics of biblical exegesis, theological reflection, and relevant experience became increasingly understood, appreciated, and employed by Christians.

Modernism, Liberalism, and the Rise of Inerrancy

As Protestantism entered the nineteenth century, Modernism increasingly presented new challenges. Rather than looking to Scripture as the final authority, Modernism relied on reason and science in its quest for truths that could be stated propositionally and systematized neatly. Modernism also uplifted individualism and viewed the past, including the religious heritage of Christianity and churches, as outmoded vestiges of a less-enlightened time. Even the Bible was viewed as a relic of a bygone era. With the rise of historical criticism, the Bible no longer enjoyed privileged status as inspired by God. When evaluated as any other book, the Bible was deemed by Modernists as unreliable on a number of levels, theologically as well as historically and scientifically. Christians were confronted by secular and naturalistic worldviews that replaced theistic beliefs, values, and practices.

One response to this challenge was the birth of Liberal Protestantism. Liberalism, in general, agreed with Modernist conclusions about the fallibility of Scripture, but disagreed that this required a rejection of Christianity. Instead, they argued that Christianity and Scripture must be radically reinterpreted. For example, Friedrich Schleiermacher thought that people's immediate experience of God represented the most reliable starting point for theological reflection. To the degree that Scripture aids in one's "feeling of absolute dependence" on God, it is helpful in determining religious beliefs, values, and practices. However, primacy was given to experience, rather than Scripture, in final decision making.

Evangelically oriented Christians could accept neither the secularizing tendencies of Modernism nor Liberalism's demotion of Scripture's primacy. As a result, they became increasingly concerned about defending the uniqueness and authority of the Bible. This is the time when the Princetonians developed the doctrine of inerrancy, which served to defend Scripture against both Modernist and Liberal critics. Soon thereafter the Fundamentalist-Modernist controversies arose, and inerrancy substantively became one of "five fundamentals" of the Fundamentalist movement. In a time of uncertainty, inerrancy served as a bulwark, withstanding the eroding tides of modernity. The doctrine itself certainly departs from Modernism's conclusion that the Bible was flawed. However, many suspected that inerrancy was heavily indebted to Modernist assumptions about the nature of truth, assumptions that have come under increasing scrutiny with the emergence of postmodernism.

Postmodernism and the Bible

We hope our brief historical survey of the Bible's history has shown that its use and interpretation have varied with the circumstances of each age. Advocates of inerrancy argue that, through each period of church history, this doctrine has endured as a cornerstone of Christianity. Some, however, interpret the development of the doctrine of inerrancy as influenced more by Modernism than by the Bible. Scripture does not use the language of error and errorlessness, nor was inerrancy a term that appeared with any frequency before the rise of Modernism. Thus, some evangelicals view the doctrine of inerrancy as a reaction, consciously or unconsciously, to the modern challenges to Christianity. Given the expectation for certainty, scientifically as well as other ways, Christians wanted to respond with a foundation of knowledge that was equally certain and error free. Regardless of one's opinion about the motivation behind development of the doctrine, the conceptual categories for considering inerrancy reflect the questions and concerns of a modern worldview.

Of course, the influence of Modernism is hard to detect when you are in the midst of it and it permeates the ideas of the age. However, postmodernism may provide some distance to evaluate the adequacy of earlier views of inspiration and raise new questions about how we use and interpret Scripture.

Postmodernism is a "hot-button" word in evangelical circles today. For some, it is the most corrosive influence Christianity has faced since Liberalism. For others, however, postmodernism opens promising new vistas for evangelical thought and is seen as a healthy corrective to the excesses of Modernism. Complicating all this is that its definition is even more hotly contested than that of evangelicalism, if that is possible. Perhaps the safest thing to say about postmodernism is that it is "post" the characteristics of Modernism. It questions the reliability of human reason, science, and the certainty of knowledge. Postmodernism uplifts the collective dimensions of humankind, emphasizing the importance of social and cultural interaction. It is more likely than Modernism to consider the past in a positive light; however, the heritage of Christianity and churches is understood relative to the social and cultural contexts in which they arose.

Some strands of postmodernism are extremely skeptical about truth in general, which leads to a thoroughgoing relativism. These forms have found little traction among evangelicals. However, less extreme versions of postmodernism have attracted the attention of many Christians. These postmodern strands direct their skepticism, not toward truth, but toward us. First, many would argue that Modernism's confidence in our ability to know the truth in a clear and unbiased way gives insufficient attention to the impact of sin. God's Word may be true, but those who read and interpret this Word remain subject to the limitations of human finitude and sin. Second, postmodernism reminds us that the knower always exists within a social context that influences the way we view the world. This context functions like a lens through which we see and understand our environment and the Bible. Thus, a Western, college-educated evangelical will very likely interpret Scripture much differently than a semi-literate Christian in Thailand.

We are still getting used to some of the issues raised by postmodernism and, predictably, evangelical responses to how this affects our view of the Bible are mixed. Some find inerrancy to be the only defense against postmodernism's challenge to the notion that truth is primarily propositional in nature and that Scripture's meaning can be discerned in a manner that transcends cultural influence. Other evangelicals find postmodernism's critique of propositional truth helpful and suggest that, rather than approaching Scripture as a repository of truth claims, it is better read as a grand narrative of God's interaction with creation. Within the overarching story of God's creative, covenanting, and redeeming work within history, we find numerous stories that speak of God's desire to be in relationship with us, despite our continual rebellion. Yet other evangelicals find postmodernism's awareness of our social, historical, racial, and economic context to be a helpful warning against imposing our cultural views (and hang-ups) on a Bible that was written in settings and circumstances very different from our own.

These last two approaches challenge inerrantism, not by frontal assault, but by undermining its assumptions about the nature of truth. Inerrancy is zealous to protect the veracity of Scripture's claims, regardless of what sorts of claims they might be. However, the second option above questions whether this distorts the idea that Jesus himself, not a set of propositions about him, is the pinnacle of truth. The third option acknowledges that, while we may express our beliefs about God in a propositional sense, the way we speak of God is always shaped by a cultural context. Thus, for example, modern notions of history demand precision and accuracy. Without these, a statement is not considered true. However, the cultures in which Scripture was written may have been more interested in drawing out the significance of events than in recording exact chronologies and precise numbers. What "history" means to us may be very different from what "history" meant to the author of 1 Chronicles. As this brief overview reveals, no evangelical consensus has emerged on whether postmodernism's impact on our understanding of Scripture has been positive or negative.

How Shall We Then Live?

Scripture remains the final authority for evangelical Christians in matters of what they believe, value, and practice. Evangelicals also consider Scripture to be inspired by God and a reliable guide. But the doctrine of inerrancy does not represent the *sine qua non* (Latin, "something that is absolutely indispensable or essential") for what it means to be evangelical. In fact, evangelicalism reflects a surprising amount of diversity in terms of how Scripture is understood, interpreted, and applied. If the story ended with our recognition of this diversity, it would be a rather typical evangelical story. After all, a recurring theme throughout every chapter in this book is the broad diversity within our family. However, disagreements over inerrancy have gone beyond diversity; they have often created division.

Since neither of us expects to live long enough to see disagreements between inerrancy and infallibility fade away, we want to offer two suggestions about how evangelicals might disagree in healthier ways. The first suggestion is to back away from the politically charged and incendiary language that often accompanies these debates. For example, inerrantists often claim that their view represents the "high view of Scripture" because it allows for no errors in Scripture. Similarly, advocates of infallibility argue that their understanding is the "high view" because it respects the limits Scripture imposes on its inspiration. Both imply that those who stake out an opposing position intentionally choose a low view of Scripture, which obscures the real issue. At minimum, our disagreements should acknowledge that both sides are motivated by respect for Scripture.

We also need to be aware of the consequences of "warfare" language in this disagreement. A key moment in the inerrancy debate occurred in 1978 with publication of *The Battle for the Bible* by Harold Lindsell. Lindsell couched debate over the essentiality of inerrancy in terms of a battle. The aftermath of the book's publication certainly resembled a battlefield. People lost jobs, church and parachurch groups split, and academic institutions lost accreditation over attempts to purge evangelical Christianity of those who did not affirm inerrancy. The tragedy is not just that this battle exacerbated a split among evangelicals; it was misnamed from the beginning. It was not a battle about the Bible. Both sides affirm Scripture as their final authority. Instead, the struggle was about two very closely related views of inspiration. However, you cannot get people very angry about those sorts of arguments. Thus, warfare language was used to imply that inerrantists alone are "for" the Bible and everyone else is "against" it. In the name of honesty, we need to back off from incendiary language that obscures the real issues.

Our second suggestion is directed toward inerrantists. You have a significant political advantage in this debate. Those who affirm infallibility have limited options as a result of being excluded from evangelical organizations, universities, and churches that affirm only inerrancy. But it does not work the other way around. Inerrantists are allowed to (and do) teach in evangelical universities, pastor and join evangelical churches, and work for evangelical organizations that quite consciously exclude inerrancy from their statements of faith. This leads to two observations. First, there are some consistency problems with this. If inerrancy *is* the litmus test of evangelicalism, can inerrantists in good faith work for or with "infallibility" groups? After all, if it all comes down to inerrancy, those organizations are not really evangelical. If inerrancy *is not* the evangelical litmus test, then is it not vicious and unnecessarily divisive for inerrantist groups to exclude other evangelicals from their ranks?

Our second observation falls under the category of "if it walks like a duck and quacks like a duck, then it must be a duck." For decades, we have observed what happens when those who espouse inerrancy work in evangelical organizations and churches with those who do not. Together, infallibilists and inerrantists minister to teens, defend Christian orthodoxy, pray, educate minds, plan revivals, send missionaries, feed the poor, and do a bunch of other stuff that evangelicals are supposed to do. In these joint efforts, the difference between infallibility and inerrancy exerts no apparent effect on our ability to work and pray together. Nor does one's take on these two options determine what sorts of other doctrinal positions one might take (although it might predispose you toward particular doctrines). Both groups seem to walk and quack like evangelical ducks. Therefore, unless inerrancy yields a distinct difference in what Christians believe or how they live, can we justify the carnage created by exclusionary practices?

One possible way forward was offered by a conference held in 1989. It was cosponsored by the NAE (an infallibility group) and Trinity Evangelical Divinity School (which has an inerrantist statement) to discuss evangelical Christian affirmations. The participants agreed on a set of statements to identify the movement, with primary emphasis on a doctrinal understanding of evangelical Christian identity. Notably, the statement about "Holy Scripture" does not use either inerrancy or infallibility to describe the Bible, though both terms are used as examples of "Evangelical Identity":

> In accordance with the teaching of their Lord they [evangelical Christians] believe the Bible to be the final and authoritative source of all doctrine. This is often called the formative or forming principle of evangelicalism. Evangelicals hold

the Bible to be God's Word and, therefore, completely true and trustworthy (and this is what we mean by the words *infallible* and *inerrant*). It is the authority by which they seek to guide their thoughts and their lives. [17]

The statement affirms that the words "infallible" and "inerrant" are both options for articulating evangelical Christian identity; however, one cannot conclude that they are necessary descriptions of Scripture—either alone or together! Nor can we accept the premise that all evangelicals define the words the same. However, this joint statement focuses on what all evangelicals agree on—that Scripture is completely true, trustworthy, and authoritative—and puts the words "infallible" and "inerrant" in parentheses, which should remind us that they represent intramural disagreement about Scripture's intended purposes.

In conclusion, we reject the idea that inerrancy is the sole indicator of genuine evangelical belief. This does not mean, of course, that we believe it is contrary to evangelicalism. Instead, the doctrine is a sincere attempt to express the implications of our faith that God inspires Scripture, and it is affirmed by many Christians. But this particular doctrinal formulation of inspiration is not the only one held by evangelicals. Thousands of evangelical institutions and churches across this country and the world do not affirm it. Nor has it been the only evangelical expression of inspiration historically. Indeed, the term is absent both from Scripture and from the language of the vast majority of evangelical Christians throughout history. It is a viable doctrine, one held by many Christians. However, it does not define evangelicalism.

6

Evangelicals Are Not All
Rich Americans

Usually entrenched on opposing sides of the cultural divide, the secular elites and the evangelicals of the Western world are rarely in agreement. Lately, however, certain members of these groups seem to have found common ground in their pronouncements. With increasing frequency, they proclaim that Christianity's influence is in retreat and moving toward extinction.[1] Of course, each cadre has a different response to this prediction. The secularists write about the church's erosion with a thinly concealed giddiness. As they see it, Christianity is in its twilight after enjoying a long and strong run, but now society can be rid of the past's superstitions and restrictions. Evangelicals, on the other hand, engage in anguished hand-wringing about the rapidly approaching era of the lonely Christian in a post-Christian world.

Crisis scenarios are effective attention grabbers. In this case, the crisis scenario just happens to be wrong. Both groups operate with a massive blind spot that confuses *their world* with *the world*. *Their world* is the Eurocentric world of North America, Europe, and most of Oceania—the Western world. The truth is, Christianity has taken some pretty tough hits in these regions. While the populations of Europe and Oceania are still nominally Christian, church attendance is abysmal in most of their countries. The situation is a bit brighter in North America, but the growth of Christianity there is not keeping pace with population growth. Thus, to the extent that our prognosticators of Christianity's future refer to *their world*, trends toward increased secularism in Europe and to a lesser extent in North America are hard to deny.

The problem with *their world* is that it overlooks a few continents, namely South America, Africa, and Asia. Both groups of commentators overlook the vast majority of the Southern Hemisphere, the place that about two-thirds of *the world's* population calls home, in their pronouncements about Christianity's future prospects. If they examined an entire planet consisting of two laterally bifurcated hemispheres, the future of Christianity looks very different. Right under their noses, the Christian faith is undergoing expansion and revitalization in Asia, Africa, and Latin America (hereafter referred to collectively as the Two-Thirds World, the Southern Hemisphere, or the Majority World).[2] It is no exaggeration to define Christianity's numerical increase in some regions as historically unprecedented.[3] Moreover, secular commentators would be chagrined to learn that this increase has occurred predominantly among the type of Christians they see as their greatest cultural adversaries—the evangelicals.

When it comes to the state of Christianity in the world, neither secular nor Christian observers in the West have been very observant. It is time for a reality check, and the statistical snapshots below give us an idea of some major trends within the Christian world in general and evangelicalism in particular.

Christianity

- In 1900, 80 percent of Christians were Europeans and North Americans. By 2000, Christianity experienced a distinct southward migration with 60 percent of all Christians residing in Asia, Africa, and Latin America.[4]
- Although Europe had more Christian adherents (554 million) than any other continent in 2000, according to projections based on current trends, Africa and South America will both surpass it by 2025. By 2050, Latin America will have about the same number of Christians as Europe and North America combined. Africa will have 100 million more Christians that the sum total of Europe and North America.[5]
- In an average twenty-four-hour period, Europe will gain, through birth and conversion, 2,200 new Christians; North America will gain 5,000. In contrast, Asia will see an increase of 19,400, Latin America 21,000, and Africa 24,500.[6]
- The percentage of Asians who profess Christianity almost doubled between 1970 and 2000 (from 4.7 percent to 8.5 percent).[7]
- The number of missionaries sent from North America was probably surpassed by the missionaries sent from the Southern Hemisphere at the turn of the latest millennium.[8]
- The largest Protestant denomination in the world is the Anglican communion. On any given Sunday, you will find more Anglicans at church in Nigeria than in the United Kingdom, the United States, Canada, and Australia combined.[9]

Evangelicalism

- Between 1970 and 2000, the fastest growth of all Christian groups oc-curred among independent churches (from 95 million to 385 million), those not explicitly linked with any denomination. They are almost always evangelical in orientation.[10]
- Two-thirds of the world's evangelicals reside in the Two-Thirds World, and that number is growing rapidly.
- More than 90 percent of Pentecostal Christians, the fastest-growing evangelical constituency, live outside the United States.
- In 2000, 27 percent of Latin America was Pentecostal/Charismatic, com-pared with 4 percent in 1970.[11]
- The percentage of evangelicals relative to the total population in North America has remained relatively steady over the past several decades.[12]

Dealing with statistics is always tricky, especially when referring to religious adherence and projections into the future. But even if you factor in all the am-biguities of statistical work, it is irrational to deny that seismic religious shifts are occurring in the Southern Hemisphere. To the secular elites, the message should be clear. Even if Christianity completely disappeared in their Eurocen-tric world, it would still be alive and thriving. The message to hand-wringing evangelicals who worry about the demise of the movement is more pointed. We Westerners view ourselves as the archetypical evangelical—middle-class, reasonably well-educated Caucasians—and hold the illusion that the move-ment's future rests in our hands. That is a pretty accurate portrait, for the 1950s. In the twenty-first century, however, this picture is hopelessly outdated. The future has already come and most of the West missed it. If evangelical-ism evaporated in the Western world, evangelicalism would remain a vital and growing movement on this planet. It would not be white, educated, or middle-class. At the same time, it just might be more authentically Christian and evangelical than the version we commonly experience in the West.

How Have We Missed This?

The obvious question is why secular elites, evangelicals, and just about everyone else failed to notice Christianity's explosive growth in the Southern half of planet Earth. The cultural myopia of the first group is, on the surface, hard to explain. After all, are not these cultural elites the cosmopolitan, highly informed, multiculturalists who have transcended provincialism and see them-selves as world citizens? Majority World Christianity represents a major global movement, and the information is available. Could it be that it just popped up in places they do not normally go for news about the world? Is it just that they did not pay attention because it is not the sort of news they wanted to hear? Both may be part of the explanation, but the main reason goes deeper, as we will argue below.[13]

What should be even more striking is that information about Majority World Christianity comes as an almost total surprise to large numbers of Western evangelicals. First, this is news that evangelicals are dying to hear, especially since it provides welcome ballast to reports about evangelicalism's waning influence in Western Europe and North America. Second, Christianity's growth in the Southern Hemisphere should be on the radar for evangelicals from North America and Europe because our missionary efforts have played more than a minor role in this expansion. After all, evangelicals are Great Commission, "disciple all the nations" people. In comparative terms, we give much more of our budgets for foreign missions, send more missionaries, and translate Bibles into more languages than any other segment of the church.

The missionary impulse is part of evangelicalism's DNA. Indeed, one of the first songs children learn in our churches is "Red, brown, yellow, black, and white. They are precious in his sight." Given this, our ignorance of mission field successes appears to reflect a different set of lyrics, something that sounds more like, "Red, brown, yellow, black, that's right. Let's just keep them out of sight." If this sounds harsh, we need to ask whether the term "evangelical" conjures up images of a Chinese factory worker who attends an illegal house church, an illiterate Guatemalan Pentecostal, or a Somali woman living in a Kenyan refugee camp with her three children. If not, we need to determine why they remain outside even the periphery of our vision, because these individuals are quickly becoming more typical of evangelicalism than the Western, middle-class Caucasian.

Paternalism and Other Stupid Western Tricks

We need to be honest about this. If a religious revival of this magnitude was under way in Canada, France, Australia, or anywhere else in the West, it would make headlines. So why has the West been caught flatfooted by Christianity's expansion in the Southern Hemisphere? The answer can be boiled down to some ugly one-word terms such as paternalism, racism, imperialism, arrogance, provincialism, ethnocentrism, and colonialism.

Words like these should not be thrown around lightly since they describe serious moral failure. However, we need to own up to the accusations. Our blindness cannot be passed off as factual ignorance because our ignorance of the Southern Hemisphere is willful and deliberate. After all, terms such as "Two-Thirds World" and "Majority World" have been in common usage for decades as reminders that the vast majority of our planet's population exists outside Oceania, Europe, and North America. The information about these tectonic religious shifts could have and should have been known to us. Our factual ignorance has deeper roots. We do not know because we just do not care very much about the Southern Hemisphere. The West usually does not care about the rest of the world unless we have a military or economic reason for turning our attention in their direction.

Once upon a time, Westerners could be excused for ignorance of the outside world. Prior to the age of exploration, the European world was unaware that Australia, North America, and South America even existed, and consciousness of other lands outside Europe was fuzzy. Most of Asia and Africa was far away, exotic, and almost impossible to reach. Because of geographical isolation, Europe had little reason to fear outsiders militarily, and Africa, Asia, and the unknown worlds were safe from military encroachment by Europeans. The age of exploration changed all that. Discovery of new lands, harnessed with the growth of capitalism and technological advances, created enormous economic opportunities for Europe. The result was that vast swaths of Asia, Africa, North America, and South America were conquered and colonized by Europeans. Exploration rapidly morphed into exploitation.

Prior to the colonial period, Christianity was absent from most parts of these newly colonized regions. Colonialism made it both possible and safe, relatively speaking, for missionaries to follow the colonizers. Protestants and Catholics alike clamored to bring Christianity to these lands, and missionaries soon arrived by the thousands. This link between colonialism and missionary endeavors created a messy legacy that remains with us today. On the one hand, it is impossible to deny the sincerity of the vast majority of missionaries. Almost all suffered significant deprivation; many died. In addition to the gospel, they brought education, medical care, and life-saving services to regions long neglected. On the other hand, because they followed behind the colonizers, missionary efforts were frequently bound up inextricably with Western culture. No wonder missionaries were seen by indigenous people as part of a broader colonial agenda. Since colonization was motivated by economic and political reasons, the colonized were often viewed as mere pawns in a European power struggle, and the indigenous people knew it. Since they benefited from the protection of colonial forces, missionaries and their Christianity were frequently viewed as an alien and oppressive force, even though they often sided with indigenous groups against the colonizers.

Although manifested in different degrees, the one thing shared by European colonizers and missionaries was a condescending and paternalistic attitude. This outlook is expressed clearly in the opening lines of Rudyard Kipling's poem "The White Man's Burden":

> Take up the White Man's burden—
> Send forth the best ye breed—
> Go bind your sons to exile
> To serve your captives' need;
> To wait in heavy harness,

On fluttered folk and wild—
Your new-caught, sullen peoples,
Half-devil and half-child.

Much debate has ensued about whether Kipling intended these words literally or as an ironic criticism of Western provincialism and arrogance. However,
the fact that they were so often read literally, even though first published in
1899, when colonialism had entered its twilight, is revealing of Western paternalism. Because the inhabitants of the non-European worlds were considered
uncivilized and unenlightened, it was the moral duty of the West to elevate them
from darkness and ignorance, or at least contain their "half-devil, half-child"
tendencies so they did not harm themselves or others. Through Western eyes,
evidence of such tendencies existed throughout these cultures—paganistic or
animistic religion, tribal social structures, polygamy, widespread illiteracy (if
they even had a written language), lack of formal educational institutions,
and the list goes on. At worst, these characteristics justified ill-treatment; at
best, they demanded a noble willingness to assume "the white man's burden"
and correct these inadequacies.

When the age of colonialism ended, at least in its overt forms, the Americas
were largely Christian, but Christians constituted a tiny minority in Africa and
Asia. Christianity's growth on those two continents started in the latter stages
of colonialism, but accelerated rapidly in the post-colonial era. Part of the
reason is that earlier missionary efforts took time to bear fruit. Moreover, by
the end of the colonial period, most missionaries were from the United States
and were often more effective than European missionaries, perhaps because
they were not as directly tainted by colonialism. An additional factor is that
missionaries increasingly became more sensitive to the cultures they served.
However, the biggest contributor to explosive growth seems to be that Christianity went indigenous. Instead of outside missionaries attempting to adapt
the Christian message to a culture alien to their own, Christians from within
those cultures contextualized it. These insiders took on leadership roles and,
because they lived and breathed the culture, they understood how to apply
Christianity to the local context. As this occurred, Western missionaries increasingly assumed supporting roles such as health care, agricultural training,
pastoral training, and communications.

Westerners who work in a Majority World context are keenly aware of a
vibrant evangelicalism that has emerged mostly apart from, and sometimes
in spite of, Western involvement. Meanwhile, back home in rich America,
certain attitudes have not changed much from colonial days. We might not
express our paternalism as blatantly as Kipling's poem does, but it remains
just beneath the surface. Paternalism is a hard habit to break.[14] We accept our
fellow Christians from the Southern Hemisphere as sisters and brothers, but
find it hard to envision them as equal partners, and even harder to view them
as potential teachers and mentors. As odd as it sounds, we "old evangelicals"

from the Northern Hemisphere, where Christianity is treading water, still see it as our place to be the evangelizers and teachers of the Majority World, where Christianity is rapidly winning hearts and gaining ground. In a wonderful stroke of irony, we have failed to recognize that the flight paths of our missionaries cross those of missionaries from the Southern Hemisphere called to evangelize the lost in Europe and North America.

It Is Not Just There. It Is Here.

While the West often views itself as the sole exporter of Christianity, the reality is that the Majority World likely has surpassed the West in the number of missionaries sent. They are going to points around the globe, including the United States. As a result, you do not need to cross twelve time zones to get the flavor of the new global evangelicalism. You may only need to cross the street. In fact, I encounter it every day. As I write, a Chinese evangelical church is remodeling a building less than a mile from my house. Just one month ago, this was a Lutheran church.

This church is not an exception. Examine the church signs in almost every United States city. In big letters, you will find the name of the congregation that built the structure fifty years ago and still worships there on Sunday morning. In smaller letters toward the bottom of the sign, however, you will see the name of a congregation that meets in the same building on Saturday night, Sunday afternoon, or some other part of the week. In many cases, you will not be able to read the smaller sign because it is written in the language native to the Korean, Armenian, Hmong, Indonesian, or Latin American group that congregates there.

Even though global evangelicalism is present almost everywhere in this country, it remains largely invisible to most of us. The primary reason is that these congregations are more likely to reflect the religious expressions and flavors of their birth cultures than those of middle-class white America. Their ministries are often carried out in their native language. Many, probably most, of these congregations are independent, so they are not included in denominational counts. Since they are not readily identified as evangelicals by traditional metrics, their votes, if they are eligible to vote, are not tabulated as part of the mythical "evangelical voting bloc." Some segments of the immigrant church have significant numbers of undocumented aliens. Because of cultural, economic, and linguistic barriers, you will not find them at the usual evangelical hangouts such as Women of Faith conferences, Christian bookstores, church basketball leagues, or accredited seminaries.

Taken individually, these groups are small, independent, and culturally diverse. Viewed collectively, they represent millions of evangelicals who escape the notice of just about everyone, including the evangelical mainstream in this country. It remains to be seen whether these immigrant churches will assimilate into the broader American evangelicalism as they get beyond the first and second generations of members. Perhaps they will, but one might question whether that will be detrimental to their spiritual vitality. It may even be preferable that American evangelicalism, as typically defined today, assimilate toward the evangelicalism of the Majority World. This is just another way of asking whether rich American Christians might learn from global evangelicalism. Before we address this question directly, we will offer some highly generalized descriptions of Majority World evangelicalism.

This Doesn't Look Like Our Evangelicalism

Cultural context inevitably has a strong influence on how one's faith is understood and expressed, so it should not surprise us that Majority World evangelicalism will assume different forms from those we associate with the United States. Donald E. Miller sums up nicely how Majority World circumstances shape the new global evangelicalism:

> In contrast to the western Church, which is considerably relatively affluent, global Christianity is made up mostly of the poor. . . . When these Christians worship, they come to God with different concerns than do their North American and European counterparts, and this affects their style of worship. They are oftentimes less cerebral in their worship. They have a different attitude toward the miraculous. And they are sometimes more conservative in their theology and moral views, offending the sensibilities of Enlightenment-saturated western Christians.[15]

To set the stage for how "old evangelicalism" might respond to its recontextualized offspring, we need to expand on Miller's summary.

As the numerical dominance of evangelicalism shifts from white to red, brown, yellow, and black, the economic status of the movement has undergone a profound shift. Instead of finding its home in middle-class small towns and upper-middle-class suburbia, as in American evangelicalism, Majority World evangelicalism is overwhelmingly rural and urban, and overwhelmingly impoverished, at least in economic terms. As a result, the issues perceived as priorities—style of worship, manner in which faith is enacted, leadership structures, willingness to challenge social mores, and how the Bible is read in the Southern Hemisphere—will all have a close link to economic status.

A glance at this book's chapters reveals how affluence has defined the evangelical agenda in this country. Eschatological formulations, political agendas, safeguarding the doctrine of divine election or a particular formulation of God's sovereignty, protecting the pastorate from women, purging school curricula of ideas considered hostile to our agenda, or opposing gay marriage are seen as crucial battle lines, which manifest themselves in our bookstores and dominate Christian radio waves. As important as these matters of doctrine and social policy may seem in a Western social context, we cannot avoid the observation that such concerns only reach the top of the priority list because of affluence and social stability. While Majority World Christians in general would agree with American evangelicals on these matters, they are not the first-order priorities of Southern Hemisphere Christians. Because their lives are pressed by the immediate needs of simple nutrition, fundamental health care, illiteracy, dislocation, and persecution, they do not have the luxury of directing the bulk of their energies toward doctrinal or political matters. There is a greater sense of immediacy in their faith.

One manner in which this immediacy is expressed is in the experiential nature of worship. Worshipers expect to experience and articulate God's love physically. Worship is highly participatory; worshipers are engaged not primarily at the intellectual level but at the experiential level. Times of enthusiastic singing and prayer go on for uncomfortably long periods by Western standards. Speaking in tongues is commonly practiced, given the prevalence of Pentecostalism in Two-Thirds World Christianity. Within cell groups, often employed in Majority World churches, there is a level of intimacy and involvement usually lacking in the individualistic lives of Western Christians. Worship is imbued with a sense of spirit and empowerment.

Miller's description of Majority World worship as "less cerebral" is reflected in assumptions about pastoral qualifications. It is rare to find pastors or missionaries with formal theological training. At most, they may have received some training from a local Bible school. This is in part because of limited financial resources. However, evidence of conversion and a call from God to ministry, not educational credentials, are the fundamental qualities sought in pastors. Pastors of Majority World congregations are frequently "tent-makers," who work an outside trade and receive little or no salary from their churches.

Similarly, missionaries from the Two-Thirds World do not fit the Western paradigm of vocational missionaries, trained in seminaries and sent by churches and agencies with financial support. Often, Majority World missionaries are commissioned by their congregations to plant churches within their region or among expatriates from their culture who have migrated to different points on the globe. Commonly, they are given the prayers and spiritual support of their home church but generate their own financial support through outside work. Thus, while their primary motivation for going is evangelistic and missionary in nature, they are usually not recognized as missionaries in any official sense.[16]

Another characteristic of Majority World evangelicalism is supernaturalism, which refers to beliefs and practices that anticipate the intervention of divine forces in the present. In general, when Majority World Christians read in Scripture about people being healed or raised from the dead, when demons are exorcised or God speaks audibly, they expect that such practices remain valid. If God communicated his will through angelic visitations, dreams, and prophecies in the biblical era, we should be prepared to hear God's voice by such means today. Access to divine truth is not gained through rational argument or systematized propositions, but by revelation. While Scripture is divinely inspired, God also reveals through words of knowledge and in Spirit-inspired interpretations and application of God's Word.

One point in common for evangelicalism around the globe is a traditional approach to moral issues. On matters of homosexuality, chastity, marital faithfulness, abortion, and other moral hot buttons for evangelicals in the United States, you will find a great deal of consensus with their theological kin in the Southern Hemisphere. There are, however, two differences. First, while sexual fidelity, sobriety, and family responsibility are viewed as worthy ends, Majority World Christianity also recognizes that the converse is a strong contributor to poverty. As a result, it often emphasizes a moral lifestyle as a path out of poverty.[17]

A second difference in moral accent is that while Majority World evangelicalism is concerned about personal ethics, it does not display Western evangelicalism's preoccupation with these issues. Instead, it places a strong emphasis on social activism and change. Without the extensive social safety net that is available in wealthy countries, Christians in impoverished regions read passages about caring for widows and orphans, clothing the naked, healing the sick, and feeding the hungry as an essential component of preaching the good news. Drilling clean-water wells, lifting people out of illiteracy, establishing homes for orphans of AIDS or massacres, teaching more efficient farming techniques, and a host of other activities that seek to improve life are viewed as the core of the Christian message, not something Christians do in addition to evangelism.

Another characteristic form of social activism involves challenging the traditional roles assigned to women. On the surface, the story is mixed. Most Majority World societies are highly patriarchal, and many churches find justification within Scripture for limiting leadership roles for women. Other churches, generally influenced by Pentecostalism, have taken a countercultural approach and have opened up leadership possibilities usually forbidden to women. Beneath the surface, the story is different. Even in places where pastoral roles are limited to men, women have assumed unofficial but influential leadership positions as nurses, writers, teachers, Bible study and cell group leaders, and missionaries.[18]

Indigenized Christianity has found entrepreneurial ways to express the Christian message in the context of financial scarcity and social marginalization. Apart from sophisticated theologies of holistic ministry, believers have spontaneously responded to the deepest needs of those around them. Without financial resources, they are without the institutions Westerners rely on for social stability, education, housing, protection from hostile powers, health care, or the next meal. Christians who are South American émigrés to Germany, converts from Islam in Africa, or members of a minority ethnic group in Asia find that, in addition to their poverty, they are cut off from the social support of community and family. In such situations, the church is much more than a spiritual entity. By necessity it is often the only available resource for any fundamental human need. In short, "Whether it is basic education, protection of children, community organization, reconciliation following wars, empowerment of women, enhancement of family solidarity, or help in forming sustainable small businesses, Christianity in Majority World areas provides hope and care for communities."[19]

Finally, Miller's quote acknowledges that Two-Thirds World Christianity is theologically conservative. While their doctrinal statements and affirmations reflect this, poverty adds a feature often missing in Western readings of Scripture. One way this is evident is in Majority World treatments of prophetic and apocalyptic texts. In Western churches, these texts are often disarmed by spiritualizing them or projecting them into the future. In contrast, the Majority World church by and large reads prophetic and apocalyptic materials as immediately relevant. The poor and marginalized Christians find hope for the present in a God who takes their side against the powers of the age. A second example is illustrative of how Jesus is understood. Jenkins notes that about 70 percent of Christians in India come from the lowest caste, the Dalits. He says:

> Read from a Dalit perspective, the Christian Gospels are an astonishing document, as Jesus systematically flouts restrictions, taboos, and eating rules powerfully reminiscent of modern Hindu practice. In Jesus' time, as today, the critical divisions in society involve the people or groups with whom one is allowed to eat. His preference for "the poor and the marginalized, tax collectors, prostitutes and lepers" . . . portrays Jesus as God incarnate as a Dalit.[20]

The Bible is frequently viewed as a subversive text that critiques and challenges the ruling power structures.

What Can Western Evangelicals Learn from Majority World Evangelicalism?

When we ask whether Western evangelicals might learn from their Majority World counterparts, it is important that we specify what this entails. Unless we become very selective about which Majority World evangelicals instruct us, our teachers will most likely be Pentecostals, since they comprise the majority of Majority World evangelicals. From the beginning, this flags a potential stumbling block because, quite frankly, many Western non-Pentecostal evangelicals do not believe that *Western* Pentecostalism has much to teach them. When you throw in a healthy dose of residual paternalism, it seems even less likely that they might be open to learning from Christians who are both Majority World *and* Pentecostal.

If we ask why many non-Pentecostals are reluctant to admit kinship with their evangelical cousins (except when we need them to bump up the evangelical statistics), it is difficult to find any historical or theological reason for it. Pentecostals pass muster on the theological filters most evangelicals use to define themselves, and Pentecostal history can be traced directly back to the Holiness branch of evangelicalism that dominated (at least numerically) nineteenth-century America. It seems more likely that many evangelicals distance themselves from Pentecostals because of sociological factors.

While the demographics are changing, Pentecostals have traditionally come from the "wrong side of the tracks." They are more likely to be non-Caucasian, and their social and political positions frequently do not square with those of other evangelicals. Pentecostal worship often appears chaotic to outsiders, and many practices seem rather unsophisticated, verging on primitive. Many pastors lack formal theological education. Worse yet, many are uneducated *and* female. They just do not seem very interested in the deep theological issues of the day. Instead, the core of their faith appears very experiential, maybe even subjectivistic. To put it bluntly, many non-Pentecostal evangelicals feel a sense of cultural, educational, economic, and social superiority, and it is difficult for most of us to believe that our inferiors have anything to teach us.

If Western evangelicals would get over themselves and start taking global Pentecostalism more seriously, we could gain something crucial: a new connection with our own history. If you exclude certain specifics of its theology (such as speaking in tongues), the parallels between current Pentecostalism and evangelicalism's beginnings are striking. In its early stages, evangelicalism gained its greatest traction among poverty-stricken political and cultural outsiders who gave priority to experiential expressions of faith over doctrinal formulae. More established Christian groups criticized them for excessive enthusiasm in their worship and reliance on uneducated clergy. They were conservative in their theology, but pragmatic and entrepreneurial in their methods, responding quickly to a whole range of social, physical, educational, and spiritual needs that had been overlooked by other Christians. In sum, if we can cut through the fog of theological and cultural variations, Majority World evangelicalism allows Western evangelicalism to see a younger version of itself.

To call Majority World evangelicalism a "younger version" of Western evangelicalism risks the impression that we are comparing a juvenile with a mature adult, which brings us back to the paternalistic attitude we seek to avoid. Neither, however, do we intend to equate the "youth" of Majority World evangelicalism with some romantic ideal, a point we develop below. Instead, glancing backward through the lens they provide into our history helps us determine whether we have lost or are in danger of losing something valuable, even essential, to our identity. We will mention three elements where Majority World evangelicalism might help reinvigorate its Western counterpart and remind us who we are.

First, while many evangelicals in the United States have become increasingly strident about protecting (their version of) doctrinal purity, the Majority World church largely has avoided a preoccupation with nailing down all the theological specifics. We spend an inordinate amount of time defending our theological and denominational traditions and writing apologetics books that will be read only by other Christians. In contrast, the Majority World church's focus on expressing God's love in concrete ways allows energies to be directed toward service and evangelism. Western evangelicalism would benefit from following their lead on this.

Second, and related to the point above, many Christians in this country fret over the "scandal of the evangelical mind," concerned that we have sacrificed intellectual rigor in the name of a mushy headed and subjectivistic piety. As academics, we share this concern. It is nothing less than scandalous that evangelicals have often interpreted their faith in a manner that sanctifies stupidity. However, our history, as well as the Majority World church's example, remind us that the evangelical message is not reliant on a theologically trained clergy and a properly educated laity. Instead, the fundamental condition for spiritual vitality is an inner spirit transformed and oriented toward God. The "evangelical mind" may indeed be a scandal, but perhaps we have an even bigger scandal in American evangelicalism—what one might call the "scandal of the evangelical spirit." The Christianity of the Southern Hemisphere can remind us that our core mission is to call people into a renewing and discipling relationship with the God who brings salvation.

A third lesson to be learned concerns our understanding of power. Many Western evangelicals assume our witness would be enhanced if we made better inroads with the power corridors of business, education, and politics. However, our history, and the activity of the Majority World churches, may indicate just the opposite. Perhaps affluence and power are not the solution to the malaise in American evangelicalism, but are part of the problem. In earlier times, evangelicalism was forced by a lack of political, social, and financial resources to rely on divine resources. A similar movement seems to be afoot in the Majority World churches. In earlier times, evangelicals lived, worked, and ministered on the fringes of society. They were usually outsiders, and that is still largely the case in the Two-Thirds World. Today, Western evangelicals tend not to know too many outsiders. We have moved out of the margins and into the suburbs. The Majority World church can remind us of where evangelicalism was most effective in the past.

This lesson about power takes on an additional dimension if we broaden the scope to look at church history as a whole. What Christianity in the Southern Hemisphere teaches us is that Christianity gets along just fine without Christendom. By Christendom, we are referring to a form of Christianity that is bolstered, explicitly or implicitly, by political structures, military power, and/ or financial clout. Since Constantine proclaimed religious toleration in the Roman Empire (AD 313), most Christians have lived under Christendom's institutionalized power that made it safe to be an adherent (and often very unsafe not to be). Christianity was exported to the Majority World under the protection of colonial Christendom, and many predicted that Christianity would evaporate in those regions when the colonists pulled up stakes and went home. Contrary to the doomsayers' prophecy, however, Southern Hemisphere Christianity did, and is doing, quite well without Christendom, despite the fact that believers were (and still are) often persecuted and even martyred after the military protection of the colonialists was gone.

What happened? Perhaps it is too simplistic, but the answer seems to be that without Christendom, the Two-Thirds World church focused on being the church. It had no option of building itself in dependence on economic, military, or political power, so it depended on spiritual resources. It went indigenous and found ways to express God's love in holistic and culturally contextual ways. Wherever there was a need that diminished a person's humanity, it responded as it could. Where it could not prevent suffering, it shared suffering.

It is hard to overstate the unique nature of our situation. While virtually every Christian expansion over the past 1,700 years has come as a result of military conquest and political protection, Christianity's explosive growth in the Southern Hemisphere has occurred by Word and not by sword. Where it has grown in the midst of violence and hostility, Majority World Christianity has almost always been the victim rather than the perpetrator. Instead of relying on financial, political, or military power, these impoverished Christians have grounded their efforts in spiritual power.

It has been a long time since we have seen the church function without the power props provided by Christendom. Majority World evangelicals demonstrate that Christianity gets along just dandy without these props. Their witness, if we are paying attention, can help wean us from our unholy reliance on Christendom's levers of power. Majority World churches remind us that Christianity thrives when it seeks to be the church and relies on forms of power that are unique to believers. If nothing else, this suggests that the energies of evangelicals in this country might be better directed toward becoming a Christian *church* rather than a Christian nation.

A final lesson to be gleaned from Majority World Christianity is that evangelicalism is at its best when its goals and aspirations are truly significant. There is reason to suspect that so many in the West disdain the evangelical label precisely because it projects no vision of greatness. American evangelicalism's preoccupation with matters of personal morality, political positions, institution building, and doctrinal squabbles seems a pale definition of the transformation that we proclaim as our goal. Arguments about whether it is permissible for Christians to drink beer or whether states should allow gay marriage simply do not excite the imagination of Christians who want to make a difference.

When we pull our camera back to get the wide-angle view of global evangelicalism, many find a more exciting set of priorities. Not only do they preach and study the Bible with vigor, they find creative ways to express the gospel in concrete ways. Thus, Christianity in the Majority World can mean that AIDS orphans are adopted in Africa, children are rescued from the streets in Brazil, those otherwise consigned to poverty by illiteracy learn to read, and people are saved from death or blindness by basic medical care. Christianity in the Two-Thirds World also has a costly side. Conversion can mean estrangement from family members, exile, imprisonment, and even death. All this serves as a reminder that evangelicalism has been at its best when it ministers to those in hopeless conditions and places itself in precarious situations. Movements die without the oxygen provided by a significant mission. If Western evangelicalism does not recapture its ambitious vision for holistic transformation in the name of Christ, it cannot justify its continuing existence. Perhaps the American evangelical agenda could be reinvigorated by looking at the ministries and priorities of its counterpart in the Southern Hemisphere.

Conclusion

We fall into false assumptions about the nature of evangelicalism when our range of vision is limited. If we look no further than the Western world, we will naturally conclude that the prototypical evangelical is indeed American and rich (relative to the average person on this planet). As the last few pages have demonstrated, however, this composite is highly misleading if our scope is global. It is as likely that the average evangelical is African, Asian, or Latino/a as North American, and the typical evangelical is poorer than the global norm. Moreover, since the vast majority of evangelicals live outside the Northern Hemisphere, whatever evaluations we might make concerning the health and future prospects of the movement will also be misleading if we draw our data only from Western countries.

Our intent is not to romanticize Majority World evangelicals. They have their share of the problems, abuses, and outright lunacies we see in any institution that consists of human beings. They have even picked up many of the bad habits of Western evangelicals, often reflecting our divisiveness, dogmatism, and provincialism. Systems of accountability are often weak or nonexistent, and a strong sense of the historical continuity of the church is a rare commodity. Thus, even though we have argued that Western evangelicals might learn from their counterparts in the Southern Hemisphere, it is not because they have avoided all our blemishes.

The point of this chapter is to challenge some deeply ingrained assumptions. When Western evangelicals, the probable audience for this book, simply use pronouns such as "us," "we," or "our," we seldom have in view the vast majority of the evangelical family. It is all too natural to include in the evangelical family only those who fit a certain cultural, linguistic, socioeconomic, theological, and racial profile. If anything, this chapter stands as a reminder that the evangelical world we so often envision is only a pale reflection of a bigger and richer reality. If we (Caucasian, upper-middle-class United States citizens) continue to speak of evangelicalism as if it is a middle- to upper-middle-class movement, if we conceive of evangelicalism as a phenomenon that is propagated and protected by Christians in the United States, then our minds remain captive to an unholy provincialism.

Breaking free of provincialism's grasp requires that Christians recognize our deepest loyalties should not be delineated by national boundaries, economic class, racial identity, or cultural background. Our primary identity comes from incorporation into Christ's body, the church. This can provide a healthy corrective to a form of nationalism prevalent within American evangelicalism, which often equates Christianity's future with our own political and social fortunes. However, an awareness of the vibrancy and expansion of evangelicalism that is increasingly independent of the United States holds the potential for self-critique of our nationalistic impulses. Moreover, when our preoccupation with North American expressions of evangelicalism is placed within a global perspective, we can move away from paternalism toward forging a true partnership with our evangelical sisters and brothers in the Southern Hemisphere.

The vitality of Southern evangelicalism should be seen as great news by Western evangelicals. Evangelicals are, after all, "Great Commission people." With the explosion of evangelicalism in the Majority World, we are now joined by tens of millions of fellow Christians from all points of the globe whose identity is shaped by the command, "Go therefore and make disciples of all nations, baptizing them in the name of the Father and of the Son and of the Holy Spirit, and teaching them to obey everything that I have commanded you" (Matt. 28:19–20). This is certainly a strong foundation for a strong partnership among evangelicals that spans the planet. Those of us in the West, however, still have a tendency to view ourselves exclusively as "goers." In our arrogance, we lose sight of the fact we are also a nation that still needs to be discipled, baptized, and taught. Arrogance is a spiritual problem that can be resolved only with a good dose of Christian humility. But humility comes hard, especially if one is rich and American.

7

Evangelicals Are Not All
Calvinists

In graduate school, I (Don) had a seminar on the Protestant Reformation. In the course, I read about the history and theology of the sixteenth-century movement. In particular, I read the writings of Martin Luther and John Calvin.

One assignment was to read *On the Bondage of the Will* by Luther. I did not agree with his strong predestinarian views, but who was I to disagree with the founder of Protestantism? Next I read *On the Freedom of the Will* by Erasmus, who was a Roman Catholic contemporary to Luther. Much to my surprise (he was, after all, Catholic), I agreed far more with Erasmus!

In the seminar, I found myself troubled by the criticism of Erasmus by so many of my classmates. Their arguments seemed based more on a dogmatic acceptance of Reformation theology than a critical assessment of Scripture and of how they really lived. Finally I stood up for Erasmus, but found myself alone in defending him. I would have given up, if not for the encouragement of my professor to defend what I believed to be true.

After class, an evangelical classmate shared some commiseration for my views. However, he could not quite understand my theological point of view. He grasped most of what I said, but he did not seem to have much of a point of reference for understanding my promotion of human freedom, or free will, whatever one might call it. Those were objectionable terms, thought to be more philosophical than biblical, and somewhat forbidding to him. He had agreed with what I said in *practice*, but in *theory* his Calvinistic background considered my views to be Pelagian at worst, or semi-Pelagian at best. Pelagianism is thought to promote works-righteousness, and semi-Pelagianism is not thought to be much different. Since both were historically considered heretical, he did not know how to reconcile his resonance for what I said with what he grew up believing in church and studying in college and seminary.

Although my friend claimed to be a Calvinist, he admitted that he was not always able to reconcile his beliefs and values, relative to Calvin's *Institutes of the Christian Religion*. He confided that he described himself as a one-and-a-half-point Calvinist. He was referring to the so-called five points of Calvinism, which will be discussed in this chapter. Basically, the five points include Calvinists' belief in (1) total depravity, (2) unconditional election, (3) limited atonement, (4) irresistible grace, and (5) perseverance of the saints. My classmate said that he agreed with the perseverance of the saints (#5). However, he only halfway agreed with the unconditional election of those who are saved (#2), but not of those who are damned— the reprobate.

Since my classmate only believed in one and a half points of Calvinism, I asked why he bothered to call himself a Calvinist. Was he not more theologically compatible with Erasmus, or possibly Arminius, the Protestant who challenged Reformed views of divine predestination? "No!" my friend said emphatically. He strongly affirmed his Calvinist credentials, despite the fact that in practice there was much with which he disagreed. He would not or could not conceive of himself as anything other than a Calvinist.

He then said to me something to the point of, "How can you call yourself an evangelical Christian, since you don't believe what Calvin says?" Now, it is a matter of debate whether even he agreed with Calvin, but he tended to identify evangelical Christianity with Calvinistic or, more broadly, Reformed-oriented beliefs, values, and practices. Such words may seem odd to some readers, yet it is an assertion I have heard way too often as I have progressed in my doctoral studies and teaching in theology.

I became increasingly aware of this narrow tendency to define evangelicalism when I read the anthology by Donald Dayton and Robert Johnston entitled *The Variety of American Evangelicalism*. In their introduction, they quote Thomas Askew, who critiqued an essay by David Wells entitled " 'No Offense: I Am an Evangelical': A Search for Self-Definition."[1] In response, Askew says:

> Wells's assertion probably applies only to a particular brand of evangelicals, those primarily associated with Calvinistic Presbyterian and Baptist networks, and especially those found in the North and West. I see the evangelical faith and motif as a much broader tradition or current in American church history, one with a dozen substreams and marked by great diversity. Fundamentalism is merely one exclusivisitic subculture within that stream.[2]

In contrast to Wells, Dayton and Johnston invite readers "to join a larger discussion that seems in no imminent danger of resolution: how are we to understand the variety of American evangelicalism?"[3]

A more ominous example of an exclusivist approach to defining evangelicalism can be found in the Alliance of Confessing Evangelicals (ACE). Like other attempts at defining evangelicalism, the ACE uses a declaration—"The Cambridge Declaration"—to assert biblical Christianity, reflective of the magisterial Reformation, especially as found in the Calvinist/Reformed tradition:

> Today the light of the Reformation has been significantly dimmed. The consequence is that the word "evangelical" has become so inclusive as to have lost its meaning. . . . [We] endeavor to assert anew our commitment to the central truths of the Reformation and of historic evangelicalism.[4]

Although the ACE claims to have broad denominational participation, a perusal of their website reveals an obvious emphasis upon Reformation societies, Reformed resources, and other forms of Reformation study. Alliance Council members include Donald Carson, John MacArthur, Albert Mohler, John Piper, Philip Ryken, R.C. Sproul, and David Wells. Now, it is not a problem to attempt to define evangelicalism and even to do so in light of one's preferred church or theological tradition. We applaud attempts to do so! The problem arises when disagreement with the ACE theses about the nature of evangelicalism does not result in differences of historical and theological opinion, which can be presented, discussed, and disputed; on the contrary, those who disagree with ACE are accused of "being dominated by the spirit of this age" and are called to "repent" from their "worldliness."[5] Open and honest disagreement does not seem welcome; agree with their declaration or be subject to judgment. In our opinion, it is almost impossible to have a fair and meaningful conversation with people if they consider disagreements with them to be evidence of sin. How can you talk logically and constructively with people when they consider you and your views sinfully corrupt? This spiritually as well as intellectually dismissive approach reminds us of the cliché: "Shoot, Ready, Aim!" Adherents of the declaration seem far more concerned about making authoritarian pronouncements than in taking into consideration that there may be more than one legitimate way to be evangelical.

Our point in this chapter is not to blast Calvinism. Far from it. We will have many positive things to say in this chapter about the Reformed tradition and its founders. Instead, our concern grows out of the observation that Calvinists seem much more likely to identify evangelicalism with (and limit it to) their specific theological tradition than do evangelicals of other backgrounds. We do not believe this observation is unique to our own experience. For example, a few years ago Roger Olson wrote a provocative article for *Christianity Today* titled "Don't Hate Me Because I'm Arminian."[6] The fact that the leading periodical of American evangelicalism would pick up such an article indicates many share Olson's complaint that non-Calvinists are sometimes perceived as being outside the realm of true evangelical Christianity.

Quite frankly, we do not find the tendency to claim evangelicalism as their sole possession among evangelicals of other traditions. Pentecostals may tell others that they are living stunted spiritual lives if they have not received the gift of tongues; Quakers may question the validity of baptism or want to convince you that all Christians should be peacemakers; evangelical Episcopalians might express disappointment that so many evangelical churches have abandoned the liturgy. Every group within evangelicalism has distinctives they would like others to adopt. But we do not hear these groups discounting the evangelical credentials of other traditions because they fail to conform to the theological distinctives of their traditions. However, we do find that some Calvinists view evangelicalism, at least *real* evangelicalism, as a sole proprietorship of the Reformed tradition rather than a jointly owned movement.

Our observation about this strand of Calvinistic exclusivism should not be taken as a blanket statement. Many Calvinists, almost certainly the majority, are quite willing and even eager to share the evangelical label with those from a broad spectrum of theological leanings. However, some within the Calvinist tradition tend to employ "evangelical" as a term that designates a particular type of Reformed Christian, one that can be distinguished both from non-Reformed Christians as well as those who adopt more liberal forms of Calvinism. Thus, our position in this chapter will be that, although Calvin and his theological tradition have profoundly and positively contributed to the development of evangelicalism, the evangelical Christian movement cannot be reduced to a single historical or theological manifestation. Instead, evangelicalism represents a maturing development within Christianity that identifies with Jesus's Great Commission, but embodies it in diverse ways. Before talking about evangelical Christianity in broader terms, let us first ask: who was Calvin?

Who Was Calvin?

John Calvin (1509–64) was a French pastor, theologian, and—most important—Reformer during the Protestant Reformation in the sixteenth century. Along with Martin Luther, Calvin helped spearhead the break with the Roman Catholic Church and the development of Protestantism. He developed a system of theology known as Calvinism, which in time came to dominate the Reformed tradition of Protestantism, in contrast, for example, with the Lutheran and the Anabaptist traditions. Calvin became a very influential religious and political leader in the city of Geneva, and Christians interested in the burgeoning Protestant Reformation came to learn from him. In turn, they spread Calvin's teachings and writings throughout Europe, particularly through his *Institutes*.

The *Institutes* were important because they represented a comprehensive, systematic presentation of Protestant beliefs and values, which could easily be reproduced, transported, and taught. Calvin emphasized the sovereignty of God for salvation and the primacy of Scripture for determining matters of faith and practice. Along with Luther and other Reformers, he rejected the Roman Catholic Church's claim to facilitating people's salvation through the sacraments and its ecclesiastical authority over Christians and local congregations. Instead, Calvin emphasized the invisible church, which transcends individual manifestations of it such as the Roman Catholic Church. All Christians are called to be ministers, and they have the right and responsibility to reform churches in order to restore them in a way that is more faithful to Scripture.

Calvin most directly influenced the development of Reformed, Presbyterian, and Congregational churches. But his influence reached much further than these denominations. Calvin influenced Anabaptists, Baptists, Puritans, and other independent or congregationally oriented churches. Again, the excellences of the *Institutes* along with other writings made his theology easily distributed, understood, and communicated in local churches as well as budding denominations. Calvin's influence spread throughout not only Europe but also the world, including the American colonies. Some of the earliest denominations and religious institutions in the country were influenced by his theology through Puritan and Congregational churches, which shaped much of the early Christian identity of the United States.

In Praise of Calvinism

On a popular level, most evangelical Christians neither know nor care about Calvin (or any other theologian, for that matter). However, on the level of scholarship, publications, and popular media among evangelical Christians, there is partiality—conscious or unconscious—toward Calvin's beliefs, values, and practices. There is a variety of reasons for this, of course, and they are commendable. The partiality, however, can also be misleading. Partiality can lead to caricatures that neglect or marginalize, sometimes with the best intentions, those who do not "fit in" with Calvinism. Yet, evangelicalism is remarkably diverse, while maintaining a recognizable family resemblance. In part, because of its worldwide growth, evangelical Christianity is becoming increasingly diverse, intercultural, international, and inclusive in ways that cause some uneasiness.

Because of the theological expertise of Calvin and others from the Reformed tradition, a disproportionate amount of evangelical Christian scholarship in the United States has been shaped by it. This is not a criticism; it is a tribute to their contributions. Calvin championed, among other things, the sovereignty of God, Jesus Christ as the sole agent of salvation, and how people receive salvation by grace through faith. The principles of *sola gratia* (Latin, "grace alone") and *sola fide* (Latin, "faith alone") became rallying slogans of the Protestant Reformation. Calvin also championed Scripture as the final religious authority—*sola Scriptura* (Latin, "Scripture alone")—and the need for its diligent study. Because of Calvin's influence on Reformation and subsequent Protestant scholarship, Christians have come to identify Calvin with Protestantism, and more specially evangelicalism. Initially, the Reformers had been known as evangelicals—those who proclaimed the *euangelion* (Greek, "gospel, good news, good story"; Old English, "godspell"). The past and present success of Reformed scholarship, however, should not confuse people into thinking that Calvin speaks for all evangelical Christians.

Despite Calvin's significance in shaping the Reformed tradition, he did not represent the totality of Protestant Reformers. There were Lutherans, Anabaptists, and other so-called radical Reformers with beliefs, values, and practices quite different from Calvin. For example, Anabaptists significantly shaped later Protestant and evangelical Christian beliefs. Their emphases on a literal interpretation of the Bible and on believer's baptism continue to influence Christians. There was also the Anglican Reformation in Great Britain that developed quite differently from the Lutheran and Reformed traditions in Continental Europe. Anglicanism maintained a greater degree of continuity with the theological ideas and ecclesiastical practices of Roman Catholicism. While affirming the sovereignty of God, most Anglicans emphasized human freedom and responsibility in ways more consistent with Roman Catholic than Calvinist teachings. Anglicanism also had a more complex understanding of Scripture and its relationship to other religious authorities. Its Anglo-Catholic approach to theology and ministry profoundly influenced the overall development of Protestantism.

Calvin did not even represent the totality of what is called the Reformed tradition. Other contributors include Huldrych Zwingli, who preceded Calvin, and other Reformers such as Heinrich Bullinger and John Knox. The Reformed tradition is itself a diverse manifestation, which cannot be reduced to Calvin's influence alone. Thus, caution needs to be used in identifying evangelicalism too narrowly with Calvinism or any other individual theological tradition, denomination, or parachurch organization.

Diversity of Evangelicalism

Most people readily acknowledge the large number of evangelical Christians, including the fact that they come in many sizes, shapes, and colors. But they often are unaware of the extent of the diversity. It stands to reason, since we are limited by the times and places in which we live, that most of us forget how provincial we have become. We tend to think that people are by and large like us, when in fact most of them are not!

Several taxonomies have been created in order to talk about the diversity of evangelical Christianity. Robert Webber presents one of the more elaborate versions in *Common Roots: A Call to Evangelical Maturity*.[7] Written in 1977, Webber's list of fourteen "Subcultural Evangelical Groups," of course, is already out of date. Some subcultures do not seem relevant today, while new ones are not mentioned. For example, one could easily mention evangelical subcultures that could include Asians, Hispanics, and other ethnic groups, Baptists, Postmoderns, Emerging Churches, and so on. The dynamic, developing aspect of evangelical Christianity testifies, in part, to the difficulty in formulating a taxonomy that applies for all time. Indeed, evangelical Christianity's adaptability may represent one of its key characteristics.

Subcultural Evangelical Groups

1. Fundamentalist Evangelicalism
2. Dispensational Evangelicalism
3. Conservative Evangelicalism
4. Nondenominational Evangelicalism
5. Reformed Evangelicalism
6. Anabaptist Evangelicalism
7. Wesleyan Evangelicalism
8. Holiness Evangelicalism
9. Pentecostal Evangelicalism
10. Charismatic Evangelicalism
11. Black Evangelicalism
12. Progressive Evangelicalism
13. Radical Evangelicalism
14. Mainline Evangelicalism

The recognition of any subcultures highlights the size as well as diversity of evangelical Christianity. Amid this diversity, why would anyone identify it with only one of the subcultures, namely Calvinism? Reformed Evangelicalism refers explicitly to only one of the aforementioned subcultures, even if it has been one of the most influential ones.

Reasons for the prominence of Calvinism, of course, include several factors: the persuasiveness of Calvin's theology, the pervasiveness of its theological and ecclesiastical influence, the historical longevity of Calvinism, Christians' general familiarity with it, its cultural connection with people in the United States, its applicability to those in various positions of power, and so on. Calvinism has influenced evangelical Christianity beyond the number of those who claim it as their theological heritage. However, how has that influence restricted evangelical Christian self-understanding?

There are many ways the narrow association of evangelical Christianity with one manifestation of it can be misleading. A number of instructive examples could be given. However, I want to focus on one of the more defining aspects of Calvinism, particularly because it is related to one of the most conspicuous characteristics of evangelical Christianity. Broadly speaking, my discussion has to do with the relationship between divine predestination and human freedom, particularly in regard to the Christian understanding of salvation. At first glance, one might wonder how this discussion relates at all to the self-understanding of evangelicalism. Yet, the relationship between divine predestination and human freedom lies close to the heart of evangelical Christianity because of the movement's emphasis on the gospel, its proclamation, the importance of conversion, and the need to evangelize.

Divine Predestination, Human Freedom, and Salvation

Calvin has been influential in the evangelical (and all Protestants') understanding of salvation, especially salvation by grace through faith. These words for conversion were epitomized in the Reformation principles of *sola gratia* and *sola fide*—grace alone and faith alone. Calvin strongly argued for the sovereignty of God and how people, because of sin, were incapable of doing anything to merit salvation. Divine grace alone and people's faith alone, which the Bible calls "the gift of God" (Eph. 2:8), are the only means by which people are saved. In emphasizing God's sovereign role, Calvin critiqued Roman Catholic beliefs and practices about salvation. He thought that Roman Catholicism minimized the severity of sin and overemphasized the role people, the church, and especially the sacraments played in people's salvation.

In everyday discourse, Protestant Christians like to talk about how "God does everything" and "we do nothing." "We give God all the glory!" On one level, these statements make perfect sense, since Christians do believe that God initiates, sustains, and completes people's salvation. They cannot merit or earn their salvation. However, on another level, how do Christians understand their role in salvation? Are they entirely passive? Automatons? Are they saved by grace exclusively, or do they have a genuine role? Of course, Calvin—like Luther and other Protestants—emphasized the need for faith. People are saved by faith, through grace (a la Eph. 2:8–9). What does it mean, though, to be saved by faith alone? Is faith passive—a gift? Can it also be active, conscious, and responsible?

There are many ways Protestants understand what the Bible, Calvin, and the Protestant Reformation say about salvation, grace, and faith. Most in the Calvinist tradition have tended toward emphasizing the sovereignty of God and the minimizing of human responsibility and freedom. Of course, Calvinists would not say that they have in any way minimized human responsibility and freedom. Instead they might say that the Bible teaches both divine sovereignty and human responsibility, and that people are responsible for the rejection of Jesus; the elect will not reject Jesus because they are new creations whose desire is to accept God's free offer of salvation. This issue is captured well in *Predestination and Free Will: Four Views of Divine Sovereignty and Human Freedom*, edited by David Basinger and Randall Basinger. The book contains four views, two of which reflect Calvinist and Reformed theology. John Feinberg, who takes a Calvinist perspective, says,

The key is not whether someone's acts are causally determined or not, but rather how they are determined. . . . If the act is according to the agent's desires, then even though the act is causally determined, it is free and the agent is morally responsible.[8]

Similarly, Norman Geisler takes what could be called a moderate Calvinist perspective. He says,

God is responsible for bestowing freedom, but humans are responsible for behaving with it. . . . This view could be called "soft" determinism in contrast to "hard determinism." The latter holds that God not only gives humans the power of choice, but God actually performs the free choice through humans.[9]

In contrast, Bruce Reichenbach takes an Arminian perspective and thinks that Calvinist views of freedom are an illusion. He says,

In sum, the compatibilist [or Calvinist] attempt to reconcile determinism and human freedom is unsuccessful. On its view freedom turns out to be an illusion. . . . We must abandon the model which sees God as the cosmic novelist; God seeks not to determine our existence, but to love us into a free acceptance of his gracious salvation and a meaningful, developing and deepening relationship.[10]

To be sure, we will not resolve these issues of divine predestination and human freedom. Great debate continues with regard to what constitutes appropriate Christian views of divine sovereignty and the role people play with regard to their salvation, at least, if not also for all events in life.

Historically, Calvin reasserted many theological ideas found earlier in Augustine. In many ways, the theology of the Protestant Reformation was influenced by a resurgence in Augustinianism, a matter of some irony since Augustine also advocated much of the Catholic theology and church practice that Calvin rejected. Augustine battled the beliefs of Pelagius, who emphasized the human role in salvation and Christian life. Pelagianism, and variations of it known as semi-Pelagianism, were condemned as heresies, reminiscent of the apostle Paul's condemnation of those who believed that salvation comes through good works or works-righteousness. Thus, any views other than those of Augustine and Calvin were often thought to be Pelagian, heretical, and to be avoided at all costs.

The problem with dividing the Christian world into Calvinist and Pelagian categories is that it oversimplifies very complex issues, historically as well as biblically and theologically. Roman Catholic and Orthodox churches, for example, are not Pelagian. They are not even semi-Pelagian. If anything, they resemble more of a semi-Augustinian view, which acknowledges that God initiates, sustains, and completes people's salvation. But that does not necessarily mean, according to semi-Augustinianism, that God excludes the need for human acceptance of God's gift of salvation, which occurs by a faith that is indeterminate and freely decided. Examples include such notable Christians as Caesarius of Arles, Gregory the Great, and Thomas Aquinas. Semi-Augustinian views continued in Anglicanism and many Protestant groups, despite the fact they had to repudiate the widely held beliefs of Calvin. The most notable example appears in the debate between advocates of Calvinism and Arminianism.

Calvinism and Arminianism

Neither Calvin nor Arminius was present at the Synod of Dort (1618–19), which was a conference of Reformed Christians held in the Netherlands, but their followers met in order to discuss at least five issues related to their theology. James Arminius had been a Calvinist, who undertook a theological investigation of divine predestination and human freedom. Initially, he sided with Calvin, but then Arminius thought that Calvin allowed for a greater degree of human freedom than was accepted by Calvin's followers. After Arminius's death, his followers sought to promote his ideas, and wanted the opportunity to discuss disputed issues. However, at the Synod of Dort, Arminian views were condemned, and many adherents fled the Netherlands.

Five issues came to summarize the differences between traditional Calvinists and upstart Arminians. They include the so-called five points of Calvinism, summarized by the acronym "TULIP," which reflects the first letter of each category in the left-hand column below.[11]

Five Points

Calvinism (or Augustinianism)	Arminianism (or Semi-Augustinianism)
Total depravity: humans begin life with all aspects of their nature corrupted by the effects of sin.	Universality of sin: fallen humanity sins and cannot do good or achieve saving faith without the regenerating power of God.[12]
Unconditional election: God's choice of certain persons to salvation is not dependent on any foreseen virtue or faith on their part.	Conditional election: election and reprobation are founded on foreseen faith or unbelief (that is, based on foreknowledge).
Limited atonement: Jesus's atoning death was only for the elect.	Unlimited atonement: Jesus's death is for all, but only believers enjoy his forgiveness.
Irresistible grace: those whom God has chosen for eternal life will come to faith and thus to salvation.	Resistible grace: grace represents the beginning, continuation, and end of all good, but grace is not irresistible.
Perseverance of the saints: those who are genuine believers will endure in the faith to the end (cf. the idea of "eternal security").	Assurance of salvation: grace can preserve the faithful through every temptation so they may be assured of salvation, but Scripture does not clearly say people may not fall from grace and be lost.

In debate between Calvinists and Arminians, more is at stake than just their views of divine predestination and human freedom. But they relate mostly to Christians' understanding of salvation. To what degree are people passive or active with regard to salvation? To what degree is salvation unconditional and irresistible? Are there conditions for which people are active and responsible in receiving God's offer of salvation? Can people resist God? Salvation?

A Brief History of Sovereignty and Human Freedom

The Synod of Dort's condemnation of Arminius's views had the effect of reinforcing the centrality of divine sovereignty and predestinarian views in the Reformed tradition. However, it did not spell the end for the position held by Arminius and his followers. One reason for this is that views such as those held by Arminius had been around for a while. This reminds us that, in our selection of the Synod of Dort as a key moment in the debate about human freedom and divine sovereignty, we have set ourselves in the middle of a longer time line.

In glancing backward on this time line, a prominent name among Calvinism's predecessors has already come up: Augustine. The fact that the Reformed position picked up and developed Augustine's views on divine election, which originated more than a thousand years before Calvin, reminds us that predestinarian views were not invented by the Reformers. They had been in the church for centuries. However, in addition to Augustine's doctrine of double predestination, Roman Catholicism also had numerous theologians who taught that, through God's grace, humans could respond to God's invitation to salvation. In fact, the latter position steadily grew in prominence throughout the medieval period.

This brief prehistory of predestination can be helpful in two ways. First, it illustrates that the church can accommodate two distinctly different understandings of the relationship between God's activity and human response. They had coexisted within Catholicism for centuries (and continue to do so). While these differing views represent disagreement, they did not lead to disunity. Second, it reminds us that the relative popularity of the various views on human freedom in relationship to divine sovereignty waxes and wanes in various historical periods. The Augustinian view had decreased in popularity throughout the medieval period, but was revived by the early Reformers. The church's theological ideas always exist within a shifting historical context, and these shifts help explain why one side or another will experience resurgence or decline in different eras.

Numerous factors—moral, political, economic, social, as well as theological—merged and created the circumstances that led to Luther's attempt to bring reform to the church. While we do not have time to trace all of these strands, one of Luther's main concerns was that many then-current practices and ideas within the medieval Catholic Church assumed that God was to a large extent accessible to human reason, and that we played a significant role in our salvation. Luther's theology sought to provide a corrective to what he viewed as Pelagianism, and his emphasis on predestination was a pivotal element in this. However, Calvin, through his *Institutes*, provided the clearest and most systematic response, placing the entire initiative on divine activity in our salvation, so much the case that our election to salvation occurs prior to creation itself. For both Reformers, free will was tantamount to heresy.

In the early days of Protestantism, predestinarian views reigned supreme. As time went on, however, Protestants increasingly emphasized human accountability and the need (and, through God's grace, the ability) for people to repent and live responsibly. Two closely related reasons might be cited for this. First, human freedom was especially important to revivalist outbreaks of the seventeenth and eighteenth centuries, for example, as found in German Pietism, British Methodism, and American Great Awakenings. Some point to these revivals as being quintessentially evangelical, since they—more than other Protestants—promoted evangelism, missions, and discipleship, activities that have become characteristic of the movement. Second, many of the movements above were reacting to Protestant Scholasticism, which had become obsessed with doctrinal precision and brought about deep divisions among some Protestants as well as a loss of spiritual vitality. As a result, the pietistic and revivalist movements downplayed doctrine and focused attention on the experiential aspects of faith, conversion, and sanctification.

In summary, Arminianism, in the centuries after Dort, experienced a resurgence of the semi-Augustinianism that predated the Protestant Reformation. The Reformers had reacted against real and perceived problems in Roman Catholicism. In time, some moderation occurred among Protestants, at least with regard to how they practiced their views of divine predestination and human freedom. In theory, they may have still affirmed traditional Calvinist and Augustinian views, but some placed much less emphasis on these doctrines and more on the experience of renewed spiritual vitality. Moreover, in view of their revivalism, many lived differently, especially in their urgent appeals for people to convert: repent now, and be saved!

My, How Your Family Has Grown

The two factors we cite above as forces that dilute the influence of Calvinism—revivalism and the increasing emphasis on the experiential aspect of faith—is joined by a third historical factor that favored the ascendancy of the Arminian perspective. Shortly after the Reformation and in the following centuries, numerous new Protestant groups, almost all of them evangelical in orientation, came into existence. Instead of tracing their roots back to Luther and Calvin, many of these groups were much more comfortable with views similar to those advocated by Arminius.

Two groups that followed closely behind the early Reformation illustrate that Calvinism was not the only game in early Protestantism. First, the Anabaptists cannot best be understood by tracing their theological and ecclesiastical lineage through Calvin. They represent an independent, distinctive Reformation alternative to Lutheranism and Calvinism. Likewise, Anglicanism, which had a significant number of evangelicals in its history and is still highly evangelical in parts of the world, does not find its theological and ecclesiastical lineage through Calvin. The Church of England intentionally developed as a middle way between Catholicism and the Continental Reformation. Certainly Luther and Lutheranism did not understand themselves through Calvin.

Similarly, later manifestations of Protestantism did not arise directly through Calvinism: the Society of Friends, Pietists, and Methodists. In many ways, the latter examples did all they could to avoid certain aspects of Calvinist theology. Baptists also cannot trace all their early manifestations through Calvin or Calvinism. Rather than grounding their tradition in the Magisterial Reformation, they sought to identify their movement as a restoration of the spirit and doctrines of the first- and second-century church. The largest segments of global evangelicalism—the Pentecostals and Charismatics—certainly do not trace their theological lineage back to Calvin but to the nineteenth-century Holiness movement, which was decidedly Arminian. Most of the aforementioned groups were aware of Calvin and Calvinism, but developed out of different Christian family backgrounds. So they cannot really be understood, evaluated, and promoted as some kind of asterisk to Calvin and Calvinism.

Our point in shaking the evangelical family tree is to illustrate one of the problems of identifying Calvinism (or any theological and ecclesiastical tradition) with evangelical Christianity. Not every branch, taxonomic subculture, or family member historically came from the same background. So, how can evangelicals accurately be understood, individually and collectively, if their theological and ecclesiastical family lineage is ignored, being inaccurately identified and evaluated by the wrong Christian genetics? Doing so seems arbitrary, and unnecessarily forces evangelical Christians to fit into the same background—like trying to fit round pegs into square holes.

A Calvinist Revival

With the widespread influence of revivalism, expressive religion, and the proliferation of new, non-Calvinistic theological groups, the latter part of the nineteenth century marked a low point for Calvinism. However, resurgence for the movement came about because of developments in the late nineteenth and early twentieth centuries. The most important of these developments was the rise of theological liberalism, sometimes referred to as Modernism. Theological liberalism challenged many of the fundamental doctrines of Christianity, such as the inspiration of Scripture and the divine nature of Jesus. In addition, it had a highly optimistic perspective of human possibilities, which tended to define sin as ignorance rather than willful rebellion against God.

Many strands of evangelicalism, to be honest, did not have a sufficiently developed theology to mount an effective scholarly response to liberalism. The main exception was Calvinism, which had maintained a robust intellectual tradition that stretched back to Calvin's *Institutes*. Most notable in the defense of evangelical theology was the faculty of Princeton Seminary, a school firmly rooted in the Reformed tradition. Although this simplifies the story in many ways, Calvinism's service in addressing the doctrinal questions posed by theological liberalism fueled a revival of its influence in the evangelical world that continues into the present.

To pick out a single case study to illustrate how this influence has played out, it is informative to examine the history of the penal-substitutionary theory of atonement. For more than a century, this doctrine has been promoted as a cornerstone of evangelical theology. Calvin promoted this theory, which emphasized that Jesus represented the perfect substitute for humanity, dying for people on the cross, paying the penalty of human sin, and thus satisfying God's judgment and wrath.[13] Following Calvin's lead, the Princeton theologians made penal-substitutionary atonement central to their response. This doctrinal position was later included in *The Fundamentals*, which considered the penal-substitutionary theory of the atonement essential to fundamentalism, and today many consider it essential to evangelical Christianity.

In the twentieth century, the theory was used to counter the moral influence theory of the atonement, which was thought to be representative of Liberal Protestantism and a works-righteousness view of salvation. This, in a sense, created the impression that Christians had but two choices. One could adopt theological liberalism, with its skeptical view of many Christian doctrines and its belief that humans were progressively able to gain salvation, or one could choose (maybe that's not the right word) Calvinism, with its affirmation of historical Christian doctrine and its insistence that salvation occurs solely on the God-ward side. However, the penal-substitutionary and moral influence theories were not the only views of the atonement held by Christians. Scripture uses a variety of words to describe the atoning work of Jesus, for example, sacrifice, ransom, redemption, reconciliation, expiation, and propitiation. From these biblical terms alternative theories of the atonement arose, prior to and subsequent to Calvin. They were generally complementary to the penal-substitutionary theory, but not always. However, the theological traditions that championed these alternative views often neglected to teach them to their followers. As a result, the alternative views themselves were neglected and, in time, marginalized or discriminated against as viable evangelical doctrines. This marginalization had negative consequences for Arminian theology because the idea of free will had become identified with the Moral Influence view of atonement.

Before we move forward, an observation about strengths and weaknesses of both the Calvinist and the pietistic/revivalist strains of evangelicalism will help frame our discussion. The later nineteenth and early twentieth centuries are a hinge in evangelical history. Prior to this time, evangelical groups whose strength was in mounting a response to the immediate social and spiritual needs of people grew rapidly in number and outreach. These groups, often of recent birth and highly entrepreneurial, formed Bible societies, built orphanages, and organized huge revivals. They also built schools, but these schools were usually oriented toward training students to meet the direct and daily needs of the people they served. Often, the leaders could look back into a recent past in which they had been pulled from a life of sin into the experience of salvation, and they were energized by the urgency that others be confronted with the gospel. In general, these groups were strongly Arminian in orientation. Some of them had a coherent theology, but rarely was it clearly propagated among the general membership.

All this worked well until the rise of theological liberalism. When a new battle opened on this front, the more experientially oriented evangelicals lacked the resources to address new issues. They had not sent their theological roots deep enough to respond directly on intellectual grounds. However, the Calvinists had a real strength here; they possessed deep theological moorings nurtured by a long-standing commitment to intellectual reflection. Through historical confessions and careful catechetical instruction, it had done a good job of communicating its theology to the laity. To be sure, Calvinists had been involved in ministry in the trenches as America had pushed its frontiers westward, and they had their share of important revivalists. Yet at the end of the nineteenth century, their theology was not the main strand informing the American evangelical spirit. But when liberalism became a threat to historical Christian faith, they were prepared to play an important role.

While we will return to this topic later in the chapter, we will sum up our observation by stating that the vast majority of evangelicals do not view doctrinal orthodoxy and spiritual vitality as an either/or proposition. The ideal for which we strive combines both. However, not every theological stream that feeds the river of evangelicalism puts the same accent on both. Many of the non-Calvinistic streams had good theologians, but their strengths were in fostering a warmhearted faith that focused on practical, everyday ministry to the pressing needs of people. Their conviction that people, with the assistance of the Holy Spirit, could repent and believe propelled their efforts in ministry. The Calvinists had their share of warmhearted believers, but their strength was in theological reflection. They did theology better than any evangelical group, although many evangelicals would argue against that opinion.

Calvinism in the Fundamentalist-Modernist Controversy

Our survey thus far has sought to illustrate how Calvinism regained its mojo after a low point in nineteenth-century America. Our next step takes us to the center of this chapter's thesis, that it is invalid to identify evangelicalism with Calvinism. As part of this, it is important to understand why Roger Olson and many other Arminians believe they deserve a place at the evangelical table. The short answer is that Calvinists are more likely to retain certain characteristics of Fundamentalism than are other evangelical traditions. Many Calvinists will bristle at this because they want to make a clear distinction between themselves and Fundamentalism, and rightly so. However, certain segments of the Reformed tradition share characteristics in common with Fundamentalism. The most specific of these is a strong commitment to doctrinal purity that often manifests in a tendency to categorize people as either in or out.

As we return to the emergence of theological modernism, it is helpful to recall that what ensued is generally referred to as the "Modernist-Fundamentalist" controversy, not the "Modernist-Evangelical" debate. In many ways, the evangelicalism of nineteenth-century America, which pushed for abolition of slavery, built rescue missions, sent out thousands of missionaries, and ran revivals, was overshadowed by Fundamentalism. Rather than seeking to transform culture, as nineteenth-century evangelicals had, Fundamentalism tended to condemn and reject it. Its response to the world was to retrench in the basics of doctrine. The clearest expression of this was the publication of *The Fundamentals: A Testimony to the Truth*, a twelve-volume rebuttal of theological liberalism. It was published in 1909 and sent free to three million pastors, missionaries, and other Christian workers. The content of these volumes was summarized in five points, generally referred to as the "five fundamentals."

- Scriptural inerrancy
- The virgin birth and deity of Jesus
- Penal-substitutionary atonement
- The bodily resurrection of Jesus
- The authenticity of Christ's miracles[14]

We want to be clear that the Fundamentalist movement was not limited to Calvinist advocates, especially within Presbyterianism. Many from Arminian-oriented groups were also involved. Moreover, these "five fundamentals" include nothing distinctive to Calvinist theology (although Calvinists would be more likely than other groups to affirm inerrancy and penal-substitutionary atonement). Fundamentalism's connection with Calvinism is not so much with any particular doctrine, although Fundamentalism's doctrines were more in sync with Calvinism than with other evangelical traditions—in the inclination to frame the primary response to threatening forces in terms of doctrine rather than action. Because Calvinism's doctrines were more systematically expressed and widely propagated than those of other groups, Calvinism gained in popularity within the Fundamentalist camps.

In the early part of the twentieth century, it was often hard to differentiate between evangelicalism and Fundamentalism. Both found common cause in resistance to Liberalism. However, evangelicals, who were at the forefront in working to bring social change in an earlier period, became more ambivalent about such ministries because, in many ways, they appeared to mirror what many Liberal Christians advocated in the "social gospel." If the Liberals are running soup kitchens and advocating for the rights of the poor, is that something an evangelical should do? In reaction to Liberalism, many evangelicals began to absorb Fundamentalism's separatist tendencies and withdrew from engagement with culture. This disengagement was encouraged also by the growing influence of dispensationalism, whose views of an imminent destruction of this world put a damper on efforts for social improvement.

Toward the middle of the twentieth century, many evangelicals began to notice that Fundamentalism's influence had taken them in directions they did not want to go. First, they had second thoughts about political and social disengagement and became less willing to leave social expressions of ministry to the liberal wing of Christianity. Second, many evangelicals became frustrated with the divisiveness of Fundamentalism and its doctrinal narrowness. Out of these concerns came the birth of what many have called Neo-evangelicalism, with the founding of several flagship organizations such as the National Association of Evangelicals and the Evangelical Theological Society, which we have mentioned elsewhere.

What Do Evangelicals Fear?

Today, most evangelicals are clear that they do not want to be identified as either Liberals or Fundamentalists. At the same time, they divide on which pole of this spectrum they fear the most. Evangelicals with an Arminian-tinged theology recognize that they part ways with Liberalism on doctrinal questions, but they have deep distaste for Fundamentalism's divisive and exclusivistic attitudes about doctrine. In addition, they find common theological real estate with Liberalism in concerns about how Christians can minister toward transforming life in the here and now, and want to preserve a place for human responsibility in this process. Thus, it might be said that Arminian evangelicals are certainly not Liberals, but they would rather be called that than Fundamentalist.

In contrast, Reformed evangelicals even today are more likely than other evangelicals to sign off on all five of the "fundamentals" of Fundamentalism. They may disagree vehemently with Fundamentalist inclinations toward splintering over minute matters of doctrine and Fundamentalists' hostile attitudes toward those outside their boundaries. They do not like Fundamentalism's anti-intellectualism, and are often unhappy with its failure to address the big social questions. But what they fear even more is the threat to orthodoxy represented in Liberalism. If theology is the first line of defense against Liberalism, and Calvinism is your theology, then it may just be possible that those who hold a different theology are either Liberals or on the slippery slope in that direction.

In many ways, the Modernist-Fundamentalist debate still shapes evangelicalism. A glance at Webber's taxonomy of evangelical groups seems to indicate most American evangelicals do not fit in the Calvinistic category. Nevertheless, Liberalism is still the greatest perceived threat for most evangelicals. Too often evangelicals fear that the only extreme to which they are vulnerable is the direction of liberalism, humanism, and secularism. However, that is not the case. They are equally vulnerable to Fundamentalism's sectarian tendencies, isolationism, anti-intellectualism, and retreat from today's world. Veering too far right, so to speak, is just as dangerous as veering too far left.

Our decades of studying and working in evangelical educational institutions provide almost daily examples of how a reflexive fear of Liberalism pervades evangelical culture. For example, when students hear religion faculty teaching about the Bible and theological topics that are new to them, it sometimes feels uncomfortable, especially if the new knowledge seems contrary to, or even just different from, things that were familiar to them before they left home, family, and their other supports in life. If students consider themselves to be "conservative," more or less, then their inference is that new things they learn must be "liberal." On one level, everyone knows that all new ideas, including ideas about the Bible or the Christian life, are not necessarily liberal. However, if students lack sufficient background in religious studies or the maturity to question that which they cannot easily understand, they may leave class complaining about how liberal the professor, class, and university are. (We do not hear students complaining that their professors are Fundamentalist.) Parents are called. Pastors are consulted. Rumors are spread. Constituencies complain, and administrators are not always well equipped or able, in a timely manner, to respond to complaints against the institution. To some readers, this scenario itself seems alarmist. But anyone who has long taught in an evangelical Christian college, university, seminary, church, youth group, Sunday school class, or parachurch ministry is excruciatingly aware of how problematic accusations are of the "L-word." (And we're not talking about lesbianism here; that's in a later chapter.)

Our point is certainly not that we should ignore the problems of theological liberalism. We are evangelicals, not Liberals, because we believe that Liberalism is theologically deficient in many ways (although, like almost every evangelical in a visible role, we have been accused of Liberalism a few times). Instead, we want to remember that evangelicals are *neither* Liberal *nor* Fundamentalist. When we become preoccupied with the dangers of

Liberalism, we often fall into Fundamentalist tendencies that are every bit as corrosive as anything in Liberalism. In our desire to be doctrinally correct, we become arrogant and judgmental. Instead of seeking to understand theological views that differ from ours, we simply attach the dreaded "liberal" label to it and congratulate ourselves on winning the battle. The damage caused by this sort of behavior is evident in evangelical circles. Reputations are damaged, pastors are fired, people leave church and never come back, non-Christians are repulsed by our bickering and divisiveness, and evangelicals, who should be allies, expend far too much of their energy expelling each other from the family.

There is a valid place for holding each other accountable for doctrine and similar claims to "propositional truth," but there is also a proper way to go about it. Before becoming modern-day heresiologists, people need to check with everyone involved in a complaint, and then discuss it—at least—with those who are knowledgeable about and have some wisdom with regard to the issues involved. Matthew 18:15–20 is always a helpful passage to consult when considering heresy hunting. Uncovering misperceptions, miscommunications, and misunderstandings can go a long way toward resolving problems interpersonally as well as theologically. It also would not hurt to remember that our actions should be guided by love.

Theory and Practice

You do not have to be too observant to recognize that people are wired differently. For example, some people gravitate toward theory. They love to think through ideas, the tougher the better, and see how they link up with related ideas. Others, however, are geared for practice. They see tasks that scream for attention and relish the thought of figuring out how to do them better than anyone else has done them. Sometimes, when "theory people" have to get along with "practice people," they can drive each other crazy. However, they need each other.

These categories, rough as they are, also apply to theological traditions. Some have strengths in constructing doctrinal systems and thinking comprehensively. Calvinism is a good example of a theory-oriented evangelical tradition. Historically, Calvin provided a systematic theology that helped the burgeoning Protestant Reformation put things together theologically in a rapidly fragmenting world. His theology was rationally clear and persuasive, and it helped the movement self-identify and grow in contrast with the ecclesiastical and cultural hegemony of Roman Catholicism. Other evangelical traditions, especially those that emerged in a very different historical context, have a more practical orientation. They keenly feel the hurt and lostness of people and, moved by the love of God, quickly jump into the fray. Arminian theological traditions overwhelmingly populate the "doer" groups.

Of course, our categories above are huge generalizations, and potentially misleading. No individual or group falls exclusively in the "practitioner" or "theoretician" column. Theological traditions that carefully nurture their intellectual systems sometimes come through with flying colors in acting out their faith. Likewise, the "doer" groups often have clear, coherent, and fully developed theological infrastructures behind their activity. However, our generalization may help bring focus to two issues within the broader evangelical movement.

First, it reminds us why Calvinists and Arminians often drive each other crazy over the doctrine of predestination. Arminians, with their strong practice orientation, often believe that Calvinist theology might be a nifty system, but is completely disconnected with the way we actually function. For example, the Bible seems to be shot through with verses about human responsibility, indeterminate choices, and the idea that all people, not just some (Calvinists' limited atonement), have the possibility of responding, with God's help, in repentance and a faith that leads to salvation.

Of course, this sort of argument makes good Calvinists want to tear their hair out. After all, the Bible is full of passages that speak of God's election and sovereignty. Moreover, if God is indeed sovereign, is it not completely illogical to believe that God could fail? Therefore, if Christ died for all and all have the possibility of coming to faith, but some do not, what else can we conclude but that God has failed to do something he desires. Finally, what part of "by grace *alone*" is so hard for those Arminians to understand?

It is not hard to see how these different perspectives solidify into divisive caricatures. Arminians, for example, often simply cannot conceive of how Calvinists would frame a coherent understanding of evangelicalism, completely ignoring the reality that many of Protestantism's greatest revivalists have come from this tradition. On the other hand, Calvinists often accuse Arminians of selling out divine sovereignty, even though evangelical Arminians do not seem to have banished this topic from their understanding of God's nature. All too often, each group accuses the other of being selective in the use of Scripture.

A second way in which Calvinists and Arminians drive each other nuts is in their differing perceptions of the biggest danger confronting Christian faith. If we look back to the quote from David Wells at the beginning of the chapter, two key words pop out: "truth" and "orthodoxy." For him, as for many Calvinists, maintaining biblical truth and orthodoxy is the defining task of evangelicalism. If people find their roots in the doctrinal struggles of the Magisterial Reformation and/or the Fundamentalist-Modernist controversy, this concern makes perfect sense. However, many other evangelical groups, most of them Arminian in theology, focus on times in our history when Protestants were persecuting, executing, factionalizing, condemning, excommunicating, and going to war with other Protestants—all in the name of truth and orthodoxy. These groups just cannot comprehend how Calvinists fail to see all the wreckage caused by an inordinate focus on propositional truth and absolutes. In contrast, some Calvinists are incredulous that other evangelicals can be so unconcerned about challenges to truth and do not see the necessity of scheduling annual apologetics conferences.

A lot of the discussion in this chapter focuses on differences within evangelicalism that constantly threaten to become divisions. However, if we draw in what we have said above, perhaps we can see an important benefit of evangelicalism. Sometimes historical circumstances require renewed focus on questions of truth and orthodoxy. In the past, some segments of evangelicalism were not in a position to meet these challenges because they had been neglectful of the long-term task of developing their theology and nurturing an intellectual culture among their pastors and laity. That is dangerous, and we need people who will remind us of it. At other times in history, evangelicals have been dogmatic, divisive, and just plain ugly to each other in their quest to preserve orthodoxy. That is also dangerous, and it is important that Christians step up and challenge these tendencies.

Churches talk a lot about the need for Christians to have others who hold them accountable, identify their blind spots, and encourage their faith. It is a good idea. It is also a good idea for different theological traditions. Various theological groups have their strengths, but these can result in imbalances that need to be brought into view. We develop cultural or racial insensitivities, which is why evangelicals need to listen to sisters and brothers of various races and nationalities. Our churches or denominations can become socially or politically homogeneous, so we need the mirror of evangelicals who experience the world differently. We deal with these in greater depth in other chapters. However, because every theological tradition has blind spots, we need outsiders to free us from the echo chambers of our own group. When we identify evangelicalism with any single tradition within the movement, those who do not fit our stereotype feel neglected or marginalized. It is no wonder that a growing number of evangelical Christians choose to not identify with the movement, despite bona fide credentials. For example, some prefer just to call themselves Asian, Black, or Hispanic Christians, or Anabaptist, Wesleyan, or Pentecostal Christians. When these groups distance themselves from the broader evangelical family, we lose important avenues to accountability.

Conclusion

A theme that runs between the lines of this entire book is the ambiguity of the term "evangelical." We are often frustrated by lack of precision, and rightly so. When words can mean anything, ultimately they mean nothing. However, there are also dangers in defining terms too narrowly. In doing so, you can leave out certain things that are properly included in the category. Our concern throughout this chapter is that there are theological and ecclesiastical forces at work among evangelical Christians that seek to narrow, specify in clear-cut propositional statements, and perhaps control what are and are not acceptable beliefs. In their view, if the beliefs of some who claim to be evangelical are not acceptable, a reckoning is needed for the sake of "true truths" and "absolute absolutes."

We do not have a problem with truth and absolutes, and we are big fans of Christian orthodoxy. We do, however, have problems with a vocal minority within Calvinism who believe that their specific version of truth and orthodoxy alone qualifies a person rightly to claim inclusion in the evangelical ranks. Calvin represents one of the best and most influential fountainheads of evangelical Christianity. But he by no means speaks for all, or for even the majority. The very term "evangelical" defies identification with a particular person or theological movement, other than the Bible. Certainly family resemblances are recognizable among people, churches, theological traditions, and other institutions. Likewise, the understanding of evangelical Christianity should not be so broad that it makes the term incoherent and unusable. Finding a *via media* (Latin, "middle way") may be no easy task, but it is better to approximate a moving target than to settle for an identifiable but misleading bull's-eye.

The free-will-versus-predestination debate has been around for centuries. We suspect that it is not going away any time soon. There have been some unfortunate chapters in the controversy. At the Synod of Dort, it was not enough to agree to disagree. The views of Arminius were condemned, a political leader who supported him was beheaded, another was sentenced to life imprisonment, and two hundred Arminian pastors were stripped of ecclesiastical orders. What is ironic is that, except for theological differences on these questions, the Arminians and Calvinists were closer theological kin to each other than any other groups.

If history offers some tragic examples of how these theological debates have divided Christians, it also provides snapshots of times when disagreement did not lead to division and condemnation. Great things have been done in joint efforts despite the theological differences. The eighteenth-century relationship between Calvinist-leaning George Whitefield and Arminian-leaning John Wesley provides an instructive example of how this has worked. Together, they led the revival in the British Isles and became two of the pivotal promoters of the evangelical movement. The two men had a decades-long relationship that began in their student days and lasted until Whitefield's death, when Wesley gave the funeral oration. We do not want to sugarcoat the situation. Many times the relationship was strained by disagreements between Whitefield's Calvinism and the Arminian theology that arose from Wesley's thoughts. However, the bigger mission of evangelizing the lost and encouraging holy lives in believers continued to draw them back together.

Examples such as these, in which we witness the fruitfulness of transcending theological distinctives to tackle important tasks, help explain why we so strongly resist the temptation to draw our theological wagons into ever-tighter circles. We do not advocate "big tent" evangelicalism for the sake of a big tent. We do it because experience has shown us that great works have been done when those transformed by God's grace reach across theological divides. We also think history is on the side of the "big tent." The story of evangelicalism is not the story of any one ecclesiastical or denominational group. It consists of countless stories of Christians from across the theological spectrum united in concerns about both orthodoxy and orthopathy, true doctrine and right-heartedness.

More than anything else, we want to celebrate the breadth and depth of evangelical Christianity. Are there identifiable markers of the movement? Yes. In fact, in our final chapter, we reproduce some of the most frequently cited theological summaries of evangelical belief (and none of them include either free will or predestination in their definitions). But in seeking to recognize and communicate the family resemblances, one may err on the side of narrowness as well as breadth. Admittedly, in this book, we are more concerned about narrow, caricatured definitions of evangelicalism than of broad, insipid definitions. But we do not think that evangelicals need only fear growth in the direction of Liberalism, humanism, and secularism. There is also the danger of Fundamentalism, anti-intellectualism, and other characteristics adverse toward biblical, historical Christianity. Wedding one's definition of evangelicalism too narrowly to any one person, church tradition, or set of doctrinal boundaries robs the movement of its historical breadth and depth. To flourish, evangelical Christianity needs to be recognized by its family quirks and unique contributions as well as by its family resemblances.

Evangelical Christians owe much to Calvin and the tradition of Calvinist and Reformed beliefs, values, churches, denominations, and other institutions. Calvin remains one of the giants not only of the Protestant Reformation but also of evangelical Christianity. His writings and role model have shaped evangelical Christianity through the development of Protestantism to the present day. Neither historically nor theologically can one talk about evangelicalism without mentioning Calvin's contributions. On a personal level, we the authors are sincerely grateful for his legacy. However, we must respectfully disagree with some of Calvin's modern-day followers. Evangelicalism is not the sole domain of the Calvinists.

8

Evangelicals Are Not All
Republicans

When all of the sociological, behavioral, and theological factors are tallied, I (Steve) have a pretty impressive evangelical pedigree. I grew up as a farm boy from the buckle of the Bible Belt, with Sunday School perfect attendance pins to prove it. My vehicle is a pickup—a big, beefy one, not one of those little wannabe models—and I have a big, beefy hound dog who rides around in it with me. My postsecondary degrees are from evangelical institutions, and I teach at a self-described evangelical university with an evangelical statement of faith. I have been the husband of one wife for three decades, with two children who attend Christian schools. We all go to an evangelical church together. Even with the mandatory two-point deduction for not homeschooling, my evangelical purity index is above the 90th percentile.

If none of this convinces you that I am a real evangelical, my ace in the hole is that I am a registered Republican. Not just a garden-variety Republican, but what political wonks call a "broken-glass Republican," as in "willing-to-crawl-on-my-knees-through-broken-glass-to-vote-Republican" type of Republican. Alas, although my coauthor easily passes muster by the grids typically employed to determine evangelical credentials, he fails this last test. Therefore, unlike the other chapters in this book, this one is written in first person singular because only a Republican has any hope of credibly advancing the major thesis of this chapter: evangelicals are not all Republican.

Given the drumbeat of American political discourse concerning the close marriage between evangelicals and the GOP, some explanation is in order about what we mean by the statement, "Evangelicals are not all Republican."

To borrow a well-worn political phrase, it depends on what the meaning of "is" is. Numerically, a majority of evangelicals *in this country* do express an electoral preference for the Republicans. However, the Republicans' share of evangelicals is not as large as most believe. "Pollster evangelicals" are not the same breed as actual evangelicals, as we will see below.

Ultimately, however, the statement, "Evangelicals are not all Republican," is not about counting noses. It is about the essence of evangelicalism. While more American *evangelicals* are Republican than Democratic, *evangelicalism* is not Republican. Evangelicalism is a worldwide movement, and labels such as "Democratic" or "Republican" have little application to evangelicals in Ecuador, South Korea, or the Ivory Coast. It is also a historical movement that predates the existence of any American political party, or the existence of the United States. Finally, political parties are about this world's kingdoms. Christianity's main concern is the kingdom of God. As a segment of the Christian world, evangelicalism can never allow itself to be defined by political categories. Because this world's kingdoms have a God-given legitimacy, Christians cannot ignore their role and duties within them. However, those who seek first the kingdom of God must remain captive to God's aims or their goals will be hijacked by those governing earthly kingdoms. As Christians, our earthly lives are characterized by dual citizenship in which our duties to earthly kingdoms should be subsumed under and defined by the heavenly kingdom.

It is in this "kingdom overlap" that things get tricky. Any time Christians begin a sentence with "I am a(n) . . . ," we wade into the perilous waters of overlapping kingdoms. No matter what descriptor we put in the blank, no matter how good and worthy the affiliation, it always threatens to co-opt our faith. This certainly does not mean we should avoid those affiliations, whether they are interest groups, alumni/ae associations, church memberships, family loyalties, pet owners clubs, or political associations. These good things stem from our God-given social nature. However, the greatest spiritual dangers come from good things used badly, and political affiliations hover somewhere toward the top of the list of good realities that hold great spiritual danger.

This is a necessary chapter because the danger that evangelicalism can be co-opted by political agendas is not just theoretical. Some Christians link particular government policies with the gospel in such a manner that the dividing line between them is indiscernible. Since evangelicals most often make these claims from the Republican side of the political divide, I will focus my attention here, although non-evangelical Christians and evangelical Democrats are equally as guilty. Along with this, we need to recognize that many perceive evangelicalism as a wholly owned and operated franchise of the Republican Party. Both factors—identifying Republican positions with the gospel and outsiders' perception that evangelicalism is the Republican Party at prayer—represent significant threats to our effectiveness, integrity, and unity. These three concerns reside both in and between the lines of this chapter. Therefore, before we move on, I want to outline briefly how the identification of evangelicalism and Republican represents a hindrance to evangelicalism's effectiveness, integrity, and unity.

If evangelicals want to communicate the gospel effectively to the world, it is critical that others recognize this goal as our fundamental loyalty. However, as noted above, millions of non-evangelicals have little or no perception of the evangelical movement except in its political manifestation. This creates a major barrier to our effectiveness as gospel witnesses because the majority of these outsiders have political views that differ, sometimes quite sharply, from the principles and goals of the Republican Party. Thus, if people have strong political leanings toward the Democratic end of the political spectrum, will they have good reason to assume they will not be welcome at your church? Should evangelicals suppose that one must undergo a political "conversion" before we trust the validity of their religious convictions? It is not difficult to see how outsiders will be reluctant to respond positively to the gospel when they (or we) assume that it drags a load of political baggage behind it. If they know nothing of us but our party affiliation, do you think they will love our Jesus if they believe he is a Republican?

A fundamental definition of integrity is that one's actions are consistent with what one claims to be. The Christian's main task is mediating God's love to the world, but it is not difficult to find inconsistencies between this message and the usual course of political activity. We claim that Jesus is the sole redeemer of a lost world, then act as if our fortunes ride on the success of a particular law or candidate. Words about loving our neighbors, and even our enemies, are drowned out in misrepresentations of those on the opposite end of the political spectrum. We talk *ad nauseam* about how Jesus challenges us to a radical new ethic, but our political discourse too often defaults to the same old power tactics of politics. To the extent that evangelical Christians of any political tribe engage in these sorts of political strategies, or even remain silent about them, we forfeit our integrity.

Finally, we need to wake up to the unfortunate fact that politics is one of the most potent causes of Christian disunity. This disunity provides one of the best tests for determining the extent to which our political loyalties have displaced our primary allegiance to Christ's work. Craig Payne states it well: "It is a disquieting truth that liberal Christians seem to have more in common with liberal non-Christians, and conservative Christians with conservative non-Christians, than either Christian group has with the other."[1] If we stake our identity on political inclinations and find greater unity with non-Christians within our party affiliations, we betray our claim to be followers of a Lord who makes us one.

Crunching the Numbers

Baseball and politics have a few things in common. Both have seasons that never seem to end, which may be why baseball seasons are sometimes called "campaigns." Perhaps more relevant is that baseball and politics are both about winning, and numbers play a fundamental role in clarifying why one team comes out on top while another retools for the next season. Because Christianity requires a different definition of winning than politics and baseball, the metrics we apply to determine how well we are playing the game will also be different. We need to crunch the numbers in the light of our faith to evaluate how we might better represent Christ in our civic involvement. Therefore, we will examine some statistical data about evangelical political involvement and consider the theological implications of these numbers.

Pollsters tell us that evangelicals comprise about 25 percent of the American electorate, which puts them on a par with Catholic voters. These are the two largest voting blocks, together comprising about half the voters. Catholics often split evenly between Republican and Democratic in national elections, making them a bellwether for predicting election outcomes. This is not the case for evangelicals. When voting patterns are broken down, evangelicals have gone overwhelmingly to the Republican side in recent contests. About two-thirds of evangelicals voted for George W. Bush in 2000, a number that went up to about three-fourths in his 2004 reelection. While many evangelicals considered Bush a strong ally, they were generally thought to be more ambivalent about John McCain. Nevertheless, McCain pulled in about 74 percent of the evangelical vote in the 2008 presidential election.[2]

These figures *appear* to prove the prevailing notion that evangelicalism is strongly identifiable with Republican politics. However, this is not as accurate as it seems for the simple reason that when pollsters speak of the "evangelical vote," they almost always leave out an important adjective: "white." As a result, more than one-quarter of Americans who identify themselves as evangelical to pollsters are omitted simply because they are not Caucasian, with African-American (15 percent) and Hispanic (5 percent) evangelicals comprising most of the uncounted remainder. The significance of this is that both of these constituencies are overwhelmingly Democratic in their voting patterns. If their numbers are incorporated, it quickly becomes evident that "evangelical voter," as used by pollsters, is a misnomer. Including Hispanic and African-American evangelicals in tallies of party loyalty significantly reduces the differential between evangelical and non-evangelical voters.

In almost every poll, evangelicals are identified by self-description. If one calls him- or herself "evangelical" or "born again," into the evangelical demographic slot they go, as long as they are white.[3] The obvious question is why "pollster evangelicals" come up about 26 percent shy of the actual number of self-identified evangelicals. Gallup pollsters explain that they exclude minorities from this count because "at least 9 in 10 blacks vote for the Democratic candidate for president each election. So, the inclusion of blacks in the group of 'evangelicals' being defined for analytic reasons obscures analysis to the degree that the purpose of defining the group is to measure their influence on political life in particular."[4]

This rationale is odd because it starts from a preconceived notion of how evangelicals vote and excludes those who deviate from the assumption, despite their self-identification. It is also a problematic rationale because these "analytic reasons" undermine the significance of respondents' religious commitments. An individual's voluntarily offered description of a spiritual commitment is at the heart of one's identity. If that is trumped because it goofs up pollsters' predetermined political assumptions (racial profiling?), both minorities and whites who identify themselves as evangelicals are arbitrarily redefined as political entities.

The problem for evangelicals arises when we, perhaps unconsciously, start to think of ourselves as the pollsters do—as political partisans. Americans of all races should be united by faith in Christ, even when they embrace differing political affiliations. However, when "evangelical" morphs into a political designation rather than an indicator of spiritual commitments, we lose the unifier (the primary reality) and underline our political allegiances, a secondary reality that stresses our differences.

The effects of defining "evangelicalism" as a political designation are devastating. If the next presidential election follows the pattern of the last few contests, the evening news may show video of a Democratic candidate in the pulpit of an African American church followed immediately by a story describing a suburban megachurch's efforts to distribute voter guides intended to mobilize members toward Republican candidates. Will outside observers see Christians in those respective churches as sisters and brothers committed to furthering God's kingdom together? Or will the lingering image be one of insurmountable division that pits "evangelicals" (but only the white ones) against the "black church" (even though the vast majority in the "black church" self-identify as evangelicals)? Even more trenchant is the question of how members of the two churches will view each other across the political divide. Will I, a Republican in a mostly white, evangelical, suburban megachurch, view my African-American or Hispanic counterpart as a co-worker in God's mission or as a political adversary? How will members of those churches see me?

Outside entities have reasons, analytical and otherwise, for attaching political, social, cultural, or racial definitions to evangelicalism. If we buy into this, alien definitions will shape our self-understanding and leave us in danger of forgetting the essential focus of evangelicalism. This perpetuates racial and social divisions that have no place in God's kingdom. The "Evangelical Manifesto" recognizes the divisive force of these alien definitions and wisely reminds us that, "contrary to widespread misunderstanding today, we Evangelicals should be defined theologically, not politically, socially or culturally."[5]

While our first statistical "remix" examined how recasting evangelicalism as a political category jeopardizes Christian unity, our second statistical consideration questions an assumption embedded in the phrase "evangelical voter." When poll-takers employ this phrase, it implies that "evangelical" is the salient factor in how we vote. However, a second element, the so-called God-gap, challenges this interpretation. The "God-gap" refers to the observation that frequency of attendance at religious services, regardless of one's religious affiliation, is one of the most reliable predictors of voting tendencies. For example, those who attended religious services once a week or more— evangelical, mainline Protestant, Catholic, Jewish, or Muslim—voted Republican in presidential elections by significant margins in both 2000 (63 percent) and 2004 (64 percent). In contrast, those who rarely or never attended religious services voted for Democratic candidates by almost equal margins (61 percent in 2000, 62 percent in 2004).[6]

The "God-gap" suggests that evangelical alignment with the Republican Party does not grow out of our theological particularities but is linked with something shared by all frequent worship attendees. That "something" appears to have a lot to do with the importance placed on tradition. The Religious Landscape Survey reveals a strong correlation between frequency of attendance and desire to conserve[7] tradition.[8] "Conserve" and "tradition" go together rather naturally. All religions are deeply grounded in tradition, and strongly committed adherents will desire to conserve and pass on that tradition. The God-gap provides an explanation for why consistent worship attendees, evangelicals as well as adherents of other religious expressions, are attracted to a more conservative political party such as the Republican Party. Phrases such as "traditional values" or "traditional marriage" resonate positively with individuals who believe that the best answers are anchored in tradition. Similarly, those with a less-than-positive view of tradition will have negative responses to any noun modified by "traditional."

If the nexus between evangelicals and the Republican Party is a shared desire to conserve tradition, this holds dangers for evangelicals, who often use "conservative" as a synonym for "true" or "good." To the extent that we conserve that which is genuinely Christian, I have no problem with this. However, we often fail to distinguish clearly between Christian tradition and political or historical tradition. We must take care to not confuse the eternal with the temporal. For example, American political conservatism emphasizes the individual's freedom to dispose of property with minimal interference by external entities. It is more ambiguous, however, whether this conserves a Christian position on property. Certain political traditions may indeed be worthy of preservation. However, in the past, evangelicals have challenged traditions such as slavery and the subjugation of women that have perpetuated evils. Simply put, not all traditions are Christian traditions. If our national or historical traditions do not fall under the judgment of Christian tradition, what we conserve will be a form of idolatry.

The second question for Christians is whether governmental policy or law is the proper means of conserving the Christian faith. To use a fairly clear-cut example, the vast majority of Christians would not support laws that punish those who refuse to convert. History has demonstrated that conversion by political coercion is not a very good idea. Matters are less clear on other issues, however. For example, a large majority of evangelicals believe that same-sex marriage is wrong. Yet there is divergence within evangelical circles about whether Christians should look to laws as a means of conserving our views on marriage. In short, evangelicals have valid reasons for wanting to conserve certain ideas and practices. The question is if political actions are the best means to do this. This raises the question to which we now turn: how should we properly understand the interaction between the church and government?

Government, Nation, and God

Our discussion to this point has started at the end of a much bigger story about the interaction of God's people and government. Both entities have been around for a long time, and Scripture is filled with accounts of the dealings of God's people with government. However, when we go to Scripture to understand how Christians should handle political engagement, we immediately notice two important factors. First, direct analogues between the governmental, social, and economic systems of Scripture and those of modern nations such as the United States are nowhere to be found. Scripture describes a diverse variety of governmental systems—tribal clans, theocracies, monarchies, and empires, to name a few. However, the modern nation is, well, modern. Even newer is the belief that broad swaths of citizens have the right (and duty) to participate in government by means of political parties. Throughout Scripture, indeed throughout most of postbiblical history, the overwhelming majority of citizens simply responded to government. Similarly, economic systems such as socialism and capitalism are newcomers on the historical stage. A two-party, modified capitalistic, participatory, democratic nation such as the United States is not found in the governmental or social configurations of the Bible.

My second observation is that the relationship between God's people and the prevailing political powers has been a dynamic affair. A few snapshots offer a glimpse into the variety. The tensions between Abraham's landless clan and the kingdoms in which they pastured their flocks (e.g., Gen. 13:1–14:17) and Abraham's concern about self-preservation with Pharaoh in Egypt (Gen. 12:10–20) are good indicators of how tenuous was the nomads' political standing. On the other hand, the Davidic kingdom put God's people in a politically powerful status. For most of the period between Solomon and the birth of Jesus, God's people were dispersed or minor vassals of a succession of empires—Assyria, Babylon, Greece, and Rome. At the church's birth, the Roman Empire alternated between general toleration of Christians and periods of persecution. A catalog of relationships between government and God's people over the past two thousand years would only reinforce the examples above. Scripture offers no single model of how God's people have interacted with governments.

We cannot simply transcribe biblical models into our present government and economic circumstances, as some Christians want to do. To take the Bible's call for individual financial responsibility as a direct support of capitalism or to read our current government's welfare safety net into Scripture's call to care for the poor overlooks the fact that these systems have no direct analogues in the worlds of Abraham, Jesus, and Paul. This is not to say that support for a relatively unfettered capitalism or expansion of our welfare structure are illegitimate political stances for Christians. However, we cannot make that determination from direct parallels drawn from Scripture. We will need to do some careful theology to understand how Christians should engage in the form of government we currently have.

Some Principles

Because Scripture does not provide a ready-made script for American Christian political involvement, we must rely on some broad theological principles for guidance. For the sake of brevity, we will consider four such principles, realizing that others could be added. Because they are broad biblical standards, few Christians should find them debatable. The debates will begin later, when we see how, even with complete agreement about these theological guidelines, Christians disagree strongly on their boundaries and the means by which we enact them.

Our first theological principle is that God ordains for secular governments a legitimate role in human society. Romans 13:1–7, perhaps the most extensive passage that addresses church-state relations, tells Christians, "Everyone must submit himself to the governing authorities" (NIV) (cf. Titus 3:1; 1 Peter 2:13–15). However, this is immediately followed by an important qualifying phrase: "for there is no authority except that which God has established." No matter how any government views itself, it is not self-legitimizing.

This single verse contains two enduring tensions that mark a Christian's relationship to government. First, while governments have valid authority, it is a derived and limited authority. A believer's ultimate authority is God, and submission to government authority follows from religious motives. Moreover, because governmental authority is both derived and limited, Christians must resist government's demands when it oversteps its proper limits. A second tension is more implicit, but nonetheless present. While government is authorized by God, it imperfectly reflects God's will for civic life. When Paul penned his letter to the Romans, he was keenly aware that the government he told Christians to submit to was the same one that crucified Jesus and often made his own life extremely trying. These two tensions should induce a great deal of reflection for Christians who are called to exhibit loyalty and obedience to governments that are capable of, and will inevitably participate in, great evil.

What we have said above leads rather directly to our second principle: governments can and do claim powers that overstep their authority. Scripture does not provide an unambiguous accounting of government's realm of authority, although it specifically legitimates levying taxes and punishing wrongdoers (Matt. 22:21; Rom. 13:4–7). Christian thinkers have often condensed these ideas into two broad areas of government authority—the restraint of evil and provision for the common good. However, authority and power are two different things, and because few institutions have the resources to curb governments, authorities may employ brute strength or legal force to claim powers that God does not authorize. No other collective entity has the legal right to imprison you, execute you, mandate certain types of education for your children, seize property that you legally own, determine minimum wages for employees, send you to war, and countless other actions that can have a profound effect on people's lives. Because government claims power in so many areas, it has ample opportunity for trespassing its rightful authority, and Christians must be vigilant about government encroachment.

Governmental trespassing is always a possibility because states share the field with other divinely ordained institutions. As Ron Sider points out, "The fact that God has divinely instituted other institutions in society (e.g., the family, the church) demands a limited state. God, not the state, creates and establishes family and church and gives them freedom and authority to carry out their responsibilities independent of the state. Only if the state is appropriately limited can other institutions in society flourish as God intended."[9]

The third principle of Christian political theology is that redemption occurs solely through the work of Jesus Christ. Some governments do a commendable job of minimizing the incidence of crime, providing workable transportation systems, and fulfilling other responsibilities that fall under the general headings of restraining evil and providing for the common good. Nevertheless, no governmental program, law, or policy can directly address the problem of sin and bring us into saving relationship with Christ. Governments can legislate rules about keeping our grubby hands off other people's property or treating people justly in employment opportunities. Nevertheless, no law or policy can mandate that these behaviors are motivated by the love of Christ, something at the heart of the gospel.

The prophet Jeremiah wrote to the exiles in Babylon, "Seek the welfare of the city where I have sent you into exile, and pray to the LORD on its behalf, for in its welfare you will find your welfare" (Jer. 29:7). This brings us to our fourth principle. Christians are not simply to obey government authorities and avoid wrongdoing. We are to work for the betterment of all society, not just our specific religious group or family. Moreover, the context of Jeremiah's command is critical. Israel is in exile; it is a captive people in a hostile society. Regardless, God's people are to work for the welfare of the city. This duty is behind the idea of vocation, or calling. Christians are not allowed to view their work as only a job, but as a response to God's call to minister by contributing to the common good. Thus, the concept of vocation provides the framework for our political involvement, which should seek to provide for the needs of all.

Interpreting Principles and Party Alignments

The lines separating governmental authority from the proper realms of the individual and other institutions are fuzzy. As a result, Christians are often divided over the proper scope and use of government authority. For example, some evangelicals question the right of governments to declare wars or execute criminals, arguing that God alone holds the legitimate power over life and death. Others doubt government's authority to dispense birth control to minors without parental notification on the basis that this trespasses on the family's rightful domain. Christians may gravitate toward the positions of a specific political party as a result of such issues of interest. At other times, our political commitments are not built on a particular plank in a party platform, but are oriented toward a broader philosophy. Below, we will return to our four theological principles to show how Democratic and Republican philosophies might interpret them differently. To speak of these political perspectives so broadly requires a great deal of generalization. However, these generalizations help us understand how evangelicals can agree fully on the theological principles but find themselves on opposite sides of the political spectrum.

Principle #1
Governments are authorized by God to punish wrongdoers and provide for the common good.

> Republicans: Interpret these two principles narrowly. Government should be limited to tasks that transcend the abilities of individuals, families, or communities, such as military defense or interstate highway systems.
>
> Democrats: Interpret the common good more expansively and expect government to be more active in matters of distributive justice.

Principle #2
Governments inevitably abuse their powers and extend them beyond roles authorized by God.

> Republicans: Since abuse of collective powers such as government has much more potential for catastrophic results, we should always be wary of investing too much power in centralized hands.
>
> Democrats: When our focus is on our individual interests, selfishness and divisiveness will rule. Democratic and centralized structures that express the common good help take the edge off individual selfishness.

Principle #3
Salvation occurs through Jesus alone.

> Republicans: Salvation is not mediated by laws, but the majority has a right to express its moral views in the laws.

> Democrats: We live in a pluralistic society and should thus craft laws that protect the rights of minority groups and avoid the tyranny of the majority.

Principle #4
Christians should work for the benefit of the society in which they reside.

> Republicans: Individual, family, community, or church efforts allow us to address social problems close to the source and are the key avenues of caring for needs and improving society.

> Democrats: Social problems are systemic in nature. Christians should engage in broad-based approaches that resolve underlying causes rather than just treating symptoms.

Evangelicals in a Two-Party System

Contrasting of responses to our four theological foundations helps explain how evangelicals might align with different political parties. These parties are a necessary part of our discussion because political decisions do not occur in a vacuum. No matter what society Christians find themselves in, they act within an existing framework. In the United States, that framework is provided by the two major parties. Thus, we need to examine how these political parties function and how their decisions have shaped (and could reshape in the future) evangelical political loyalties.

Given the diversity of this country's population, both major parties are coalitions of folks who otherwise have little in common. Compromise is necessary to mesh inner-city minorities with social science professors in the Democratic Party. Likewise, it requires significant give-and-take to bring together Alabama Baptists and country club executives at the Republican Convention. The two main political parties engage in careful calculations to make their views inviting to large numbers of citizens. If a party's positions do not attract a large enough coalition, its candidates do not get into the power positions. When one party has too few people in elected position, the other party decides what happens to your money, whether you go to war, and whether you can be fined for smoking a stogie on the beach.

As demographics change, parties revisit their commitments and choose those people they want to attract. Each party's leaders make these choices knowing they may alienate those already aligned with them. This is directly relevant to understanding the strong identification between white evangelicals and the Republican Party, because this alignment is of rather recent vintage. Many recall 1976, dubbed the "year of the evangelical," because of the emergence of evangelicals as a potent political force. Less often remembered, however, is that the Democratic candidate Jimmy Carter enjoyed a 25 percent margin of the evangelical vote over Gerald Ford, the Republican candidate.[10] Every presidential campaign since that has seen the white evangelical vote go decisively to the Republican candidate. Until that time, evangelicals tended to line up with the Democratic Party, especially in the "Solid South," so called because of its solidly Democratic inclinations.

This dramatic and rather rapid realignment is evident in changing party preferences. In the 1960s, Democratic evangelicals outnumbered Republican evangelicals in the South by more than a 3–1 margin (69 percent vs. 21 percent). By the 1980s, white Southern evangelicals made an 18-point swing toward the Republican Party (51 percent vs. 39 percent), a gap that has widened in the past two decades. In the North, evangelical Republicans outnumbered evangelical Democrats in the 1960s (57 percent vs. 35 percent), but increased the spread considerably over the next two decades (72 percent vs. 22 percent).[11] While numerous reasons can be cited, the realignment boils down to this. The Republicans have been more effective than Democrats in crafting positions attractive to white evangelicals. Keep in mind that I am not dealing with the question of whether evangelicals *should* be attracted to the Republican Party's positions. The point is simply that the two major parties have made decisions over the past few decades, and these decisions have resulted in shifting loyalties.[12]

It is sometimes implied that the imbalance of evangelical party affiliation is problematic. Perhaps so, but if the Democratic Party wants to bring more evangelicals over to its side, this would not be hard to do. I have three suggestions almost guaranteed to cause millions of evangelicals to change their political registration to Democratic. First, Democrats' willingness to reach out to evangelicals cannot end on the first Tuesday following the first Monday in November in years divisible by four. Maybe it should not be this way, but if a group plays a significant role in putting candidates into office, they expect to be players after the election. As we mentioned above, the evangelical vote was a major factor in Jimmy Carter's election. After the victory, however, he appointed almost no evangelicals to political positions. Similarly, while President Bill Clinton made frequent references to his Baptist upbringing and employed language that resonated with evangelicals, they were excluded from his administration.[13] To date, President Barack Obama has placed no evangelicals in significant power roles.

In contrast, many self-identified evangelicals have been significant forces at the highest levels of national Republican politics as viable primary candidates (Mike Huckabee) and vice-presidential (Sarah Palin) or presidential (George W. Bush) nominees. Moreover, all three Republican presidents from Reagan forward have appointed outspoken evangelicals to their administrations.[14] We can debate whether the Republicans have done evangelicalism any favor by including us in government. However, political parties know the rules of the game. If a group helps you gain political power, it wants a voice in how that power is used. If you ignore their contribution after the election, it is difficult to persuade them to vote for you the next time around.

Second, the Democratic Party should be more respectful toward people of faith. Many dismiss as paranoia the perception among evangelicals that there is a discernable undercurrent of hostility toward them in the Democratic Party. However, polls indicate that this perception is grounded in reality. Democrats were only half as likely to have a positive evaluation of evangelicals as Republicans (31 percent vs. 63 percent). It does not stop here. Democrats have less favorable views toward all religions (except Scientology) than do Republicans. In fact, Republicans have significantly more positive views toward Jews (70 percent vs. 51 percent) and Catholics (68 percent vs. 51 percent), even though these two groups are more likely to vote Democratic.[15] You do not need a PhD in political science or behavioral psychology to figure this out. If Democrats want people of faith to hop under their big tent, they need to love on them a bit more. This is particularly true when they woo evangelicals. When more than two-thirds of Democrats harbor unfavorable views toward them, it is understandable why many evangelicals are suspicious of Democratic overtures.

Finally, one simple decision would guarantee that millions of evangelical voters would join the Democratic Party. All Democrats have to do is change their position on abortion, and really mean it. On the majority of domestic or foreign policy issues, evangelicals poll very close to the composite for the entire population. For example, the Religious Landscape poll found that 52 percent of evangelicals favored strict environmental regulation as compared with 55 percent of the American population at large. Similarly, 55 percent of evangelicals said the government should help the disadvantaged, about the same as the general population.[16] We find similar outcomes on health reform, loss of jobs to overseas workers, terrorism, and a wide range of other political matters. However, when the same poll asked about abortion, the numbers diverge noticeably. Almost 70 percent of evangelicals said that abortion should "always be illegal" or "legal in few circumstances," more than 20 percentage points higher than the general population.[17] Because evangelicals do not skew too strongly left or right on most political issues, many would find the Democratic Party quite amenable if it changed its abortion position.

For many readers, my point above simply confirms their view that evangelicals are one-issue voters. I think it is too simplistic to put it this way, but let us grant that this is the case. If Democrats know that millions of evangelical votes could be available to them (and millions more Catholic votes, since this group also polls high on the pro-life side) and they say they really want evangelicals to join their party, why not simply change to a pro-life position? No one who pays attention to American politics believes this will happen, at least in the immediate future, for an obvious reason. A change on this single position would result in the Democrats alienating tens of millions of their present constituents. Why? Because a whole bunch of Democrats are also one-issue voters (if we are going to grant that for evangelicals, it is only fair to grant it here also) who put a very high priority on preserving a pro-choice position. By adopting one position on abortion and rejecting another, both parties have chosen which group of single-issue voters they want to include and which they will exclude.

The discussion above is not about whether it is healthy to be a one-issue voter. Instead, the question is why many evangelicals have moved rather decisively toward Republican loyalties over the past few decades. My answer is pretty basic. Republicans have opened key political positions to evangelicals (although nowhere close to the proportion of their vote), maintain a positive view of people of faith in general and evangelicals in particular, and reflect the beliefs of most evangelicals on abortion and other "values" questions. Democrats could do all these things and recapture a significant percentage of the evangelical vote, but they choose to appeal to other constituencies instead. Nothing wrong with that; every political party has to make these decisions. However, when Democrats adopt positions they know will alienate many evangelicals, no one should be shocked when evangelicals align with the other party.

The Problem of Friends in Political Parties

Despite what I have said above, I am convinced that the Republican Party represents a greater danger to the spiritual well-being of evangelicals precisely *because* it has accommodated itself to evangelicals. We know from experience that we find it easier to gloss over the faults and shortcomings of those with whom we agree. However, Christians must always maintain a countercultural edge. If evangelicals become too comfortable with the Republican Party, and I believe this has often been the case, we are in danger of having our faith co-opted for political ends.

Although the Republican Party may be supportive of some causes near and dear to evangelical hearts, we should not fool ourselves that they do so for the reasons or goals that should characterize Christian social engagement. To illustrate, let us return to the four theological principles above. I noted earlier that these theological touchstones should be relatively unproblematic for Christians. However, they would be completely foreign, even repulsive, ideas to many people in any political party, the Republican Party included. Because of the need to establish a broad constituency, political parties must exclude these principles of Christian political engagement from their platforms or philosophy statements. Thus, evangelical Republicans should recognize that millions of fellow Republicans believe that "we, the people" constitute governmental authority, not God (as our first principle states). Although Republicans generally advocate limited governmental power, many would be baffled by our second principle's claim that boundaries on government are established by God. Similarly, while Republicans are reluctant to view government as the source of salvation (in whatever way we define it), their mantra of self-reliance does not fit comfortably with the Christian confession that redemption occurs through Jesus alone.

Our fourth principle—the idea that God's people have a mandate to work for the benefit of all—requires a bit more investigation. Most Republicans (and Democrats) truly believe their policies seek the good of the whole. However, the concept of the common good is ambiguous. Thus, secular Democrats and Republicans alike might define "the good" primarily in terms of financial gain, military power, individual freedom, greater access to educational resources, or a number of other goods that political activity can bring about. However, no single political aim—economic, intellectual, psychological—satisfies the aim of Christian political theology. God has created us as multidimensional beings, and narrowing our definition of the common good to a single aspect of life is reductionistic.

If we are not single-dimensional beings, we are obligated to consider a wide range of issues when we go to the ballot box. Thus the *Evangelical Manifesto* affirms commitment to "the sanctity of every human life, including those unborn" and the "holiness of marriage as instituted by God between one man and one woman." However, it continues, "we must follow the model of Jesus, the Prince of Peace, engaging the global giants of conflict, racism, corruption, poverty, pandemic diseases, illiteracy, ignorance, and spiritual emptiness by promoting reconciliation, encouraging ethical servant leadership, assisting the poor, caring for the sick, and educating the next generation."[18]

While the preceding paragraphs have focused on how the Christian's motives and aims will differ from those governing political parties, we also need to say something about the means, the way Christians engage in politics. We cannot overlook the fact that those who campaign and advertise on your party's behalf will do so with uncharitable tactics. Blatant mistruths, manipulative half-truths, questioning of motives, and other unethical means will be used toward what is portrayed as a noble end. Candidates and parties will frame their ideas with an eye to strategic advantage, but with blindness to the question of truth. All too often, we excuse such methods because they are omnipresent in politics and are done in the service of policies or people we may support. In the face of such tactics, Christians need to assume a prophetic stance, challenge these methods, and engage in repentance when we have been guilty of collusion. Prophets are seldom popular, and a call to a radically new way of conducting campaigns is a surefire way to alienate political allies. However, if we forsake kingdom values for insider status, the cost is too high.

Conclusion

Although a significant majority of evangelicals may *vote* Republican, we can never *be* Republican in the same sense that we are Christian. No candidate is a Savior. No platform replicates Scripture. No political party finds its fundamental impulse in a desire for God's kingdom. Therefore, no Christians can find their identity in their political commitments. The political term for those who totally identify with a party against their best interests is "useful idiot." As harsh as this is, the theological term "idolatry" carries even more wallop. Because no party shares the aims, motivations, or means of God's kingdom, an unqualified, unreserved allegiance to any political party sets up a false god. Our vote always represents our feeble attempt to discern the better option from a range of incomplete and imperfect choices. Thus, an evangelical's political participation should be tinged with a certain degree of sorrow.

Developing a thoughtful approach to Christian political involvement is part of a broader quest to become the people God has created us to be. So how do we know when we are on the right path? Without a doubt, a number of good indicators could be applied. However, my pastor set before our congregation an intriguing "thermometer" for helping us to gauge whether we bring glory to God and light to those around us. The challenge was this: how can our congregation minister in such a way that if we ever decided to relocate, the surrounding community would rise up with such loud protest that we would be compelled to stay put?

To put it mildly, this is an evocative challenge because our community is highly diverse. It is racially and economically mixed. There are a lot of folks in the neighborhood who do not care much for our brand of Christianity, or any brand of Christianity. More than a few would be happy to see us disappear simply because of the traffic we bring to the area. The circumstances tempt us to believe that my pastor's goal is impossible. However, the very impossibility of it makes it a perfect goal for God's people, who are called to strive for the humanly unachievable.

With little modification, my pastor's challenge is a fitting goal for evangelical political engagement in a pluralistic society. How can we carry on political discourse in such a way that everyone, even our political opponents, would feel the loss if we were no longer in the arena? Are we able to communicate to people at every point on the political spectrum that we are not just deeply concerned about the things that hinder their lives, but are actively engaged in seeking resolution to those problems? Can we challenge the methods, goals, and motives of political allies in a way that causes them to question their primary allegiances?

This sounds impossible, and it is, as long as we rely only on the tools offered by the current political game. Fortunately, Scripture points the way to an alternative form of politics. The politics of God's kingdom is defined primarily by love. Love is the basic impulse that should propel Christian action, and the Bible offers no escape clause when it comes to politics. Without love, Christians, regardless of their political persuasion, are unfaithful to their identity as citizens of a different kingdom.

Given the rancor and divisiveness of the current political context, talk about love sounds quaint and naïve. However, the very fact that the most basic of all Christian virtues seems out of place in politics is an indictment of how deeply we have compartmentalized our political behavior from the rest of our lives. If we are looking for places where we need to engage in serious repentance, this would be a good place to start. However, repentance falls short if it does not blossom into movement in a new direction, and a return to the way of love offers an incredible opportunity. As Amy Black puts it, "If Christians view politics as a means for demonstrating love in action as a witness to the world, the nature of political discourse could change."[19] Christians are called to be world-changers, and the world of political discourse, which suffers from a severe love deficit, would be a good place for Christians to get to work.

A final word on love brings closure to our discussion on why evangelicalism is not Republican. Those who are driven by love can be clear about *why* they act, but love is not as clear about *what* a lover ought to do. I, like the majority of evangelicals, view a Republican philosophy as the best expression of Christian ideals. However, many committed and loving evangelicals disagree with me. It is not out of line for me to offer arguments about why I believe they are politically wrongheaded, but this comes well down a list of priorities. My top priority is to ensure that my political loyalties reflect my primary allegiance to God's kingdom, and to do so in a way that causes you to join in this reflection as well. I am a Republican, but I am never a Republican in the same way that I am a Christian. My faith should demote my political loyalty to a secondary status and radically shape my association with the Republican Party. If you are an evangelical, it is likely that you share my political inclinations. However, as an evangelical Christian whose life falls under the lordship of Jesus Christ, I hope it is clear why we conclude, "Evangelicalism is not Republican."

9

Evangelicals Are Not All
Racist, Sexist, and Homophobic

When I (Don) attended Stanford University as an undergraduate student, I got hooked up with an on-campus ministry called Campus Ambassadors. I joined because different Christian organizations that worked on campus such as Campus Crusade and Navigators divided up the frosh dorms and—by luck or providence—Campus Ambassadors ministered in my dorm. Throughout my university career, I worked with the various ministries of Campus Ambassadors and became a student leader. However, what I did not know was that, in becoming a student leader, the director expected me to attend one of the Baptist churches that supported Campus Ambassadors. So, for my last two years of college, I went to a large Baptist church.

The youth pastor in the Baptist church was both a budding theologian and a debater. He also seemed to enjoy challenging Stanford students. I am not sure whether it was because he doubted the sincerity of our Christianity, or just because he liked testing us. Anyway, when the youth pastor found out that I came from a Free Methodist background, he challenged me theologically about everything from divine election and free will to the doctrine of entire sanctification. Although historically entire sanctification represented an identifying doctrine of Wesleyanism, I was clueless about it, since the doctrine was not much emphasized in my home church. The youth pastor took great pleasure, publicly and one-on-one, arguing for the superiority of Baptist theology over Methodist theology. It seemed that he considered anyone other than Baptists to be misguided at best, or flat-out wrong.

Frankly, I felt picked on. I had not yet studied theology and was woefully at a disadvantage in debate, though—as they say—I gave it "the old college try." Be that as it may, I learned a great deal about what Baptists, at least this Baptist church, believed and practiced. One of the things that intrigued me was that, in public worship, women were not allowed to speak from the pulpit. They could sing or play a musical instrument in front of the congregation. However, if a woman stood up to give a testimony or an announcement, then a man had to stand beside her. After noticing this phenomenon, I asked the youth pastor about it. He said that women are not permitted to lead men in church, nor are they permitted to stand in positions of public leadership without being under the authority of a man.

Call me ignorant, but that perspective of women in church was new to me. Throughout my life, I had seen women preach sermons, lead evangelistic revivals, and fulfill all sorts of leadership positions inside and outside churches. My aunt Naomi, in fact, had been a missionary in the Philippines for more than two dozen years and was an ordained minister in the Free Methodist Church. She had been one of my spiritual role models!

When I asked about the rationale for why women were not permitted to lead in church, I received a biblical diatribe from the youth pastor. Unable to keep up with his knowledge of Scripture, I retreated from debate. However, I regularly studied the Bible in my personal devotions. So, I undertook a study of what it said about women in ministry. To the novice, what Scripture said about women was disheartening. I admit that, for the first time in my life, I was confused about what Christians should believe about the leadership roles of men and women. On the one hand, much in Scripture seemed to discourage leadership roles for women in the church. On the other hand, I had witnessed firsthand the gifted and effective ministries of women such as my aunt Naomi.

Over years of biblical, historical, and theological study, I have spent a great deal of time attempting to understand the roles of women and men in the church. Having weighed the evidence, I affirm egalitarian views that undoubtedly would have confirmed the extent of my fallenness to the Baptist youth pastor. However, I am not alone in my beliefs and values, which affirm women in leadership, including women in ordained ministry. Certainly the biblical, historical, and theological evidence is contested; there is no doubt about that. There is also little doubt today that there is no consensus among evangelical Christians about the issue.

Little did I know that during those college years, I had become a small part of a much bigger discussion about gender roles that has only intensified over the intervening decades. Although questions of race and homosexuality did not come up much during my years at the Baptist church, big changes were brewing in those areas as well. For younger readers, who have grown up in the midst of discussions about race, gender, and homosexuality, it is often difficult to recognize the seismic cultural shifts that have occurred in a relatively short period of time. However, in historical terms, we have experienced massive social changes and are still trying to digest the meaning of these revolutions. A couple of snapshots will remind us of how radical and sudden these shifts have been. In 1950, just over one-third (33.9 percent) of women age sixteen and older were employed. In 2010, that number is projected to be almost two-thirds (62.6 percent).[1] In 1955, it was simply assumed that a black should and would give up a bus seat for a white passenger. That year, Rosa Parks opened a new phase in the civil rights movement when she refused to obey the bus driver who ordered her to do just that. A few years ago, if you were homosexual, you spoke of it only in hushed tones among your most trusted friends, and probably not at all to your family. Now we have gay pride parades and homosexual marriage propositions on ballots.

Attitudes and beliefs about race, gender, and homosexuality that had been set in concrete for centuries with very little discussion are now being challenged in an unprecedented way and in an extremely compact time frame. Viewed from this historical vantage point, it should not surprise us that emotions rise dramatically when we raise these issues. Quite often, Christians did not join these conversations until they were well under way everywhere else. When these discussions move into the church (which usually happens some time after they are well under way in society), the temperature of these debates notches up even higher. After all, many long-held views now under scrutiny are not thought simply to be a matter of cultural heritage but grounded in God's eternal truth. Before we move on to our conversations about racism, sexism, and homophobia, we need to make some initial observations about potential potholes we face along the way.

Mr. Obvious Makes Three Observations

Obvious Observation #1: Most of us would really rather not talk about racism, sexism, and homophobia. These are, as we have said above, emotional issues. Given the combustible nature of these discussions, many people would rather have a colonoscopy than dive into them. For the sake of avoiding discomfort and general annoyance, it seems smarter and safer just to work around contentious issues such as these. That might be prudent, except for a couple of factors. First, we need to talk about gender, race, and sexuality precisely because there are angry, hurt, and confused people on all sides of this issue. Second, this discussion is imperative because a lot of these folks are angry *at*, hurt *by*, or confused *because of* Christians. Evangelicals have often made grave errors about how they relate to people, particularly those who are different racially or sexually, with terrible personal, social, and evangelistic repercussions. Even in cases where we have not been a cause of the problem, we often lack the sensitivity to understand the real pain and anger of others. As those called to be agents of healing and peace, Christians should not be lagging, but at the forefront of bringing reconciliation wherever possible. There is much that we—collectively speaking—need to consider, discuss, respond to, and possibly repent.

Obvious Observation #2: Sexism, racism, and homophobia are not simply variants on the same topic. Each of these issues has its unique features and facets and deserves more direct attention than we can give it in a single chapter. Even though we will address race, gender, and homosexuality separately below, we want to acknowledge that each represents a unique challenge for Christians that is more complicated than we can discuss adequately here. However, there are common threads that offer some justification for bringing homophobia, sexism, and racism together. First, people have been treated unfairly and inhumanely because of all three forms of prejudice. Women have been viewed as property, humans have been enslaved on account of their race, and people have been taunted, excluded, or murdered because of their homosexuality. Reasonable people should not have any problem agreeing that these are all forms of bigotry and that they are just plain wrong. Second, all three areas represent our struggle to know how to interact "Christianly" with those who are different from us. Difference pushes us out of our comfort zone and often leaves us feeling vulnerable and fearful. Thus, since all three areas in this chapter confront us with "otherness," we also will see similarities in the responses we will encounter.

Obvious Observation #3: It is difficult to separate perception from reality on matters of race, homosexuality, and gender. All three areas represent moral discussions in which gaps can arise between what people actually believe and how others perceive them. This can be extremely frustrating since most people believe they have no intentions toward bigotry and, instead, take principled stands on these issues. Nevertheless, they are often perceived by others as racist, sexist, or homophobic. To bring it closer to home, *evangelicals* are rather widely perceived as racist, sexist, and homophobic. This creates a challenge we should not ignore because people's perceptions are their reality. If, therefore, others perceive evangelicals as biased and discriminatory, it reflects poorly on Christianity. Moreover, it broadens the idea that evangelicals are hypocrites, speaking of love at the same time they harbor bigoted and hateful opinions of others.

We face twin obstacles in attempting to separate false perception from reality when it comes to bigotry. On the one hand, these forms of bias do exist, and they cause palpable and severe damage to those who are the victims. On the other hand, we have no measurable means by which we diagnose these conditions. We do not even agree on how to define them. To be sure, there are extreme situations where we could find a strong consensus that an act crossed the line into sexism, for example. However, in other cases it is not clear where the boundary separating false impression and true reality lies.

Dancing through the Minefields

The fact that we can easily be perceived as sexist, racist, or homophobic without any intention of being so is a frightening thing, and this brings us full-circle to "Obvious Observation #1." It is hurtful to be accused of something for which you are innocent, and particularly hurtful when the accusations deal with serious moral deficiencies, which racism, sexism, and homophobia are.

As a result, we avoid these topics because they leave us feeling as though we are tap-dancing our way through a moral minefield, never quite sure of when we will trip some unseen fuse that will bring accusations of discrimination down on our heads. Sometimes mistaken impressions arise because we confuse issues and view different opinions on related matters as evidence of bigotry. Although it is not a complete list, we identify below five places where our discussion of these topics can get crossed up and lead to false perceptions.

1. Honest disagreement about ethics or theology. Sometimes people are offended by evangelical Christians just because they have different opinions or ideologies, and this can often lead to the conclusion that they are biased. It is not hard to see how this occurs. The issues of race, gender, and sexuality are obviously moral questions, and these sorts of issues touch us where our nerve endings are closest to the surface. Thus, when individuals arrive at different conclusions about the sensitive issues, accusations often fly.

This sort of conflict is inevitable because questions of race, gender, and sexuality are at the forefront of so many discussions today. No one gets to sit on the sidelines. Christians must weigh in on the matters because there are proverbial lines that people ought not to cross. These boundaries exist because God loves all people and desires their flourishing. Crossing these boundaries is sinful because it hinders the best of what God has in mind for us. In addition, Scripture does not always fit into what is culturally acceptable or fashionable. Much of what Scripture says is countercultural, regardless of whether one talks about first- or twenty-first-century culture. If the world and its culture are inextricably bound up with the finitude and sin of people, they are bound to conflict with biblical teachings. Of course, Christians are not the only ones offering moral evaluations about these topics. All people make judgments, regardless of whether they are religious. In fact, the variety and volume of moral pronouncements about race, gender, and sexuality might be the best counterevidence that moral relativism is not all that prevalent in our society. Although we hear frequently of a postmodern context wherein everyone's voice or story is welcomed (and ostensibly tolerated), no one acts as if all views are morally or theologically equivalent.

Although everyone takes moral stances on these burning questions, not everyone comes to the same conclusions. As a result, evangelicals may offend those who differ because of their heartfelt religious or moral convictions. Thus, for example, a view of women thought to be honoring and respectful by one individual may be judged as sexist by another. The belief that homosexual behavior is wrong is often dismissed as homophobic by those who disagree. Of course, these disagreements emerge on all fronts. Evangelicals come to different positions on these three areas of concern, and do so from strongly held theological principles. Where these divergences occur, we need to see them for what they are rather than interpreting them as evidence of bigotry.

2. Honest disagreements about the best means of dealing with these issues. We are reasonably satisfied that the vast majority of people are not out to oppress others and want to inhabit a world in which people are shown proper respect. However, the consensus splinters when we get to the question of *how* we achieve this ideal world. Does it involve ballot measures? If so, which ones? Those that affirm traditional views of marriage or those that allow for homosexual unions? How about affirmative action programs? Are they effective in opening new opportunities for minorities or do they perpetuate the belief that minorities only get positions because of preferential treatment? Sexual harassment training? Does this raise awareness of real problems or does it create problems by making people hypersensitive to every word, joke, or gesture from co-workers? Responses that some believe are fundamental reforms are viewed as politically correct drivel by others. People of good will and motives often find themselves at opposite ends of the spectrum in their understanding of the best way to rid our society of denigrating behaviors and attitudes. However, differences concerning the means to solve a problem do not necessarily indicate divergence from a desire to root out discrimination.

3. How big are the remaining problems? Most people agree that important strides have been made in correcting some of the more egregious failings in the treatment of others. We do not often see eye-to-eye on exactly how far we have come, however. Some would argue that the forces of racism, sexism, and homophobia are still quite vital, even if not as overt as before. They would argue that remaining forms of these biases are embedded within systems and institutions, where they are much harder to identify and change. Others have a more optimistic view of our progress, and believe that following policies constructed on concepts such as institutionalized racism, for example, is like hunting for ghosts. If you believe the ghosts of racism roam our institutional hallways, you can always find evidence, although that evidence will never be conclusive to all observers. These optimists argue that current laws and attitudes are sufficient to guarantee that doors are open to all. Of course, this evaluation opens them to the charge that they are biased because they benefit from the system. This charge usually incites the optimists to bring the countercharge that the pessimists are simply engaging in reverse discrimination. Each side may judge the other as biased when the real issue may simply be that they disagree on how far we have advanced on resolving bias.

4. These issues have become politicized. One major obstacle to coolheaded discussion of these topics is that race, gender, and homosexuality have become political weapons. By political, we mean political in both the electoral sense as well as in other ways that individuals and groups seek to gain power for themselves. Indeed, it is sometimes hard to know whether certain policies may be, for example, racially biased or if a person is simply playing the "race card" to shut down an opponent. It is difficult to discern when ideas or practices truly victimize a group or if a group is using the charge of victimization to gain leverage for its agenda. Real bigotry occurs; trumped-up charges of racism, sexual harassment, and homophobia occur. It is not always easy to tell the difference. Ironically, evangelicals generally associate the use of group identity as a political bludgeon with minority groups, feminists, and the homosexual coalition. However, many evangelicals employ the same claim to victimhood at the hands of media or government. Again, it is not always easy to determine how much validity there is to this. However, if evangelicals feel they have been shoved to the margins, it should cause us to be more sensitive to the claims of groups who have at times suffered from discrimination.

5. Our experiences with racism, sexism, and homophobia differ. The authors are a couple of highly degreed, upper-middle-class, heterosexual white guys. We bring a much different set of life experiences to this discussion than those from different circumstances. Some would argue that, precisely because of our own experiences (or lack of them), we have no business speaking about these matters. Instead, we would be better off if we would shut up and listen to those who have felt the sting of discrimination firsthand. They have a point, and a good one. We have thought and read about these issues and have had honest and sometimes painful conversations with those who have endured discrimination, but that is only a pale reflection of living with inequity on the personal level. However, the underlying issue in all this is how people can live together in a healthy way, without any voice being excluded. We all have our stories and sensitivities, and no one leaves those behind in these conversations. Often, offense and mistreatment of others occurs because of ignorance that comes from separation and neglect—individual, social, cultural, ethnic, gender, sexual, or religious ignorance. Ignorance, of course, can only be an excuse for so long. When ways exist for overcoming it, we fall into sin when we fail to take the opportunity to do so. In short, followers of a Suffering Servant have an obligation to listen and respond to the stories of others' suffering.

All five factors above represent potential choke points in the hard and necessary discussion about race, gender, and sexual preference or orientation. A common thread that runs throughout these five obstacles is that so much that shapes these conversations happens on the subterranean level. They involve beliefs, motives, goals, experiences, and fears—factors that have a powerful influence on how we act, even if they are not immediately evident to others, and sometimes not clear even to ourselves. When others dismiss, misconstrue, or ignore our beliefs or experiences, the gulf between people grows instead of contracting. Similarly, when others attribute fears or motives to us that are unfair and false, we have to work hard to avoid acting in kind. These discussions often go nowhere because they deal only with surface positions and fail to see the important impulses behind them.

While we are not naïve enough to believe that we can ever completely close the perception/reality gap, there are a few steps that evangelicals can take. First, we need to talk directly with thoughtful people who disagree with us instead of responding to caricatures. Too often, we select the extremist screamers from the other side and portray them as the normative voice of the opposition. This is usually a great tactic for rallying people to a cause, but it just happens to be dishonest and immoral. When we fail to acknowledge that those who have sincere disagreements with our diagnoses and positions have moral or theological reasons for their views, we create animosity toward our own views. We need to listen carefully to those who disagree. Second, when evangelical Christians do speak, we should be prepared to make the best public argument possible, realizing that we need to be sophisticated apologetically in presenting our position, arguing our case, and implementing policies. Too frequently, we have not framed our responses about race, gender, and sexuality in a coherent and thoughtful manner.

Perhaps most importantly, many of the negative perceptions about evangelicals could dissolve if we were more humble in these discussions. Christians have, at times, been guilty of egregious acts of racism, sexism, and homophobia, even though we were certain that God was on our side. We need to willingly 'fess up to our past shortcomings. Moreover, every now and then, Christian views about racial, gender, and sexual relations change. This should make us more humble when it comes to considering the variety of views people have, and should cause us to be less dismissive of people's ideas just because they are new, different, or held by people other than ourselves! Because evangelicals tend to have a strong respect for tradition, we normally resist change. However, at times, traditional views have supported unhealthy attitudes toward other people. To the extent that this occurs, Christians must become the champions of change.

If we allow our discussion to remain at the level of how we deal with misperceptions of Christianity on matters of sexuality, race, and gender, we might fool ourselves into thinking that our only concern is a marketing problem. That lets us off the hook too easily. First, we need to ask where we are guilty of jumping to hasty and false conclusions about the views of others. To what extent have we overlooked the beliefs motivating those who hold different positions? Is our disagreement really about right and wrong, or do we simply diverge on the steps necessary to treat people in a Christian manner? Do I use these issues to advance selfish agendas? Have I listened empathically to those who believe they are denigrated or marginalized?

The second part of this is more difficult, because it involves honestly asking whether there is reality underlying the perception that evangelicals are homophobic, sexist, or racist. Stereotypes do not materialize out of thin air, so we need to ask whether we continue to harbor views about others that require correction. Like any other exercise in which we engage in soul-searching to eradicate sinful views and attitudes, this is not a lot of fun. However, in view of the seriousness of our subjects, it is a necessary process.

Paving the Road to Hell?

Most evangelicals believe they have the right intentions when it comes to dealing with questions of race, gender, or sexuality. Moreover, they would argue that these intentions are grounded in a foundational principle that seeks fair treatment for all people. Thus, for example, evangelicals might note that Scripture demands equitable consideration of others and condemns favoritism, prejudice, and chauvinism. They understand that favoritism, for example, disrupts relationships for people, family, churches, and society on multiple levels. Moreover, they view this principle as one rooted in the nature of God, who does not show favoritism (e.g., Deut. 10:17; Rom. 2:11; Acts 10:34–35; 15:7–9) and is portrayed as unbiased toward all people, classes, and races (e.g., 2 Chron. 19:7; Matt. 5:45; Gal. 3:28; Col. 3:25).

Starting from this point, it seems that we should have no problems. We have a principle that seems sufficient to avoid bias, discrimination, and bigotry, and people who intend to follow the principle. But can we be racist, sexist, or homophobic without intending to be? In short, the answer is yes. As the old saying puts it, "The road to hell is paved with good intentions." The unfortunate fact is that those who enslaved people of other races, viewed women as property, or confined homosexuals in insane asylums intended to do what was good, or at least claimed to do so. However, their good intentions created hellish circumstances for vast numbers of others.

It is important to note that almost no one throughout history has claimed that racism, homophobia, or gender discrimination is good *per se*. Instead, they argued that different treatment is justified because whatever made "the other" different also made him or her inferior or unsuited for certain opportunities or roles. Thus, when women have been denied an education, Africans enslaved, or homosexuals institutionalized, it was generally justified by claiming that because of their gender, race, or actions, they lacked the intelligence, temperament, or moral qualities required for equality or freedom. Religion brings an additional dimension to this. If God creates people with these differences, then it is a short step to the conclusion that giving certain individuals full rights and opportunities is contrary to the nature God imparts to them. Differences between races, sexual activities, or genders were not viewed as incidental variations but as indicators of a fundamentally different nature that justified different treatment.

Our intention to follow good principles is a good start, but it does not absolve us of participation in racism, sexism, or homophobia. Through ignorance and error, we can justify systems that deny others full expression of their humanity. The ignorance that supports our unholy trio of sexism, racism, and homophobia is not easily dispelled for several intertwined reasons. First, it becomes embedded in systems and traditions. Few saw anything unusual or unseemly about slavery because it was business as usual for centuries. Second, this business-as-usual arrangement worked to the benefit of those who held power. Despite claims to good intentions, bias toward our interests made it difficult to see the results of oppression clearly. We are inclined to see what we want to see.

A third element that causes a tunnel vision that blinds us to the sufferings of others is that the systems that perpetuate racism, sexism, and homophobia separate us from "the other." Interactions with those who were different were not viewed as equal-to-equal engagements because those in power dictated the opportunities and freedoms of those pushed to the margins. Thus, our ignorance of suffering resulted from ignoring the others as persons and thinking of them either as instruments for our own benefit or a problem to be controlled. Finally, since systems marginalize groups, marginalized people create their own cultures that differ from those of people in power. Since the powerful assume that their cultural expressions are the norm, any divergence is viewed as inferior or deviant. This brings us back to where we started. Because of the differences in the ways racial groups, women, or homosexuals lived and viewed the world, others believed they were justified in treating them as inferiors.

The previous paragraph was written primarily in the past tense because we find the most blatant examples of such prejudice in our history. However, we should not assume that these problems are behind us. All the factors that led to oppression in the past are alive and well today—systems of power that favor certain groups, the inclination to put our interests above those of others, segregation into groups and subcultures, and the tendency to judge others as if we and our ways constitute the norm. Because they all are powerful engines behind oppression, we need to test our attitudes and beliefs carefully to determine whether they become our justification for racist, sexist, or homophobic mind-sets.

Racism and Human Diversity

Racism is an age-old problem, and religions in general, and Christianity in particular, do not have a clean record. It would take far too long to recount the injustices perpetrated by Christians against others over racial, ethnic, cultural, and religious differences. The usual suspects come to mind: religious violence, religious warfare, crusades, inquisitions, colonization, coercive missionary tactics, even genocide. The last one is a particularly ugly form of racist activity because it goes far beyond the subjugation of others and seeks instead the eradication of an entire group. Moreover, this ugliness has been justified by appeal to Scripture (e.g., Num. 31:7–18; Deut. 7:2; 13:15; 20:17; Josh. 11:19–20; 1 Sam. 15:3). While we can rather easily distance ourselves from episodes as extreme as genocide, it is more difficult to disentangle our attitudes from colonialism and its residual effects.

Colonialism represents one of the more noteworthy ways in which European and American countries subjugated other countries militarily, politically, economically, culturally, and religiously. Through oppressive means, lands around the world were colonized, often with the best of religious intentions. "Manifest Destiny" and the "white man's burden" motivated colonization, emphasizing the superiority and benefits of Western Christian civilization.

Colonialism not only hurt the reputation and authority of the West, it hurt the reputation and authority of Christians, missionaries, and churches because Christianity and Western civilization were viewed, often by both sides, as a package deal.[2] The memories and hurt continue, and Westerners would do well to think long and hard about why their beliefs, values, and practices are so often rebuked and hated today by Two-Thirds World countries. While overt colonialism is mostly gone, latent colonialism persists via Western governmental policies and military incursions, imperialistic tendencies of economic control, and the cultural domination of other countries (e.g., movies, music, art, and literature). It is not a stretch to imagine that this is accompanied by more than a little latent racism.

Racism is certainly a part of our history. However, relative to the rest of the world, the United States has made notable progress in fighting attitudes, language, and other actions that make race a primary determinant of the supposed inherent superiority of one race over others. We can point to a number of benchmarks as measurements of advance—integration of schools, laws barring discrimination on the basis of race, and a number of other visible indicators. Surely the election of an African-American to the presidency, something almost unthinkable a few decades ago, is a decisive signal that our society has changed. After Barack Obama was elected president, some religious and political pundits announced that racism is dead, that we no longer need to be concerned about racial issues.

Does this mean racism, at least in this country, is no longer a problem? To modify Mark Twain's response after reading his own obituary, it may well be that reports of the death of racism are exaggerated and premature. First, if our goal is integration, then we are a long way from hitting that mark. We live and work side-by-side, but this is very different from living and working together. Second, racism involves more than overt acts of discrimination, segregation, and violence. Covert racism is insidious since it is less immediately evident and more easily ignored, especially in highly politicized public forums wherein economic, corporate, and religious interests can take over otherwise equitable dialogue. Less overt racism occurs variously in institutional racism (e.g., economic discrimination, redlining), state racism (e.g., unfair governmental policies and laws), racial profiling, and so on.

Third, the temptation to pronounce racism dead often relies on defining the problem too narrowly. So-called black/white issues have dominated much of the country's struggles with racism; the United States has weathered fighting over abolitionism and civil rights, and has even elected a black president. However, to understand racism as a two-dimensional issue makes the simple error of failing to look out our windows. Society is much more colorful than the "black and white" world often assumed in our definition of racism. Our society includes racial, ethnic, linguistic, and national groups with labels such as Asian, Hispanic, Mideastern, Native American Indian, and so on. Moreover, within each of these designations is a complex of diverse national backgrounds, languages and dialects, and cultural traditions. The United States is indeed very diverse, and the diversity is increasing. Perhaps this is why racial issues may not soon go away. The world is becoming smaller, so to speak, and issues of diversity stand to become more complex as well as widespread.

Finally, our often-constricted definition of racism ignores the fact that racial tension often manifests itself in ethnic, cultural, linguistic, national, religious, or economic dynamics. For example, some face steep obstacles to participation in certain environments because the apparel traditional to their native culture or required by their religion makes co-workers or customers uneasy. While race is not the obvious factor here, such cultural or religious differences are found predominantly among minority groups. Thus, racism encompasses more than skin color, but is bound up in cultural differences that can become stereotyped or feared because of their unfamiliarity.

Partiality and Impartiality

Theory is often much easier to master than practice, and the early church did not wait long before it faced the question of how its theory should be applied in a case of ethnic difference. On Pentecost, the birthday of the church, the Holy Spirit came upon Jews from every nation and cultural background. This would seem to establish the principle that God's new work transcends racial and ethnic lines. However, a problem arose shortly about what should be done with Gentiles, those avoided and despised by Jews for centuries, who were becoming followers of Christ. How should they apply their theory? The apostles did what Christians have been doing ever since: they held a conference. After much discussion, Peter sealed an agreement when he said, "And God, who knows the human heart, testified to them [the Gentiles] by giving them the Holy Spirit, just as he did to us [the Jews]; and in cleansing their hearts by faith he has made no distinction between them and us" (Acts 15:8–9).

Peter's argument was built on a theoretical foundation established at Pentecost: the Holy Spirit does not stop at ethnic or cultural boundaries. However, the apostles themselves hesitated at these old borders. Why? The simple answer is that after centuries of separation, stereotypes, and animosity, many Jewish Christians were still baffled by the idea that God's kingdom would include Gentiles as full and equal members. Nevertheless, the doors swung open for those who had previously been despised and feared. Perhaps we find ourselves with our own version of "the Gentiles." On our theoretical and theological level, we know that God's plan includes people of all races, without limitation or reservation. However, because of lingering stereotypes and unfamiliarity, we face the difficulty of envisioning and enacting this reality to its complete extent. God's Spirit flows freely across racial lines, but we are often slow to follow.

Of course, another apostle, Paul, makes clear that racial barriers are not the only walls God intends to dismantle. Gentiles as well as Jews were to be accepted into the church; slaves as well as those who were free were to be accepted in the church; and women as well as men were to be accepted as being "one in Christ Jesus" (Gal. 3:28). We will focus more directly on the gender issue in short order, but we need to look at the economic and political implications in Paul's statement that slaves have a full stake in God's kingdom, certainly a radical idea in his day. As noted above, the Bible has much to say about the need for impartiality, fairness, justice, and care for social outsiders such as slaves, aliens, widows, orphans, and the poor in general. In fact, Jesus seemed to advocate on behalf of partiality for the poor—those who are impoverished in various ways. After all, he preached the gospel to the poor (Matt. 11:5; Luke 4:18), cared for the poor (Matt. 25:31–46), and said that the poor are blessed (Luke 6:20). This advocacy is sometimes referred to as Jesus's "preferential option for the poor." While we acknowledge that the issues of poverty are not identical with those of race, strong correlations exist between the two in our society. Therefore, we will have a hard time extracting our response to one issue from our response to the other.

The question of illegal immigration provides an illustration of difficulties in bringing our theories of the equality of all into sync with our practice. Political kingdoms such as the United States may be fully justified in denying full equality to non-citizens. However, God's kingdom has different citizenship requirements. So what are our obligations as Christians to those who live at the margins of society precisely because they lack certain protections and opportunities that citizenship would afford? This is a difficult issue, and we will not presume to give the authoritative answer on this question. However, the question offers an opportunity for some probing self-reflection on our perception of minority groups. First, we should ask whether our response to the plight of the undocumented would change if they were of the same racial origin as ourselves. If our answer changes on account of this factor, we might be seeing traces of racism. A second area for self-reflection deals with our motives. Are our views of how we as Christians should address undocumented aliens guided by compassion and a sense of shared humanity, or by selfish concerns or fear?

The question of motives is harder to answer than it appears, because we are not always clear (or honest) about what impulses guide our actions and beliefs. This question becomes particularly difficult in times of economic crisis, when people from other racial or ethnic groups seem to threaten or thwart one's own financial well-being, or during times of social and militaristic upheaval, or when there is fear that terrorists may attack. I can remember that after the terrorist attacks against the United States on September 11, 2001, there was a great deal of fear, finger-pointing, accusation, and discrimination against perceived enemies. The discrimination occurred on governmental levels, tragically, as well as on individual and interpersonal levels. Evangelical Christians were not exempt. In the latter case, Muslims were targets of people's fear, allegations, profiling, and overall intolerance. It did not matter whether there was any truth to the fears; it did not even matter whether they targeted the right people! For example, because Sikh men wear turbans, they were subjected to scorn and harassment on the assumption they were Muslim and potential terrorists, even if they were longtime citizens of the United States. The point is that all our lovely theories about the equality of all people, regardless of race, fly out the window when ignorance and fear shape our practices (or reactions).

Overcoming Racism

Racism does not generally top the list of social problems that concern evangelical Christians and for which they advocate. It was not always this way. For example, evangelicals founded Oberlin College in 1834, the first college in America that admitted both blacks and females as full students. Its first and foremost commitment was decidedly evangelical, "to make the conversion of sinners and the sanctification of Christians the paramount work." However, as the outgrowth of this commitment, the college was dedicated also to the cause of abolitionism and equality. Needless to say, this went against the grain of society at the time and the fledgling school encountered severe criticism from many quarters, including other evangelicals.[3] Nevertheless, Oberlin is but one example of the early work of evangelicals to advance racial justice. While the record was often spotty, whenever one came across an eighteenth- or nineteenth-century society or group that called for the end of the slave trade, the abolition of slavery, or the education of slaves or former slaves, it was likely to have evangelically oriented leaders, churches, and denominations at the helm.

However, after the turn of the twentieth century, social activism among evangelicals diminished and attention was diverted from racial justice. This is often attributed to the rise of dispensationalism and the Fundamentalist-Modernist controversy, which we examine elsewhere in the book. In general, however, conservative strains of Christianity pulled back from society and became more concerned with self-preservation than outreach and social change. With a few courageous exceptions, white evangelicals were often the obstructionists during the civil rights movements that started in the middle of the twentieth century. To sum it up, in the last century evangelicals have acted like Cain, who asked, "Am I my brother's keeper?" (Gen. 4:9), rather than following Jesus's admonition to "love your neighbor as yourself" (Mark 12:31; cf. Rom. 13:9).

Perhaps, while the twenty-first century is still young, evangelicals need to dust off the noble theories they espouse about impartiality and place them front and center. In order to better love their neighbors as themselves, evangelical Christians need to educate themselves about the nature, pervasiveness, and insidiousness of racism. Too often racial issues fall off their theological and ministerial radar screens, which may well make problems of racism worse. On the theoretical level, we acknowledge that the kingdom of God is a colorful place; Christians of all races worship the same God. However, our monotone congregations rarely reflect this. Everyone knows the cliché that "the most segregated hour of the week occurs at 11:00 a.m. inside churches on Sunday mornings." Evangelicals are not totally ignorant of the fact that something is wrong when our congregation does not look much like Christianity on this count, although overcoming internal segregation is no simple feat. Racial reconciliation movements among evangelical Christian leaders, churches, denominations, and parachurch groups have increased, which is a positive sign. But more positive signs are needed.

Ironically, Martin Luther King Jr. should be one of the great role models for racial reconciliation among evangelical Christians. He was an evangelistic preacher whose sermons would warm the cockles of the most ardent adherents of the Great Commission. Yet, as a part of his evangelically oriented Christianity, King also felt the theological conviction needed for prophetically challenging racial and other social injustices in the United States. The two were not mutually exclusive; indeed, he considered justification and justice inextricably bound up with one another. It is no accident, after all, that the root meaning of "just-ification" and "just-ice" is the same! Both are important to God, and so both should be important to evangelicals. King represents a dynamic role model of dealing constructively with a breadth of biblical priorities sadly lacking today, inside and outside churches. Fortunately, evangelical Christians are known for our ability to adapt quickly. Perhaps it is not too late to recapture our racial reconciliation mojo in the twenty-first century and reestablish evangelicalism at the vanguard of racial justice.

Sexism and Women's Issues

Sexism refers to devaluation and unjust treatment based on gender. Historically, women have suffered much from sexist attitudes, actions, and social structures. Sometimes women were considered inferior or the property of men, stereotyped as intellectually inferior, objectified, and persecuted for assuming roles traditionally thought to be proper only to men. Of course, sexism involves more than overt oppression or persecution. It can involve a variety of intangible and indirect manifestations, ranging from neglect to marginalization, in the very language people use as well as in other thoughts and actions. For reasons such as these, people are increasingly concerned to use inclusive language with regard to men and women so that the words, phrases, and concepts they use do not inadvertently exclude women. Often people think that sexism is a result of ignorance. Again, it is important to remember that the root for "ignorance" is "ignore," and too often people intentionally ignore issues related to sexism, which is in itself sexist! It is a "male privilege" (or a feature of a male privilege–oriented society) to ignore the concerns, including the pleas, of women. To this extent, evangelical Christians are as guilty as most of contemporary society, which systemically continues to ignore many women's issues.

Has improvement occurred with regard to women's issues? Yes. We are well beyond barring women from owning property and voting or forcing them to relinquish jobs when they get married. But matters are far, far from where they need to be, if for no other reason than the fact that evangelicals, instead of taking the lead in discussing the issue, have often been pulled along by outside forces. Too many people dismiss women's issues as PC (political correctness), which is used as an excuse to exclude further care or consideration about sexism. People who refuse to consider the history, nature, and extent of sexism, including evangelical Christians, do so at their peril. Why?

- Females constitute slightly over 50 percent of both this country's and the world's population. This by itself should alert us to the necessity of a thoughtful conversation about the issue. We are talking about a large number of people, created in God's image.
- Few will disagree that these people created in God's image have been unfairly treated in the past and continue to suffer oppression around the world for no other reason than their gender. As Christians, we cannot simply shrug off oppression, especially on this scale. We need to identify causes, determine where it still occurs, repent, and vow that it never happens again.
- As realization has grown about the depth and extent of oppression in the past, much anger and resentment has come as a result. More than a little of this has been directed at Christianity, and we need to frame a coherent and sensitive response.
- Women and men do not live in isolation from each other. God's plan is for us to live together. If men act in ways that deny women full dignity, this harms everyone, not just women. To the extent that one gender is not allowed to flourish as God intended, whether by law, religious teaching, social expectation, or some other cause, the other gender suffers as well.
- When we speak of "gender issues," we are not dealing with abstractions. No one is generically male or female. We are talking about people to whom we are intimately related—spouses, mothers, daughters, grandmothers, sisters, aunts, and cousins. These are not simply people with struggles and aspirations; these are people whose struggles and aspirations we share.

Hierarchy and Equality

While the problem has not been as widely discussed on the popular level, a great deal of evangelical Christian literature has been and continues to be written in academic circles on the subject of gender issues. The intention of these scholars is to write that which they believe best reflects biblical teaching about the subject matter, taking into account historical Christian views on men and women. They also have in common an attempt to consider the rational, experiential, and cultural angles of gender issues. However, evangelical scholars often come to very different conclusions about how to resolve these issues.

One sign of progress is that the vast majority of evangelicals have abandoned older views that saw women as of lesser humanity (e.g., Thomas Aquinas refers to women as "misbegotten males"). Instead, most evangelical views can be placed under two broad categorizations—what we will call hierarchical (or complementarian) and egalitarian. Proponents of hierarchical views often prefer to call themselves complementarians, since it emphasizes the positive aspects of the relationships between men and women. Both views affirm that females possess the full value and dignity of humanity, but differ on what roles are proper to the sexes.

The complementarian view emphasizes an obvious observation. Females and males are not exactly alike (otherwise it would be a bit silly to have two different gender designations). In fact, we are different enough that we can, in most cases anyway, distinguish male from female with a glance. We differ biologically and, more controversially, we seem to be able to identify differences in forms of communication, psychology, interests, and other areas. The big question is, what does God intend for us to conclude from these differences? Complementarianism says, as the name implies, that male and female complement and complete each other by bringing their differences to the table. These differences are manifested in terms of roles God intends each to fulfill. In general, males are thought to play the more public role—providing for the financial needs of the family and giving leadership in organizational and ecclesiastical affairs—while the role of females was oriented toward the home and the nurturing of children.

Traditionally, those who adopt the complementarian approach see a hierarchical relationship between men and women. The overwhelming majority of biblical teachings suggest a hierarchical structure in the world, which God intentionally created, and the orderliness of God's creation extends to the relationship between men and women, parents and children, and so on. Some consider the order of creation to be God's ideal, while others consider hierarchy a safeguard put in place by God as a result of the fall. In any case, the God-ordained chain of command between people is thought to exist for the benefit of women as well as men. The hierarchical relationship empowers both men and women, and it complements and enhances every interaction the genders have with one another. Over and over, the New Testament testifies to hierarchy (e.g., John 4:7–30; 1 Cor. 11:2–16; 14:33–35; 1 Tim. 2:9–15; 5:11–16; Titus 2:3–5). Thus, Christians should help women to experience fulfillment through submission and dependence in marriage, family, and—correspondingly—society (e.g., Eph. 5:21–22, 25; 1 Peter 3:1–6).

Egalitarianism, on the other hand, is a more recent term, which gained widespread usage with regard to gender issues only during the latter half of the twentieth century. As the name implies, egalitarians promote full equality for men and women, not only in terms of human dignity but by espousing open access to all roles in society. Although this position looks similar to secular approaches to gender equality, evangelical Christians who advocate this view do so on theological grounds and consider their views wholly compatible with the Bible. In general, egalitarians acknowledge that individual passages in Scripture appear to support a hierarchical structure. However, they argue that we often overlook portions of Scripture that point to full equality.[4] For example:

- Biblical principles promote equality (Gen. 1:27–28; Gal. 3:28).
- The subordination of women occurred as a result of the fall, which we seek to overcome in all other ways (Gen. 3:16).
- Scripture promotes the creation of a just society, free from any kind of marginalization or oppression (Ps. 103:6; Micah 6:8; 1 Peter 2:13–17).
- Scripture offers numerous positive female role models in addition to those of men, for example: Deborah (Judges 4–5); Esther (Esther); and Priscilla (Acts 18; Romans 16).
- Hierarchicalism is not consistently present in Scripture, for example, in the writings of Paul (1 Cor. 11:4–5, 16, vis-à-vis 1 Cor. 14:33b–35).
- Headship may refer to the "source" of one's life rather than "authority" over one's life (1 Cor. 11:3; Eph. 5:23;); of the principle of mutual substitution in Ephesians 5:21.
- The Holy Spirit equally gifts males and females, and denial of the exercise of these gifts hinders God's work (Acts 2:17; 1 Cor. 12:4–11).

In addition to scriptural and theological arguments, both sides appeal to evangelical tradition and history to support their positions. Evangelicals tend to have greater respect for tradition, and many find in history strong support for the complementarian view. They argue that the role differences found in Scripture also have been reflected in social structures in virtually every society. By this interpretation of history, complementarians argue that egalitarianism is a dangerous innovation that overturns time-tested social roles and threatens the stability of the family and culture.

However, students of evangelical history recognize that egalitarianism has a long history within the movement. While many assume that feminism is a secular idea that popped into existence only a few decades ago, various strands of evangelicalism, going back to the beginning, saw greater roles for women as the logical outgrowth of evangelical renewal and revival. Indeed, women were often in the lead in these movements.

To name just a few examples, Margaret Fell was an early leader in the Society of Friends—the Quaker Movement. She represents one of the earliest advocates for women's rights, in the seventeenth century, and is especially remembered for her pamphlet on "Women's Speaking" (or "Women's Speaking Justified"), which provided biblical argumentation for equal rights for women, including women in ministry.[5] During the eighteenth century, John Wesley affirmed women in leadership in Methodist societies, the primary organ of ministry within the movement. In roughly the same period, several hundred female preachers were active between the First and Second Great Awakenings. In the nineteenth century, Phoebe Palmer was one of the most prominent evangelists of the age, and Catherine Booth cofounded with her husband the Salvation Army, which empowered both women and men in ministry. During this century, women were a main engine in American missionary efforts, establishing, funding, and administering numerous organizations. Historian Douglas Sweeney says that by the early twentieth century, the women's missions movement "proved so powerful . . . that by the early 1930s male denominational leaders sought to co-opt its institutions."[6] In the twentieth century, Pentecostals were at the forefront of empowering women in church leadership roles. Aimee Semple McPherson was an itinerant Pentecostal preacher who founded the International Church of the Foursquare Gospel. Other evangelically oriented denominations, in addition to Pentecostals, affirmed women in all levels of leadership, including ordination.

These historical examples indicate that the promotion of women in leadership is not the exclusive province of secular feminism and non-evangelically oriented churches and denominations. In fact, evangelicals were often ahead of the curve. This often-overlooked (suppressed?) record of countercultural tendencies, in which evangelicals have bucked traditional views of women's roles, reminds us that in addition to disagreements about interpreting Scripture on the legitimate functions of women, we disagree about how to interpret our history. So what do we make of the fact that throughout much of evangelical history, women have had pivotal and groundbreaking ministries? Is this a sign of the Spirit's anointing and gifting or an aberration of God-ordained roles? Are these cases in which Christians rightly and successfully confronted unholy hierarchies embedded in social norms, or do they represent rebellion against traditions that reflect God's will for family and society? These are two very different interpretations, but each has a long history within the evangelical family.

Paradigm Shift?

Paradigm shifts often take a long time, and I expect that women's issues are no different. If it took more than a century for Christians to deal with the abolition of slaves, there is no reason to suspect a faster resolution of the debate between hierarchical and egalitarian views. In fact, there is no reason to expect that the debate will ever be resolved. That includes debate among evangelical Christians. Both sides appeal to Scripture and history, and both have the best of intentions with regard to how they treat one another—both men and women.

What is to be done in the meantime? We certainly do not expect to advance debate on the issues. But we do want to draw some tentative conclusions. First, there is no unanimity among evangelical Christians with regard to the relationship between men and women. So, it is woefully inadequate to claim that one view speaks for all. Second, to the degree that all evangelical Christians recognize unjust, discriminatory treatment of women, such injustice needs to stop. Finally, we encourage evangelicals to become proactive, advocates on behalf of women's rights and the treatment of women, regardless of whether they hold hierarchical or egalitarian views. Almost every evangelical Christian with whom I have spoken, heard speak, or read, talks about how Jesus was progressive in how he treated and related with women. How wonderful it would be if evangelicals became known for their advocacy on behalf of women as well as for God, family, and children!

Homophobia and Homosexuality

Are evangelical Christians homophobic? Do evangelicals become so irrationally fearful of homosexuality and homosexuals that they become adverse to or discriminate against them? It should sadden us to know that more than nine out of ten (91 percent) of non-Christian young adults perceive Christians as homophobic.[7] Sadly, I find it difficult to deny that this perception has a strong correspondence to reality. Nor do I feel any compulsion to defend evangelical Christians on this charge. Homophobic attitudes, jargon, and bigotry against homosexuals is inexcusable, and it has occurred far too often. Is society at large much better? Not really. Perhaps one could say that evangelicals are no worse than anyone else. But for Christians, who should be characterized by love and compassion, to claim that we are no worse than anyone else sets the bar far too low. However, I discovered firsthand that even the most minimal of expressions of love and compassion can be risky business within the evangelical community.

In 1996, I wrote an article for *Christianity Today* titled "Revelation and Homosexual Experience."[8] Two articles were written under the same title, the other article by Wolfhart Pannenberg.[9] In the articles, both Pannenberg and I stated that homosexuality is contrary to biblical teaching and thus sin. Of course, I want to think that I included a great deal that extended Christian empathy and compassion to all who consider themselves homosexual. Be that as it may, I was clear in stating my position about sexual sins, including homosexual behavior. However, more than ten years later, long after publication of my article, I was accused by some colleagues of accepting and promoting homosexual behavior, even though the article made clear that the opposite was the case. The mere fact that I would express compassion for those who considered homosexuality was more than enough to make me suspect. Now, this might seem like an unfortunate misunderstanding, if not for the fact that rumors were spread, false accusations were made, and I was asked to submit written proof to administrators that I did not controvert university policy on the subject. Potentially, my job was on the line!

Why is homosexuality such a radioactive issue for evangelicals? Perhaps one response is that most of us have a significant degree of empathy toward those who commit adultery, steal money, tell lies, or engage in other activities that fall short of Christian ideals. We understand the temptation of these sorts of things because, to varying degrees, they also tempt us. However, for the majority of people, sexual desire for members of their own gender is not a temptation at all. It seems alien, perverse, and even repulsive. Since it is not part of our human experience, we have to resist the urge to treat those who are sexually attracted to the same gender as subhuman. In large part, this is why responses to homosexuals are described as a "phobia" or fear; it is so far outside our realm of experience that our reactions tend toward the irrational and reactionary. It also helps account for why we frequently put homosexual activity into a special category of sin, despite the fact that Scripture does not do so. When it comes to how Christians respond to homosexuals, there are hurdles to love that we do not encounter in other areas.

Although discussions have only recently moved into the open, homosexuality and homosexual behavior seem to have occurred throughout most of recorded history. It is not just a passing fad. References occur in many ancient sources, including the Bible. Generally, homosexual behavior was condemned for various reasons. Only about a half dozen verses deal with homosexual behavior, and even those verses are increasingly contested by biblical interpreters (e.g., Gen. 19:1–9; Lev. 18:22; 20:13; Rom. 1:24–27; 1 Cor. 6:9; 1 Tim. 1:10). Of course, the Bible says a great deal more about sexuality than just homosexuality. The Bible is surprisingly frank and open about sex, much more so than most Christians. After all, sexuality as well as procreation seem to be blessings from God. Sex is good and to be enjoyed appropriately. As with all goods provided by God, however, abuses can and do occur. Many sexual behaviors are condemned among men, women, animals, and so on. Nevertheless, homosexual sins are not treated with greater severity in Scripture than other sexual sins.

Complexity of Issues

Issues related to homosexuality, homosexuals, and homosexual behavior—however you want to refer to the subject—have become more complex, and we need to recognize some of these complexities. First, our binary language of heterosexuality and homosexuality is a rather blunt instrument for understanding the issues. This is evident from a number of coalitions that designate themselves as LGBTIQ—those who advocate on behalf of those who are lesbian, gay, bisexual, transgender, intersexed, and queer (or questioning).[10] There is strong evidence that the dynamics of male (gay) and female (lesbian) homosexuality differ significantly, and both have a different character from bisexuality. Transgendered individuals believe that their gender identity does not match their biological or genetic gender. This can occur in both male and females, and transgendered individuals may or may not attempt to change their biological makeup by surgical or pharmaceutical means. *Intersexed* (or *intersexual*) people are born with chromosomal and/or physiological anomalies, or ambiguous genitalia. The term "queer," long used in a derogatory manner against lesbians and gays, has been embraced by many homosexuals as an ironic challenge to discriminatory attitudes, actions, laws, and policies that unjustly affect them. Some gay and lesbian Christians advocating on behalf of the full acceptance of homosexuals and homosexual behavior describe their beliefs, values, and practices as queer theology. Thus, the LGBTIQ alphabet soup reminds us that nonheterosexuals do not fit into a single convenient category. However, the fact that these disparate subgroups have banded together in a coalition shows that they have a common bond in being marginalized by society.

A second matter that complicates our discussions is that not all are in agreement about the causes of homosexuality. Traditionally, it has been assumed that homosexuals suffered from a mental disorder[11] or were simply heterosexuals acting in rebellion toward social norms. However, scientific studies increasingly challenge age-old opinions about the biological as well as sociocultural nature of homosexuality. A growing number of scientists and behavioral specialists argue that same-sex attraction is biologically determined. They can no more prevent themselves from being homosexual, at least in nature, than others can prevent themselves from being heterosexual or determine their height, weight, and skin color. Others continue to have strong doubts about whether individuals have a predisposition toward same-sex attraction. Of course, there is no contemporary consensus on the matter of sexual orientation, and we probably should not expect consensus anytime soon. In view of what we have said about the varieties within the LGBTIQ coalition, it may be that no one-size-fits-all explanation works for the question of sexual orientation. However, for those who have listened to homosexuals who, because of the social alienation they experience, say they would give anything to be free of same-sex attraction, it is hard to dismiss the possibility that some individuals are born with an orientation they did not and would not choose.

Third, if we grant that certain individuals have a homosexual orientation, what is the proper response from evangelicals? Can sexual orientation be a sin? The Bible does not condemn people for having homosexual tendencies, feelings, or temptations (although there are sinful ways to entertain such tendencies or feelings) any more than it condemns heterosexuals for these. Its focus is more on certain behaviors or actions. Some evangelical groups do not consider such an orientation sinful per se, but believe that, with counseling, some (few groups say "all") may experience a change in orientation. Other evangelicals believe that such a "re-orientation" is not possible. Thus, they would encourage those who have a homosexual orientation to live celibately. They argue that the single homosexual is essentially of the same status as the single heterosexual. Both have sexual impulses that in themselves are not sinful, but become so only if these impulses are acted upon outside marriage. Of course, the difference is that the single heterosexual has the possibility of marriage, and thus the potential for legitimate sexual expression that is not available to the homosexual. As hard as it is to say, we all have certain predispositions we are not allowed to act upon. Widespread data seem to indicate that boys are more aggressive than girls and that some individuals are born with a strong genetic predisposition toward alcoholism. This certainly does not give males a pass on acting violently, nor does it mean that those predisposed to alcohol have a license to abuse alcohol. However, it may mean that we should be more merciful toward those who have challenges that are not part of our experience when they fail in those challenges.

A fourth complexity in framing an evangelical response to homosexuality is the extent to which it should be opposed by political and social means. Historically, the vast majority of evangelicals have considered homosexual behavior to be contrary to the teachings of Scripture, and thus sin. However, we also recognize that it is probably not a good idea to make every ungodly act illegal. Gossiping about a person or lying to your momma about what time you got in last night are sinful, but it is unlikely that we want legislators to write laws assigning criminal penalties for these acts. The reason is that we recognize different spheres of responsibility. The church is responsible for certain matters, the family for other concerns, and the state for yet other areas. It is not always clear where the boundaries lie in the spheres of responsibility, and that creates tension for evangelicals with regard to homosexuality. To what degree should they argue for their beliefs and values about homosexuality in the public forum, including federal and local governments, public schools, and even the media?

One of the hot issues in evangelical communities is the question of gay or lesbian marriages. Many evangelicals have taken the lead in working to defeat homosexual marriage initiatives on the grounds that such unions violate God's intent for marriage. Moreover, they would argue that the idea that marriage should be limited to male and female is not governed by the beliefs of a single religion, era, or place. It is a time-tested arrangement necessary for the stability of the family and the healthy nurture of children. On the other hand, some evangelicals agree that although same-sex marriage falls short of God's ideal, such unions should be allowed by the state on the basis of civil rights. Perhaps churches should not participate in the marriage of homosexuals because they are committed to an ideal of marriage that is grounded in Christian values. However, it is not the task of government to ensure that marriage conforms to any sort of divine ideal. Governments allow marriages between all sorts of people who engage in behaviors considered sinful by almost any religion—drug addicts, sex offenders, and people who lie to their moms about what time they got home (and evangelicals do not seem too interested in opposing these marriages). The government's job is to make certain that people receive equal treatment, regardless of their values.

Evangelical Challenges

Challenges arise when a particular belief or value becomes an excessive (or obsessive) focus of evangelical Christians, churches, denominations, and parachurch organizations. This sometimes seems to be the case with evangelical activism opposed to homosexuality. No one seems to notice—other than the rest of the world—that evangelical Christians seem to focus narrowly on homosexuality with relatively fewer qualms, at least publicly expressed, about other sexual sins. Especially to outsiders, it appears quite hypocritical for evangelicals to promote public policies against homosexuality without comparable activism against adultery, patronizing prostitutes (male and female), pedophilia, and remarriage after divorce, which many churches and denominations prohibit just as much as homosexual activity. While sexuality outside the boundaries of celibacy in singleness and fidelity in marriage may be consistently condemned, the volume rises noticeably in condemnation of gay and lesbian sexuality, especially in terms of what is said in public forums.

What is behind evangelicalism's preoccupation with homosexuality, to the near exclusion of other sins? First, most evangelicals seem to think it is a pretty safe sin to fixate on because it rarely involves them in any direct way. If you start preaching or campaigning against adultery, abusive behavior, or neglect of the poor, then you can be sure you will score direct hits on a substantial percentage of your congregation or constituency. Evangelical congregations have chased off most of their homosexual members, and those who remain know they are wise to hide it. So they are safe targets for industrial-strength attacks.

Second (but closely related to the first point), many homosexuals have become rather strident in their opposition to Christianity, especially the evangelical variety, and have become vocal and aggressive in pressing their political agendas. Some of what they have to say is pretty mean-spirited and in-your-face. It is always a temptation to react to this sort of behavior with similar venom, and too often evangelicals have succumbed, producing alarmist literature appealing to exaggerations, caricatures, and conspiracy theories about how gays and lesbians are taking over the media and then the government and society. (I'm not talking about communications from the "God hates fags" groups, whose crazy actions verge on domestic terrorism.) These are well-known evangelical Christian ministries and political action groups that talk a lot about truth and love, but rely on fear, intentional misrepresentation, and borderline hate-mongering in their fund-raising appeals to evangelical insiders such as me.

In view of these circumstances, it does not require much insight to recognize that evangelicals have quite a challenge if we want to be Great Commission people to those in the homosexual community. To put it bluntly, this challenge exists because so many of our current responses reduce homosexuals to depersonalized abstractions or faceless enemies. As a rule, we, especially older evangelicals, do not know homosexuals well enough to view them as flesh-and-blood people. However, as a result of broader openness among younger homosexuals, younger people do know them. They know them as siblings, relatives, classmates, and friends, and they see them in all their humanity. That is why, as we stated at the beginning of this section, 91 percent of young non-Christians view evangelicals as homophobic. We have depersonalized people they love. Thus, by our actions and attitudes, we not only alienate millions of homosexuals, we alienate those who love them the way we should be loving them. So how do we become the face of Jesus to a large group that now views evangelicals as homophobic?

David Kinnaman, coauthor of *unChristian*, recounts the following conversation with Mark, a gay friend, who asked, "So, David, do you still think I am going to hell because I am gay?" In response, Kinnaman started by apologizing if he had communicated this attitude. He acknowledged his belief that homosexual behavior was a sin, but added that we all experience brokenness in our sexuality. The key for everyone was what we decide about Jesus. His friend Mark responded, "David, here is what you need to know about my life. I was incredibly lonely. I hated myself. I could not figure out what was wrong with me, and it was eating me alive. I almost dropped out of school. It was awful. I know guys who have committed suicide because of the deep conflicts that exist between who they are and what religion says is right and wrong."[12] Unless we all start having these sorts of conversations with those in the homosexual community, evangelicals will view a large segment of the population as abstract entities to be feared. In other words, we will be homophobic.

Conclusion

The extent of injustice, pain, and suffering in the world can sometimes seem mindboggling. In this chapter, we discussed only three problem areas confronting people today: racism, sexism, and discrimination against homosexuals. Other injustices could be added against those who are very young or old; those who are challenged physically, mentally, and emotionally; those who represent different religious (or nonreligious) beliefs, values, and practices; and so on. Everyone can be discriminated against, and reverse discrimination can also occur, when those who have been privileged in the past become discriminated against in the present. In fact, we hear evangelicals with increasing frequency express the belief that they are becoming acceptable targets of discrimination. No one likes it when they are the victims, and they shouldn't. God has programmed us to respond negatively to unjust treatment.

So if our call as Christians is to do battle against any form of unjust treatment, where do we go from here? First, we should listen and educate ourselves, especially if we have escaped relatively unscathed from the forces of discrimination. It is easy to confuse reality with our limited experience of the world. However, when we hear other voices, our view of the world expands. We recognize that others confront hurdles that thwart their desire for freedom and respect, hurdles that we will never fully understand.

Second, we need to engage in careful and continual self-examination to determine where stereotypes and caricatures linger and shape our attitudes and language. Our actions and beliefs can be motivated by a fear that drives us toward a tribalism that looks at power as a zero-sum game (in which someone always has to win and all others must lose) and views competitors for that power as enemies. This perspective is unacceptable for people of God's kingdom, which seeks to include "every nation and every tribe."

A third challenge is to better learn how to respond instead of reacting. A lot of people are very angry at evangelicals because of how we have treated them, or how we are perceived to treat them. Too often, we react with similar anger. We need to remember that anger comes from pain. When we have been responsible for that pain, we need to admit it and make amends. When the pain grows out of misperception, we need to carefully and lovingly set the record straight to the extent that we can.

Fourth, we need to put things into perspective. As we noted at the beginning of the chapter, even when we can agree that we should be about the business of eliminating racism, sexism, or homophobia, we are bound to run into disagreements about how best to do the job, or how much of a job remains. Too often, evangelicals have approached these discussions as if every question is an all-or-nothing matter. Evangelicals will be better Christians and less hurtful toward others when they accept that changes have occurred, and that many have been beneficial. Thus, evangelical Christians need to affirm what is central, be willing to give up what is peripheral, and be loving toward others, even if they have divergent beliefs, values, and practices. To this extent, they would reflect the wisdom of Meldenius, the seventeenth-century Lutheran pastor who advised: "In essentials, unity; in nonessentials, liberty; in all things, charity."[13]

Perhaps this can be summed up by reminding ourselves how far bigotry is from the values of the kingdom of God. Bigotry has to do with "a person obstinately or intolerantly devoted to his or her own opinions and prejudices; *especially*: one who regards or treats the members of a group (as a racial or ethnic group) with hatred and intolerance."[14] Obviously, hatred is diametrically contrary to love, the most fundamental of Christian virtues. However, while hatred can be expressed in overt acts, it also can be found in covert forms such as neglect, indifference, separation, and depersonalization. Our battle against the perverse forces of racism, sexism, and homophobia cannot be at arm's length if it is shaped by Christian love. Instead, it requires us to come face-to-face with those who are different, and sometimes quite angry with us. It will involve individualizing and personalizing those who in many cases are known to us only as abstractions and thought of as undifferentiated members of a group. We need to get close enough to discern the image of God in all.

Postscript

Occasionally, on my way out of church, I (Steve) pause in the doorway of a room where a Chinese congregation meets each Sunday for lunch after their worship. (Apparently, church covered-dish meals are an international phenomenon.) I feel a kinship with them because they worship the same Lord I do, not to mention that they seem to enjoy eating as much as I do. Along with this kinship, I also sense the difference. They certainly do not look like my German and English forebears, and because they speak Mandarin, I am clueless about the conversations, except for the smatterings of English I hear from the younger ones. Despite the language barrier, a glance around the room will tell anyone what is going on. Grandmas are holding infants, fathers watch energetic kids out of the corner of their eye while trying to hold a conversation, teenagers giggle in the corner, and expectant moms compare notes on their pregnancies. Human life, with all its love, aspirations, and anxieties, is happening here.

I always survey this scene a little longer than I might otherwise because my daughter is of Chinese birth. Odd as it may seem, I rarely see a Chinese girl when I look at my daughter. I just see her, in all her glorious humanity. What will it take for me, and for us, to look beyond the different ways in which humanity manifests itself to see people in their image-of-God humanity? The answer is deceptively simple: God loves people, regardless of their race, gender, and sexual orientation. None of these factors negates or enhances our humanity. Until all people are loved and respected, regardless of race, gender, or sexual orientation, evangelical Jesus followers cannot let up in confronting the sins of racism, sexism, or homophobia, especially when we find them in our own lives.

10

Conclusion

People of the Great Commission

While writing this book, I (Don) tried to remember the first time I consciously referred to myself as an *evangelical* Christian. Can you think of when you first described yourself as being evangelical (if you have)? I do not remember having thought about the chronology until writing this book. As a theologian, I regularly refer to myself as being an evangelical Christian. But when did I first take this rather abstract, contested idea of evangelical and use it to describe myself?

As a kid, I vaguely remember that the Free Methodist Church in which I grew up was a member of the National Association of Evangelicals. Although I did not know what that affiliation meant, the identification was somehow self-identifying and reassuring. I was a part of something greater than just my local church and denomination. Perhaps the topic of evangelicalism was discussed, but I certainly do not remember what was said.

In 1976, *Time* magazine had a cover story with the title "Year of the Evangelical." The feature article focused on the presidential candidacy of Jimmy Carter—a Southern Baptist Sunday School teacher. It discussed the growing presence and identity of evangelical Christianity. I probably learned more about evangelicalism from that article than from anywhere else. I did not read the entire article, but it was discussed in church and by Christian friends. However, most people (even within the evangelical movement) seemed unclear with regard to its various beliefs, values, and manifestations. Still, President Carter became a noteworthy example of evangelicalism, even though I knew few Christians who voted for him.

As I progressed in my ministerial and theological studies, I am sure that the topic of evangelical Christianity arose from time to time. In retrospect, I know

189

that I attended an evangelical seminary. However, I used my denominational affiliation or Wesleyan heritage, rather than evangelicalism, to identify myself.

While doing doctoral studies in theology in 1983, I had a friend named Dan who enthusiastically encouraged me to join the Evangelical Theological Society (ETS). I was not familiar with the organization, but I trusted my friend and read the application he gave me. After reading the one requirement for membership—the doctrine of inerrancy—I told Dan that I did not use the term to describe my view of Scripture. Instead, I used the statement of my denominational affiliation, which had the language of sufficiency rather than inerrancy. From a scholarly perspective, I considered the doctrine of inerrancy to be problematic on many levels, and so I felt no compulsion to use it. Still, Dan encouraged me to join because the ETS was flexible in its understanding of the term. So, I joined the ETS and decided to attend the annual meeting in Dallas. While I was there, however, Robert Gundry was expelled from the ETS because his views on the Gospels and redaction criticism were considered incompatible with inerrancy. As soon as I returned home, I canceled my membership. I wanted to have integrity, and I knew I did not fit into the contentious culture of ETS. I preferred to pursue my evangelical scholarship in ways that were free to study the truth of Scripture as well as its relevance to the real-life needs and questions of the world.

In 1990, I published my first book with Zondervan. I initially titled it *The Wesleyan Quadrilateral: Scripture, Tradition, Reason and Experience*. However, Zondervan wanted to amend the subtitle to read *Scripture, Tradition, Reason and Experience as a Model of Evangelical Theology*. It was a watershed experience for me. I was not opposed to calling myself evangelical; I had just never done it so publicly. Once the book was published, I realized that I would forever be identified with evangelical Christianity and what it might mean for me professionally as a theologian. Although I was and continue to consider myself evangelical, the identification included many Christian groups, beliefs, values, and practices with which I do not agree. Moreover, not everyone with whom I affiliated understood the term, much less welcomed it. However, calling myself evangelical was accurate, as I understood the term historically and theologically. In *The Wesleyan Quadrilateral*, I took care to describe what I consider evangelical Christianity to be, and I have continued to promote it since then. In fact, I like to think of myself as a champion of evangelicalism, which is why it is important for me to write this book.

A Socratic Approach

In the introduction to this book, we described evangelical Christianity as a contested concept. We did not attempt even a preliminary definition, given the fact that so many attempts have already been made. Indeed, a cottage industry seems to have arisen among evangelical publishers to put forth a defining work on the subject (the present publication not excluded!). Yet, no one definition seems to have gained widespread acceptance, although some definitions have been deemed more adequate than others.

Thus far, our approach to defining evangelical Christianity has been, methodologically speaking, somewhat Socratic. That is, we have dialogued about various beliefs, values, and practices that have been identified with evangelicalism. Like Socrates, we think that "life without this sort of examination is not worth living."[1] So, we have discussed, analyzed, and evaluated ways that evangelical Christianity has been defined, or at least identified. Again, like Socrates, we focused on theses thought to be incorrect or inadequate to define evangelicalism. For example, is the essence of evangelical Christianity summed up in the doctrine of biblical inerrancy? Some think so; however, a great deal of historical and contemporary evidence contradicts the thesis. The same is true of other theses that attempt to define evangelicalism in terms of Calvinism, pretribulational premillennialism, and so on. Indeed, we consider the subject matter in the various chapters of this book to be misrepresentational of the whole of evangelical Christianity. It is not that these subjects do not contain elements of truth; usually caricatures arise from real-life experiences. However, caricatures do not generally represent all or even most evangelicals; that would be to the detriment of the movement. After all, who wants to be known for being sexist, racist, homophobic, mean, stupid, and dogmatic?

Of course, it is a matter of debate as to whether the Socratic method leads to genuine knowledge, or whether it is a negative method, used only to rebut false claims, for example, about evangelical Christianity. It has been our hope that in disputing false claims about evangelicals, we will be better able to understand and perhaps define the movement. In eliminating caricatures, we would be able to work more positively toward distilling the essence of evangelical Christianity. Of course, in working toward that end, we remain mindful that the more Socrates dialogued, the more he professed ignorance of the subject matter. Socrates considered himself to be wiser for acknowledging his ignorance, contrary to those who—still ignorant—claimed knowledge, especially those who claimed to have truth nailed down. We will resist the temptation to claim absolute knowledge of evangelicalism's true definition, and thus avoid the wrath of Socrates on that count. However, since we are not as wise as Socrates, we will offer our own definition toward the end, but with the proviso that it is tentative and incomplete. Along the way, we will examine different types of definitions others have attached to evangelicalism and consider how they may help us move down the road to a better understanding.

Distilling Essences

Many approaches are used to define evangelical Christianity—to distill its essence. They include definitions that are historical, theological, sociocultural, political, institutional, experiential, and so on. No one definition seems sufficient to capture the breadth, vitality, and development of the movement. In some respects, it seems a diminishment of evangelicalism to attempt a single, all-inclusive definition. It is like trying to describe yourself: Can you do it in a single sentence? Can you do it in two or three sentences? No doubt you can capture some salient aspects of who you are in a short definition. However, most of us would beg others to realize that there is much, much more to who we are than can be encapsulated in a sentence or two.

One of the problems arises from deciding what we are actually defining. Robert Calhoon, for example, makes a distinction between "evangelical" and "evangelicalism." He describes the former as "the proclamation of salvation through faith in Christ."[2] He gives other descriptors of "evangelical," which largely have to do with a distinctive understanding of religious beliefs shared by converts. These represent an attempt to define evangelical as orthodoxy (right beliefs). On the other hand, Calhoon says, "evangelicalism is a different term, an academic concept, identifying the bond between proclaimers and believers and the social energy which conversion releases into a surrounding human environment."[3] This is a helpful distinction, and one of which we are aware. It broadens our understanding of evangelicalism as a lived reality, dynamic, or movement that includes emphases on right action (orthopraxy) as well as right feelings and relationships (orthopathy). The definition Calhoon offers is consistent with our contention that evangelicalism ought not to be reduced to a particular belief or set of beliefs, values, and practices. Our intent has not been to narrow classifications of evangelical Christianity and/or evangelicalism by focusing excruciatingly on definitional minutiae. Instead, we have tried to broaden the discussion without being oblivious to important family resemblances.

Undoubtedly, there are scholars better versed than we are at articulating the multiple, dynamic dimensions of evangelical Christianity, drawing on resources from a variety of academic disciplines. We are not lifelong scholars of the topic, although we are lifelong evangelicals. So, rather than give our own definition at this time, we present to you for consideration three classical definitions of evangelical Christianity.

What constitutes a classical definition of evangelical Christianity? At this point, we can only say they are classical because we (and others) say so, which of course is not a very convincing argument! Nevertheless, there are certain descriptions of evangelical Christianity that have received widespread acceptance, inside and outside the movement. One focuses on distinctive characteristics; the second concentrates on beliefs and values; and the third majors in action, especially evangelism. We present them with commentary in the hope of doing justice to past, present, and future developments of evangelical Christianity.

First Definition

The first definition of evangelical Christianity comes from David Bebbington in a historical survey titled *Evangelicalism in Modern Britain*. Bebbington describes four main qualities or characteristics of evangelicalism:

> There are the four qualities that have been the special marks of Evangelical religion: conversionism, the belief that lives need to be changed; activism, the expression of the gospel in effort; Biblicism, a particular regard for the Bible; and what may be called crucicentrism, a stress on the sacrifice of Christ on the cross.[4]

Bebbington summarizes these characteristics by saying that they "form a quadrilateral of priorities that is the basis of Evangelicalism."[5] Bebbington's quadrilateral of priorities has received widespread support in defining the essence of evangelical Christianity. The four characteristics are easily understood—too easily, some would say. They may not suffice as an institution's "statement of faith" or "articles of religion," but they attempt to balance both the beliefs (a la orthodoxy) and practices (a la orthopraxy) of evangelicalism.

A similar description of evangelical Christianity can be found in *The Evangelical Moment* by Kenneth Collins. Collins talks about "four enduring emphases" found among evangelicals. They include: "(1) the normative value of Scripture in the Christian life, (2) the necessity of conversion (whether or not dramatic or even remembered), (3) the cruciality of the atoning work of Christ as the sole mediator between God and humanity, and (4) the imperative of evangelism, of proclaiming the glad tidings of salvation to a lost and hurting world."[6]

Roger Olson builds on the fourfold sets of evangelical characteristics above in *Reformed and Always Reforming*. Olson thinks that another characteristic is needed to focus biblical understanding of Christianity, within the longstanding fidelity of evangelicalism, on what he calls the "Great Tradition" of Christian belief. The Great Tradition includes the ancient ecumenical doctrinal consensus plus the consensus of the sixteenth-century Reformers. Olson says: "A fifth common theme of the evangelical ethos is: (5) deference to traditional, basic Christian orthodoxy within a higher commitment to the authority of God's Word in Scripture as the norming norm of all Christian faith and practice."[7] Olson is right to contextualize the definitions by Bebbington and Collins within pertinent points of church history that continue to influence evangelical Christianity.

Although the aforementioned definitions try to capture the spirit of evangelicalism as well as its beliefs and practices, it is difficult to do so in written form. Several commentators on evangelical Christianity emphasize the experiential dimension, which has variously been described as right passions (orthopathy), right heart (orthokardia), or right affections (orthoaffectus). In *Evangelicalism and the Orthodox Church*, which was published as *A Report by the Evangelical Alliance Commission on Unity and Truth among Evangelicals (ACUTE)*, equal importance was placed on three approaches to understanding evangelicalism: historical, doctrinal, and experiential.[8] The latter includes evangelical understandings and expressions of the spiritual life. Concern for the experiential dimension of evangelical Christianity can also be found in

Ronald Nash's *Evangelical Renewal in the Mainline Churches*. Nash says that the essential elements of genuine evangelical renewal include both "doctrinal renewal" and "spiritual renewal."[9]

Bebbington's definition tries to incorporate the experiential dimension of evangelical Christianity in its reference to conversionism. Although some may dislike the brevity of his definition, it is also a strength in coherently summarizing the dynamic reality of evangelicalism, which is a changing and growing movement. If we wanted a longer definition, there is seemingly no end to the number of beliefs, values, and practices some consider essential to evangelical Christianity. So we will focus on what has been, at least since the mid-twentieth century, a standard definition of evangelicalism.

Second Definition

The second definition of evangelical Christianity comes from the National Association of Evangelicals, which is an ecumenical organization established in the United States in 1942. The NAE does not represent all evangelical Christians. Many individuals, churches, denominations, and parachurch organizations that call themselves evangelical do not affiliate with the NAE. Moreover, the organization has evolved over time, nevertheless staying true to its original vision of providing a united and public witness to the gospel of Jesus Christ. Yet, the NAE epitomizes the renaissance of evangelicalism, sometimes known as Neo-evangelicalism. Its self-identifying statements do not intend to present academic, diachronic historical and theological statements that can be used as universal descriptions for all evangelical Christians. Instead they present one historical manifestation of evangelicalism—one that has been very influential in the United States as well as throughout the world. The NAE may not represent the ideal of evangelical Christianity, but it does represent the broadest consensus of evangelicalism in United States history.

Evangelical Christians from around the world organized the World Evangelical Fellowship in 1951. It represented the fulfillment of earlier hopes for an Evangelical World Alliance in London in 1846 for the purpose of launching "a new thing in church history, a definite organization for the expression of unity amongst Christian individuals belonging to different churches."[10] Renaming itself the World Evangelical Alliance, reminiscent of the EWA, the WEA represents a broader organization of evangelical Christians worldwide, but the influence of the NAE self-identifying statements remains obvious. With only minor variations in the order of affirmations and word selection, the doctrinal declaration of the WEA is the same as the NAE.

The National Association of Evangelicals' "Statement of Faith" provides a simple yet profound summary of basic beliefs and values, thought to be representative—if not essential—to members of the NAE. Of course, any documents created by committee, including ecumenical committees, are notoriously suspect for whether or not they descend to the lowest common denominators among evangelical Christians. Even if this is the case, the Statement of Faith may represent a broader, more genuinely ecumenical consensus among evangelicals. The statement reads as follows:

- We believe the Bible to be the inspired, the only infallible, authoritative Word of God.
- We believe that there is one God, eternally existent in three persons: Father, Son and Holy Spirit.
- We believe in the deity of our Lord Jesus Christ, in His virgin birth, in His sinless life, in His miracles, in His vicarious and atoning death through His shed blood, in His bodily resurrection, in His ascension to the right hand of the Father, and in His personal return in power and glory.
- We believe that for the salvation of lost and sinful people, regeneration by the Holy Spirit is absolutely essential.
- We believe in the present ministry of the Holy Spirit by those whose indwelling the Christian is enabled to live a godly life.
- We believe in the resurrection of both the saved and the lost; they that are saved unto the resurrection of life and they that are lost unto the resurrection of damnation.
- We believe in the spiritual unity of believers in our Lord Jesus Christ.[11]

The confessional statement sounds similar to historical Christian affirmations, dating back to the ancient ecumenical creeds. Statements of Faith emphasize, if not overemphasize, the doctrinal and cognitive dimensions of Christianity.

There is also a "Mission Statement" that describes the task of members in the National Association of Evangelicals. The Mission Statement emphasizes the content as well as the dynamism and relevance of evangelicalism. It says:

> The mission of the National Association of Evangelicals is to extend the kingdom of God through a fellowship of member denominations, churches, organizations, and individuals, demonstrating the unity of the body of Christ by standing for biblical truth, speaking with a representative voice, and serving the evangelical community through united action, cooperative ministry, and strategic planning.[12]

No one document seems adequate to define evangelical Christianity, yet the NAE statements together represent a discriminating constellation of beliefs, values, and practices that attempt to capture the holistic nature of evangelicalism. The NAE identifying statements have the further weightiness of representing more than fifty self-described evangelical churches, denominations, and other organizations. What they say is no mere academic exercise; they carry the authority of millions of evangelical Christians. They give no short and sweet definition but a real-life model that is exemplary even for those evangelically oriented Christians who do not formally affiliate with the NAE.

Third Definition

The third definition of evangelical Christianity comes from a familiar source—a practitioner, if not also an icon of contemporary evangelicalism—Billy Graham. Certainly Graham did not invent evangelical Christianity, but for the last half century he has epitomized so much of what the movement represents. Not only is Graham the quintessential evangelist, he is also exemplary in his ecclesiastical, scholarly, and ecumenical involvements. A longtime Southern Baptist, Graham has preached worldwide to billions of people by means of crusades, radio, and television. It is estimated that more than two million people have converted to Christianity as a result of his evangelistic ministries. In addition, Graham has written numerous books, which extended his ministry far beyond the spoken word. For the sake of this book, an important involvement by Graham was in founding and promoting what became known as the Neo-evangelical movement in the United States during the mid-twentieth century. Graham gave early leadership in the National Association of Evangelicals, helped found the magazine *Christianity Today*, and participated in other ecumenically oriented efforts to unite evangelical Christians and promote evangelism. Thus, Graham lends a great deal of weight to defining the essence of evangelicalism.

Given Graham's stature in the evangelical (or Neo-evangelical) Christian movement, it stood to reason that he would be asked to write the introduction to *The Evangelicals: An Illustrated History*, written by John Allan and copyrighted by the World Evangelical Alliance. Graham says:

> We are not meant to live for ourselves; Christ has commanded us to tell others of his saving and transforming power. Thus evangelicals have always given priority to evangelism. Evangelicals may disagree on some minor points of doctrine or practice, but they unite on their common commitment to evangelism.[13]

Graham continues his introduction by talking about the biblical imperative to evangelize, how churches lose their spiritual vitality and influence when evangelism is neglected, and how God's plan to call out people for his name is unchanging. So, from Graham's perspective, the essence of evangelical Christianity is the "common commitment to evangelism." This description is expected, given his long and successful history of evangelistic crusades around the world. But does evangelism genuinely represent the conceptual and practitioner glue that holds historical evangelicalism together?

It is tempting to consider evangelism the essence of evangelical Christianity, as simplistic as it may sound to some people, especially those interested in exhaustive definitions of the movement. Certainly no one can investigate evangelicalism for long without noticing the prevalence of evangelistic preaching, crusades, missions, revivals, altar calls, passing out of tracts, door-to-door evangelism, and a myriad of other types of evangelistic outreach. However, evangelism alone fails to encapsulate enough of evangelical Christianity to suffice as a definition, although its preeminent place in the movement must not be denied.

Evangelism does serve as a clue, nevertheless, to how we want to define evangelical Christianity. Although evangelism alone does not describe evangelicalism, it alludes to the so-called Great Commission Jesus gave to his disciples. The Great Commission goes beyond evangelism alone; it also talks about making disciples, baptism, obedience, and related concerns about continuing Jesus's mission. It is fidelity to fulfilling Jesus's mission, of course, as understood by evangelicals, that best identifies them.

People of the Great Commission

We have looked at only a few definitions of evangelical Christianity. Dozens and dozens of others could be added. Despite the earnestness, objectivity, and detail sought by many in defining evangelicalism, each attempt reflects the interests and concerns of those defining it. This has to do with that to which we referred in the introduction: agendas that lie behind attempts to understand, define, and promote evangelical Christianity. We are not different. We have an agenda as well in discussing evangelicalism. For example, as suggested by the title of the book and the subject matter of each chapter, we resist characteristics ascribed to evangelical Christianity that we consider inaccurate or peripheral to many, if not most, evangelicals. We do not like definitions that are too narrow, especially with regard to deciding who is and who is not a true evangelical Christian. Too often we—and others—have been excluded from an evangelical event, church, denomination, society, parachurch group, or some other organization because we did not fit their definition. Regrettably, evangelical Christians seem to be known less for those people they like than for those they dislike. The cliché is that evangelicals are known by who they hate (or who they damn to hell).

We also recognize the warning some give about definitions that say too little about what it means to be evangelical. Practically speaking, how can anyone know and function as an evangelical Christian without some way to determine minimal beliefs, values, and practices? Of course, opening the gates too widely is problematic for some who want to identify themselves as evangelicals. It lets in the riffraff, so to speak; it endangers people's historical or contemporary beliefs, values, and practices that are considered inviolable, at least for them. (Might it give them too few people to hate?)

The problem remains, however, that there is not sufficient unanimity among evangelical Christians to vouchsafe every conceivable belief, value, and practice. This is why the book contains so many chapters about the diversity among evangelicals. Thus, we prefer simple definitions over those that are more complex. We prefer definitions that avoid doctrinal and praxis dichotomies (or doctrinal, praxis, and experiential trichotomies), and do not even get us started about the plethora of definitions that include interdisciplinary academic investigations. What does sociology say? What do post-colonialists say? What would Freud say? All such studies are valid and helpful, but they do not always help us to distill the essence or basic impulse of evangelical Christianity.

At the expense of erring on the side of simplicity, we like to think of evangelical Christians as people of the Great Commission. Let us repeat: *Evangelicals are people of the Great Commission*. The Great Commission, of course, alludes to Jesus's last words to the disciples in Matthew 28:16–20:

> Now the eleven disciples went to Galilee, to the mountain to which Jesus had directed them. When they saw him, they worshiped him; but some doubted. And Jesus came and said to them, "All authority in heaven and on earth has been given to me. Go therefore and make disciples of all nations, baptizing them in the name of the Father and of the Son and of the Holy Spirit, and teaching them to obey everything that I have commanded you. And remember, I am with you always, to the end of the age."

Working out what it means to be evangelical relates to how Christians understand, experience, and implement this missiological directive of Jesus—of the *missio Dei* (Latin, "mission of God").

Several questions and concerns immediately arise in defining evangelicals and evangelical Christianity this way. Let us address a few of them.

1. **Do not all Christians affirm Matthew 28:16–20?** Of course they do. It is not a matter of acceptance but of priority. Historically, theologically and ministerially, evangelicals have tended to emphasize the Great Commission as basic to what they believe, what they value, and how they live. Other church traditions and movements have placed equal or greater focus on other aspects of God, Scripture, and ministry.

2. **What about Matthew 28:16–20 is most important?** There is not a single, unchanging, normative interpretation among evangelical Christians. There is not even a clear-cut exhortation to evangelize, which is a common misconception about the Great Commission. It talks about "going," "making disciples," "baptizing," "teaching," and "remembering," which clearly envisions a more comprehensive mission than just evangelism. Of course, it is difficult to make disciples without engaging in evangelism of some sort. So, Christians need to come back to the passage over and over again in order to rightly interpret, embody, and live out the Great Commission.

3. **Why focus only on Matthew 28:16–20?** Actually, evangelicals do not focus only on the Great Commission. It is a priority rather than an exclusive approach to being Christian. Nevertheless, "going," "making disciples," and so on represent the basic impulse of evangelicalism. However, not all evangelical Christians interpret and implement the Great Commission the same way. This accounts for much of the diversity and adaptability of the movement. But manifestations of evangelism represent undeniably an application of the Great Commission.

4. **What of other priorities in Scripture?** Evangelical Christians neither deny nor neglect other priorities in Scripture. They still honor other basic beliefs, values, and practices. But those affirmations do not distinguish evangelicals from other biblically oriented, orthodox Christians. For this reason, we do not think specific affirmations, for example, as found in Bebbington (conversionism, Biblicism, activism, and crucicentrism), uniquely identify evangelicals vis-à-vis other Christians. As much as conversionism may be thought to distinguish evangelical Christianity, conversion and calls to conversion are not uncommon throughout Christendom. What distinguishes evangelicalism is the priority it gives to conversion within the context of the Great Commission—going, making disciples, and so on.

5. **With regard to the mission of God (*missio Dei*), is the Great Commission sufficient?** No, evangelical Christians would not say that the Great Commission alone is sufficient for the whole of what God wants Christians to be and do. Scripture contains many important beliefs, values, and practices. Even Jesus suggests other expressions of ministry (e.g., Mark 16:14–18; Luke 4:16–21). Again, it is a matter of priority rather than tunnel vision with regard to approaching the Bible. Nevertheless, the Great Commission has primacy for evangelicals in conceptualizing and fulfilling the mission of God.

6. **Might the priority given to the Great Commission represent a distortion of Scripture?** Of course, any prioritizing of Scripture (or "canon within the canon") can lead to distortion, and evangelical Christians have been guilty of distorting the gospel along with other Christians in church history. One of the purposes of this book is to challenge evangelicals to avoid beliefs, values, and practices that frustrate the reign of God and Christianity more than help them.

7. **If you like simplicity, why do you not just call evangelical Christians people of the gospel, since that is the derivation of their name?** It is tempting to call evangelicals people of the gospel—people of the *euangelion* (Greek, "gospel, good news"). It is even more tempting to call evangelicals people of Jesus Christ, who is the embodiment of the gospel. But all Christians are people of the gospel—of Jesus Christ. Distinguishing them by the etymology of the word does not really get at what has made evangelicals distinctive.

8. **Should we not add just a little bit more content with regard to what it means to be evangelical?** We are tempted, of course, to add more to our definition. We recognize the limitations of brevity and the dangers involved with saying too little. We especially recognize it when individuals, churches, denominations, and others seek practical guidance in developing self-identifying statements that place them within the tradition of evangelicalism—for example, statements of faith, mission statements, and statements about core values. We applaud such statements and consider them essential to Christianity. However, since they are essential to Christianity, is it possible to say that statements of Christianity are exclusive to evangelical Christianity? No. Moreover, the more exhaustive one becomes in describing proposition after proposition with regard to what evangelical Christians purportedly believe, the less likely one may resemble other self-described evangelicals. The more suspicious and fearful people become, the more judgmental and divisive they become; also, the more likely one is to be excluded from the particularized descriptions of others. Thus, we prefer to err on the side of a simple definition, but one that is not simplistic.

9. **Does your definition exclude some in church history from being called evangelical?** Perhaps. It depends on how narrowly you understand the Great Commission. Consider Luther, for example. Was he an evangelical? You could argue that he was, since Luther placed so much emphasis on salvation by grace through faith, and since he experienced a conversion exemplary of evangelicalism. On the other hand, you could argue that Luther and the Reformation involved different issues than are usually associated with the Great Commission. This is why evangelical Christianity is often traced as much (or more) through the pietistic likes of Edwards, Whitefield, and the Wesleys, despite important theological underpinnings promoted by Luther and Calvin.

10. **What prevents Christians from outside historical streams of evangelicalism from calling themselves evangelical?** Nothing! Indeed, we encourage Christians from other traditions to take the Great Commission more seriously in how they understand, embody, and minister to others. To this extent, we are willing to let in more of the riffraff! The riffraff, so to speak, include Christians from historical Protestant churches as well as Catholic and Orthodox churches. Although the term "evangelical" has sometimes been used historically to distinguish between Protestants and other church traditions, we see no inherent problem with Catholic and Orthodox Christians using the term "evangelical" to describe themselves.

11. **Are more exhaustive studies of evangelical Christianity relevant or needed?** Yes, because of what we perceive as the importance of evangelicalism in the past as well as the present, ongoing studies are welcome. If evangelical Christianity is as influential and dynamic as we think, then

everyone will benefit from examination that includes historical, theological, sociological, institutional, political, economic, experiential, and other approaches. If evangelicals want to live faithfully in relationship to the Great Commission, then they should be as discerning of themselves as they are in discerning God's will for how they are to love God and others.

Not Your Father's (or Mother's) Evangelicalism

The old advertising slogan for Oldsmobile cars was: "This is not your father's Oldsmobile!" Since Oldsmobiles are no longer built, it may not be an apt illustration. (Of course, there are many makes of cars no longer being built!) But the point we want to make is that evangelical Christians and others too often work with an antiquated understanding of what it means to be evangelical.

Consciously or unconsciously, people repeatedly identify evangelical Christians in a hyphenated way: Reformed-evangelical, Charismatic-evangelical, Holiness-evangelical, Baptist-evangelical, Catholic-evangelical, and so on. But these designations reduce evangelicalism to a part of the movement, insufficient for understanding the whole. Indeed, we argue that the whole of evangelical Christianity equals more than the sum of its parts. In the same way, people consist of more than an analysis of their bodily parts, personality type, cultural context, and distinctive spirituality. It takes time to get to know someone or something in-depth. They represent more than the sum of their parts, their individualities.

We like to think of evangelical Christianity at least in terms of right beliefs (orthodoxy), right actions (orthopraxis), and right feelings, affections, and relations (orthopathy). Evangelicalism may be defined in ways that include more than these categories, but they cannot contain less.[14] Caricatures arise when people limit their understanding and appreciation (or depreciation) of evangelical Christianity too narrowly. Individual Christians, churches, and denominations may have more precise self-descriptions for what it means to be evangelical, but they need to be wary about projecting them on others or presumptuously speaking on their behalf.

Amazingly, the fluid understanding of evangelical Christianity that exists today has provided a fortuitous—if not providential—opportunity in church history for ecumenical cooperation among Christians. Although ecumenism is not a term with which evangelicalism has been identified (caricatured?), the movement has been profoundly involved with ecumenical activities. Going back to the evangelical revivals of the eighteenth century, amazing cooperation took place among the Pietists, Methodists, and Puritans, for example, in the First Great Awakening. In the nineteenth century, evangelical Christians were at the forefront in both revivalism and social activism. In the twentieth century, the rise of the National Association of Evangelicals and the Billy

Graham Crusades' interdenominational and international approach to evangelism brought innumerable, albeit diverse, Christians together for the sake of cooperation in ministry. Who knows what the twenty-first century may afford with regard to increased opportunities for Christians, churches, denominations, and parachurch groups to cooperate with one another?

Of course, caricatured views of ecumenism are just as detrimental as caricatures of evangelical Christianity. In essence, ecumenism exemplifies Jesus's prayer for his disciples that they might be unified (John 17:21). The first creeds were called "ecumenical" because the early church councils attempted to unify Christians and churches throughout the ancient world. They met in order to find ways of becoming united, more cooperative. Today evangelical Christianity may provide, surprisingly, one of the more fruitful opportunities for ecumenical cooperation among Christians. Certainly evangelicalism does not provide the only avenue to Christian unity, since there exist other ecumenical impulses around the world—some far older and more developed than those among evangelical Christians. Nevertheless, the pragmatic, dynamic, and embracing nature of the movement—at its best—provides unimaginable and perhaps yet undreamed potential for uniting Christians worldwide. Evangelicalism may not represent all Christians, but it can become a leader in bringing together diverse people, cultures, and nations. Indeed, it can even bring together people from different worldviews and religions, and not just for the sake of evangelism and missions, although such impulses lie at the heart of the Great Commission.

Loving one's neighbor as oneself represents a belief, value, and practice as much at the heart of Christianity as the Great Commission. Evangelical Christians need to explore that principle—the Golden Rule—as well as the Great Commission as they endeavor to integrate, embody, and live out both biblical charges. The mission of God includes multiple principles, precepts, passions, and plans of action. It is our hope that evangelicals lead—rather than follow—Christians worldwide in uniting and mobilizing one another for the holistic mission of God.

Beyond Caricatures

As much as we want to contribute to defining the nature and extent of evangelical Christianity, the main purpose of this book is to extricate it from caricatures wrongly and detrimentally identified with the movement. Regardless of whether you define evangelicals as people of the Great Commission, or prefer another definition, evangelical Christianity is not helped by definitions, descriptions, or characterizations that reduce it to peripheral details. Such details are, of course, important. We do not want to trivialize issues related to the Bible, important Protestant traditions, eschatological views, ethical issues, and so on. However, we do not consider them essential or defining for evangelical

Christianity. So, we want to place them in more appropriate perspective in relationship to evangelicalism. We want to get beyond caricatures!

Caricatures are inherently hurtful, of course. Certainly there are more issues that we could have discussed. For example, some associate evangelical Christians with issues related to abortion, the death penalty, war, pornography, alcohol, parenting, music, media, and so on. Of course, there are far worse caricatures with which evangelicals have been identified that are not mentioned in this book, since—frankly—they exceed our PG-13 rating. Some associations are false and defamatory; these are easy to dismiss. Other associations are too true, and so the caricatures seem more accurate than inaccurate, although we wish it were not the case. The truth can hurt, and evangelicals can be as guilty as others in living unreflective, uncritical lives. Does it hurt more or less when evangelicals are unfairly or untruthfully caricatured? Should evangelical Christians only be concerned about justified criticisms, or should they also be concerned about unjustified criticisms?

We think it is naïve and shortsighted to ignore criticism—justified and unjustified—about evangelical Christianity. In large part, evangelicalism tends to be irenic and focused on shared beliefs, values, and practices for the sake of God's reign, churches, and their various ministries. When criticisms are justifiably leveled at evangelicals, they should be honest and repentant in how they respond. Failures, sins committed, and other shortcomings ought not to be denied. Growth into Christlikeness cannot occur without honesty, critical thinking, and—of course—prayer and the grace of God. Self-righteousness is also a temptation to be avoided by evangelical Christians. They are no less subject to temptations than others. It is our hope, nonetheless, that they become increasingly victorious over such temptations, by the grace of God and the various means of grace God has given them.

Sometimes there is need for polemics that serve apologetically to defend evangelical Christianity from its detractors. Evangelicals want to present themselves and their involvements as positively and winsomely as possible. They certainly do not want to be known for what is not true about them, distracting everyone from the heart of who they are. Finally, evangelicals want the Great Commission to be fulfilled throughout "all nations."

Conclusion: A Future with Hope

Evangelical Christians are people of the Great Commission. They seek to understand what Jesus meant by his parting words to the disciples (Matt. 28:16–20). Then they seek to embody and live it out through everything that they think, say, and do. Affirmation of the Great Commission is not in any way thought to be a truncation of the gospel. On the contrary, it represents a primary component of fulfilling what God wants people to do, including all the beliefs, values, and practices that God reveals in Scripture.

Will caricatures continue? Of course, caricatures seem to be an inescapable part of life, regardless of whether the caricatures are justified or unjustified. But we encourage evangelical Christians to have a clearer understanding of who they are. Do not get hung up on those things not essential to evangelicalism—things that are peripheral to its essence and mission. Instead, focus on first things—those that are as essential to historical manifestations of evangelical Christianity as they are to contemporary expressions of it. This book intends to help evangelicals fulfill their fundamental character, emphasizing the primacy of the Great Commission in identifying and vitalizing their mission in the world. In so doing, it is our hope that non-evangelical Christians as well as those outside Christianity altogether will have greater understanding and appreciation for the movement.

We have great hope about the future of evangelical Christianity, and for that matter the future of God's reign and of the role of Christians and churches worldwide. We are not pessimistic about the future; we are hopeful about the ways in which God wants to work in and through people's lives. We think that evangelicals have an important role to play in the church universal, and we want to help them fulfill all to which they believe themselves called by God. We do not expect evangelical Christianity to diminish in its spiritual and other influences; we expect it to flourish by the grace of God. So, rather than become preoccupied with peripheral matters, we want evangelical Christians to focus on understanding, embodying, and advancing Jesus's Great Commission.

Notes

Chapter 1 Introduction

1. William J. Abraham, *The Coming Great Revival: Recovering the Full Evangelical Tradition* (San Francisco: Harper & Row, 1984), 7–8.

2. Mark A. Noll, *The Rise of Evangelicalism: The Age of Edwards, Whitefield, and the Wesleys* (Downers Grove, IL: InterVarsity, 2004). See also Mark A. Noll, *American Evangelical Christianity: An Introduction* (Oxford: Blackwell, 2001), 10–12, and *The Old Religion in a New World: The History of North American Christianity* (Grand Rapids: Eerdmans, 2002), 51–52, 55.

3. For example, see Timothy L. Smith, *Revivalism and Social Reform in Mid-Nineteenth Century America* (Nashville: Abingdon, 1957).

4. John Wesley, "Catholic Spirit," Sermon 39 (1750), in *The Works of John Wesley*, vol. 2, Sermons II, Bicentennial Edition (Nashville: Abingdon, 1985), 90.

Chapter 2 Evangelicals Are Not All Mean, Stupid, and Dogmatic

1. Sam Harris, *The End of Faith: Religion, Terror, and the Future of Reason* (New York: W. W. Norton, 2005), 25.

2. Richard Dawkins, *The God Delusion* (Boston: Houghton Mifflin, 2006), 308.

3. Christopher Hitchens, *God Is Not Great: How Religion Poisons Everything* (New York: Hachette, 2008), 17.

4. Victor J. Stenger, *God: The Failed Hypothesis* (Amherst, MA: Prometheus Books, 2007), 248. As the title implies, Stenger's book is built on the view that science has the tools to prove or disprove the hypothesis that God exists. His justification for this rather interesting hypothesis is "God is supposed to be everywhere, including inside every box. So when we search for God inside a single box, no matter how small, we should either find him, thus confirming his existence, or not find him, thus refuting his existence" Stenger (27).

5. Sam Harris, *Letter to a Christian Nation* (New York: Alfred A. Knopf, 2006), 74.

6. One of the central theses of Harris's book is that religious extremism is aided and abetted by religious moderates. Thus, he says, "the very ideal of religious tolerance—born of the notion that every human being should be free to believe whatever he wants about God—is one of the principal forces driving us toward the abyss [of world destruction]." See Harris, *End of Faith*, 15. Apparently, this advocate of tolerance believes it necessary to be intolerant of religious tolerance.

7. W. Bradford Wilcox, *Soft Patriarchs, New Men: How Christianity Shapes Fathers and Husbands* (Chicago: University of Chicago Press, 2004), 116. In case you are wondering, Wilcox is not an evangelical, but a Catholic.

8. Ibid., 119, 129.

9. Ibid., 82.

10. Ibid., 152.

11. Ibid., 184.

12. Ibid., 177, 179.

13. Lisa D. Pearce and William G. Axinn, "The Impact of Family Religious Life on the Quality of Mother-Child Relations," *American Sociological Review* 63 (December 1999): 810–28.

14. Rodney Stark et al. *What Americans Really Believe* (Waco: Baylor University Press, 2008), 183.

15. S. Philip Morgan, "A Research Note on Religion and Morality," *Social Forces* 61, no. 3 (1983): 683–91.

16. Joseph Carroll, "Americans' Personal Satisfaction," *Gallup Surveys*, January 4, 2005.

17. Arthur C. Brooks, *Who Really Cares: The Surprising Truth about Compassionate Conservatism* (New York: Basic Books, 2006), 36. A more recent Gallup survey had less of a gap (21 percent). See "Charitable Giving Differs in Canada, U.K., and U.S.," *Gallup Surveys*, December 3, 2007.

18. Ibid., 39.

19. Ibid.

20. For figures on educational achievement and income levels, see "The U. S. Religious Landscape Survey, Pew Forum on Religion and Public Life."

21. Stark, *What Americans Really Believe*, 186–89.

22. The list of nine ideas grouped under the heading of "Occult and Paranormal Beliefs" are (1) dreams sometimes foretell the future or reveal hidden truths; (2) ancient advanced civilizations, such as Atlantis, once existed; (3) places can be haunted; (4) it is possible to influence the physical world through the mind alone; (5) some UFOs are probably spaceships from other worlds; (6) it is possible to communicate with the dead; (7) creatures such as Bigfoot and the Loch Ness Monster will one day be discovered by science; (8) astrology impacts one's life and personality; (9) astrologers, palm readers, tarot-card readers, fortune-tellers, and psychics can foresee the future. See Stark, 125–31.

23. Ibid., 128.

24. The main difference is that the NAE statement, like nearly all evangelical statements of faith, begins with an affirmation of Scripture's trustworthiness as the source of all dogma. However, the Apostles' Creed and Nicene Creed assume that a trustworthy Scripture is at the foundation of everything contained in these statements. In other words, the NAE statement simply makes explicit what is implicit in the creeds.

25. A good single-volume text that examines this theological diversity is *Across the Spectrum* (Grand Rapids: Baker, 2009), in which Greg Boyd and Paul Eddy outline evangelical views on just about every theological issue of importance.

26. "America's Evangelicals: More and More Mainstream but Insecure," *Religion and Ethics Newsweekly* April 13, 2004.

27. David Kinnaman and Gabe Lyons, *unChristian: What a New Generation Really Thinks about Christianity . . . and Why It Matters* (Grand Rapids: Baker, 2007), 25.

28. Ibid., 29–30.

29. Interestingly, 48 percent of white evangelicals perceive that they are "looked down on by most Americans," almost exactly equal to the percentage of young outsiders who have a negative view of evangelicals. Ibid.

30. Philip Yancey, "Lessons from Rock Bottom," *Christianity Today*, July 10, 2000, 72.

31. The same day I wrote this section, a newswire story came out about a video game publisher who hired twenty fake religious protesters to picket the convention center where his company

was featuring the release of a game titled "Dante's Inferno." The "protesters" handed out religious tracts and carried signs with messages such as "Hell is not a video game." See "Electronic Arts Stages a Fake Protest at E3," Associated Press, June 5, 2009. In addition to illustrating our point that evangelicals are widely known for what they oppose, this event should make us aware that marketers realize the very fact that evangelicals find something repulsive will often entice others to buy the product.

Chapter 3 Evangelicals Are Not All Waiting for the Rapture

1. See Hal Lindsey with C. C. Carlson, *The Late Great Planet Earth* (Grand Rapids: Zondervan, 1970).

2. For example, see Norman Cohn, *The Pursuit of the Millennium: Revolutionary Messianism in Medieval and Reformation Europe and Its Bearing on Modern Totalitarian Movements* (New York: Harper & Row, 1957), 14; Robert Clouse, "The Apocalyptic Interpretation of Thomas Brightman and Joseph Mede," *Bulletin of the Evangelical Theological Society* 11 (1968): 182; Peter Toon, "Introduction," in *Puritans, the Millennium and the Future of Israel: Puritan Eschatology 1600 to 1660* (Cambridge, MA: James Clarke, 1970), 14, 17; and Stanley Grenz and John R. Franke, *Beyond Foundationalism: Shaping Theology in a Postmodern Context* (Louisville: Westminster John Knox, 2001), 242. Premillennialists point to this conciliar decision as evidence of the distortions thrust upon Christianity by the post-Constantinian church in the fourth century—the so-called "Constantinian captivity of the church." Ironically, such accusers accept the canonization of Scripture by the same post-Constantinian church near the turn of the fifth century. Even those churches and denominations that claim they have "no creed but the Bible" cannot avoid the awkward truth that the very canon to which they appeal had not and may never have been established without the ancient church in the fourth and fifth centuries.

3. There were differences of opinion with regard to how to interpret the Bible in general and apocalyptic literature in particular. Ancient Christians were trying to make sense of sacred writings as best they could, given the fact that a full canon of the Bible was not agreed upon by a synod in Hippo until 394. In the meantime, interpreters did the best they could given limited biblical texts.

4. An interesting twist on this is that, after the beginning of the twentieth century, postmillennialism was dominant among theological liberals. Thus, while Hodge and Warfield were very possibly the two theologians most frequently cited against liberalism, they championed an eschatological view that many came to view as an almost infallible indicator of theological liberalism.

5. Proponents of premillennialism and pretribulationism say that their beliefs go back to the time of the ancient church, and that Augustine and others superseded earlier, more accurate interpretations of Scripture. While it is true that patristic writers refer to the imminent return of Jesus and other statements about the end times, there is no development of rapture-oriented eschatology. Little was said about predicting the end times from the perspective of pretribulational premillennialism until the nineteenth century.

6. Shirley Guthrie Jr., *Christian Doctrine: Teachings of the Christian Church* (Atlanta: John Knox, 1968), 384–88. Cf. Guthrie's revision of these principles in *Christian Doctrine*, rev. ed. (Louisville: Westminster/John Knox, 1994), 381–86.

7. Since most evangelical Christians are Protestants, they seem to have no problem condemning the Christianity that led to the Crusades and Inquisition. But they are less willing to say that Christians had any complicity in the Holocaust, even though the state religion of Germany was Christian. To these examples could be added other examples of the abuse of Jews' civil rights. Have Christians in general and evangelical Christians in particular had no complicity in injustices that occurred?

8. One can argue that the statements about eschatology use "code words" for a pretribulational and premillennial view of the end times. Some argue that phrases such as the "personal," "visible," or "imminent" return of Jesus really mean the expectation of a secret rapture and the

advent of the tribulation. It is possible. My point, however, is that such language is not used. Indeed, the language in these statements usually cautions against speculation and overemphasis on eschatology. Rather than speculation, statements on eschatology focus on the need to live Christlike lives, to do the will of God in the world, and to be ready to meet Jesus anytime.

9. Statement of Faith, National Association of Evangelicals Home Page, http://www.nae.net/about-us/statement-of-faith (accessed August 4, 2009).

Chapter 4 Evangelicals Are Not All Anti-evolutionists

1. "Vatican Admits Galileo Was Right," *New Scientist*, November 7, 1992.

2. To add a bit more detail to this story, Galileo's heliocentric hypothesis was rejected by the church in 1616, but Galileo himself was not condemned. Indeed, he was allowed to continue to teach his view as a hypothesis. Two decades later, he published *Dialogues Concerning the Two World Systems* (1632), in which he gave clear preference to his heliocentric view (essentially disregarding the limits the pope had imposed on him). The following year, Galileo was put on trial, and his view was found to be contrary to orthodox Christianity. He was required to recant his views and was imprisoned. His sentence was later commuted to house arrest.

3. We will focus primarily on the creation account of Genesis 1, and leave open the difficult issue of how this squares with Genesis 2. This debate also makes a natural turn toward the debate about age of the universe and the "big bang" theory. We will only briefly touch on these questions. Similarly, disagreements about how the flood of Genesis 7 comes into play, applications of evolution to the social sciences, methods of dating fossils, and a host of other questions will not come into play, even though they are critical for the full discussion of the evolution issue.

4. "Religion," *Gallup Survey*, n.d. Survey questions were asked between June 1–3, 2007.

5. While "young earth" creationists often provide an order of events that seeks to put specific dates on aspects of creation, "old earth" creationists will commit themselves to a specific sequence within the order of creation, but are not interested in affixing specific dates or timespans to the various phases of the creation process.

6. The Institute for Creation Research, Creation Ministries International, and Creation Research Society all have websites that advocate YEC and highlight resources that support this position.

7. The most famous chronology representing the young earth creationist position is that of Bishop Ussher in 1650, who calculated right down to the day and time of creation, claiming that it occurred on October 23, 4004 BC.

8. Two websites that champion OEC and list useful resources in support of this view are Reasons to Believe and Answers in Creation.

9. The influence of this position was bolstered by its advocacy in the *Scofield Reference Bible*, first published in 1909.

10. William Jennings Bryan, famous for his advocacy of the anti-evolution position in the Scopes Trial, was an early champion of this version of creationism. Moreover, he allows that evolution probably occurred over a long period of time in nonhuman species, but that human beings were not a product of these processes. Perhaps the best known of contemporary "day-age" creationists is Hugh Ross, an astrophysicist.

11. A subvariant of the "day-age" view is progressive or "intermittent-day" creationism, which argues for a succession of twenty-four-hour days, with each day interrupted by an extended period in which the created order developed gradually. For an exposition of this version of OEC, see Robert C. Newman, "Progressive Creationism," in J. P. Moreland and John Mark Reynolds, eds., *Three Views on Creation and Evolution* (Grand Rapids: Zondervan, 1999), 105–33.

12. Prominent evangelical advocates of this view include Francis Collins, former director of the Human Genome Project (see *The Language of God: A Scientist Presents Evidence for Belief* [New York: Free Press, 2007]); theologian and biophysicist, Alister McGrath; Karl Giberson; and Darrel Falk. A useful website to learn more about TE is that of the BioLogos Foundation.

13. Popular versions of this position can be found in Daniel G. Dennett, *Darwin's Dangerous Idea: Evolution and the Meanings of Life* (New York: Simon & Schuster, 1995); and Richard Dawkins, *The Blind Watchmaker: Why the Evidence of Evolution Reveals a Universe Without Design* (New York: W. W. Norton, 1996).

14. Closely related is the distinction between *science* and *scientism*. Science refers to the endeavor to understand our universe by empirical means. This, by itself, does not make any judgments about whether truth claims about the universe include or exclude divine involvement. In contrast, *scientism* is a philosophical stance that excludes by definition any role for nonphysical realities. All who subscribe to evolutionism would be advocates of scientism, but scientism includes those who argue that evolution itself cannot explain all biological phenomena.

15. This position is held by Jonathan Sarfati in *Refuting Compromise* (Green Forest, AR: Master Books, 2004).

16. For example, Hugh Ross's organization, Reasons to Believe, affirms that the Bible is "verbally inspired and completely without error (historically, scientifically, morally, and spiritually) in its original writings," but also embraces OEC. A few other inerrantists who do not hold to YEC are Gleason Archer, James Montgomery Boice, William Lane Craig, and Carl F. H. Henry.

17. Another way that unrecognized assumptions come into play is when we presuppose that the most important truths should be communicated in ways that would be accessible to historical or scientific research. An obvious problem is that this assumption undercuts the theological significance of much in the Bible that is clearly expressed in a poetic manner. Another problem will show up on Valentine's Day when you attempt to express the depth of your affection for your most significant loved one in a scientific or historical treatise.

18. "NOMA" is the acronym for "nonoverlapping magisterial" coined by Stephen Jay Gould. See "Nonoverlapping Magisteria," *Natural History* 106 (March 1997): 16. This position was later expanded in his book *Rocks of Ages: Science and Religion in the Fullness of Life* (New York: Ballantine, 1999). Gould, a religious agnostic, argues his case from the perspective of paleontology and evolutionary biology. For a Christian expression of this model, see Jean Pond's chapter in Richard F. Carlson, ed., *Science and Christianity: Four Views* (Downers Grove, IL: InterVarsity, 2000), 67–110.

19. A nice overview of science's boundaries is provided in Del Ratzsch, *Science and Its Limits*, 2nd ed. (Downers Grove, IL: InterVarsity, 2000). See especially chapter 6. Alister McGrath does a terrific job of showing how evolutionism consistently oversteps these boundaries in *Dawkins' God: Genes, Memes, and the Meaning of Life* (Malden, MA: Blackwell, 2005).

20. One example of the partisan use of the Scopes trial is obvious in the movie version, *Inherit the Wind*. In order to make the anti-evolution side appear to be ignorant and out of touch, the trial transcript was heavily edited in a way that made William Jennings Bryan appear extremely confused, incoherent, and unwilling to confront facts. Edward Larson's Pulitzer Prize–winning book does a terrific job of putting the Scopes trial into historical context and showing how the trial has been distorted to serve the purposes of individuals on both sides of the debate. See Edward Larson, *Summer for the Gods: The Scopes Trial and America's Continuing Debate over Science and Religion* (New York: Basic Books, 1997).

Chapter 5 Evangelicals Are Not All Inerrantists

1. A. C. Dixon and Reuben Archer Torrey, eds., *The Fundamentals: A Testimony to the Truth*, 12 vols. (Los Angeles: Bible Institute of Los Angeles, 1910–15).

2. National Association of Evangelicals, Home Page, About NAE, Statement of Faith, http://www.nae.net/about-us/statement-of-faith (accessed September 23, 2008).

3. The Westminster Confession of Faith (1646), Center for Reformed Theology and Apologetics, Chapter I. Of the holy Scripture, http://www.reformed.org/documents/index.html?mainframe=http://www.reformed.org/documents/westminster_conf_of_faith.html (accessed November 9, 2009).

4. The background for the discussion above is linked to the complex relationship between evangelicalism and fundamentalism. Although members of each group are often reluctant to admit it, there is such a strong kinship between them that their line of demarcation is not always clear. The issue of inerrancy helps illustrate this. For some evangelicals, rejection of inerrancy is one of the key elements (although not the only one) that distinguishes them from fundamentalism. Other evangelicals would view inerrancy as one of the shared pieces of theological real estate and would look to other areas to distinguish between fundamentalism and evangelicalism.

5. As an illustration of the Law of Unintended Consequences, selection of inerrancy as the only requirement for joining ETS excluded large numbers of individuals who, by every other doctrinal measure, would be considered solidly evangelical, but allowed members of non-Trinitarian groups such as Mormons to join. To deal with this, a Trinitarian clause was added to membership requirements.

6. This has created a difficult situation for evangelical scholars who want to be in conversation with others but do not affirm inerrancy. Many have joined the ETS by adopting definitions of inerrancy that were never intended by the founders of the society (a friend referred to it as "mental footnoting"). Others have formed alternative scholarly societies. This occurred in part because of specific theological concerns—for example, the Wesleyan Theological Society (founded in 1965) and the Society for Pentecostal Studies (founded in 1970). However, another reason for their formation was that many could not in good conscience sign off on inerrancy but desired to be in conversation with other evangelical scholars. They had little recourse but to form their own scholarly societies.

7. See Carl F. H. Henry, *God, Revelation and Authority*, vol. 4 (Waco: Word, 1979), 211–19.

8. Article XIII of the *Chicago Statement* denies that "inerrancy is negated by Biblical phenomena such as a lack of modern technical precision, irregularities of grammar or spelling, observational descriptions of nature, the reporting of falsehoods, the use of hyperbole and round numbers, the topical arrangement of material, variant selections of material in parallel accounts, or the use of free citations."

9. While issues of accuracy on matters of science and historical fact represent most of the debate about error in Scripture, questions about other types of potential areas of error also arise. Some center on concerns about apparent theological inconsistencies, for example, whether God is unchanging, or whether God changes previous decisions. More contemporary concerns have to do with the authenticity of biblical authorship because of apparent discrepancies in the writings claimed by a single author. Still other concerns have to do with whether biblical writings were unduly influenced by aristocratic, economic, racial, or chauvinistic biases.

10. Dewey Beegle has written extensively on these matters. See Dewey M. Beegle, *God's Word into English* (New York: Harper, 1960), *The Inspiration of Scripture* (Philadelphia: Westminster, 1963), and *Scripture, Tradition, and Infallibility* (Grand Rapids: Eerdmans, 1973).

11. The fact that both sides can employ slippery-slope argumentation reminds us that this logical device is not an infallible or inerrant predictor of outcomes. When I was a kid, I was told that boys should not be permitted to grow their hair long; if so, they soon would be walking around with hair hanging down to the floor. Likewise, girls were told they should not be permitted to wear short skirts; if so, they soon would be walking around naked. Of course, when I was a kid, boys did not walk around with hair hanging down to the floor, and girls did not walk around naked. Slippery-slope arguments are appealing because there are cases where one move in a particular direction sometimes leads one toward even more radical steps down the same path. However, such steps are not inevitable and often appeal more to people's fears than to reality.

12. I. Howard Marshall, *Biblical Inspiration* (Grand Rapids: Eerdmans, 1982), 70.

13. William J. Abraham, *The Coming Great Revival: Recovering the Full Evangelical Tradition* (San Francisco: Harper & Row, 1984), 84–85.

14. "Nicene Creed," *Encyclopedia of Christianity,* ed. John Bowden (Oxford: Oxford University Press, 2005), 300.

15. The Nicene Creed (or Nicene-Constantinopolitan Creed), International Consultation on English Texts Translation, in *The Lutheran Book of Worship* and *The Book of Common Prayer* (Episcopal); Creeds.net, http://www.creeds.net/ancient/nicene.htm (accessed April 28, 2008).

16. See Don Thorsen, *The Wesleyan Quadrilateral: Scripture, Tradition, Reason and Experience as a Model of Evangelical Theology* (Grand Rapids: Francis Asbury Press for Zondervan, 1990), 21–24.

17. Kenneth S. Kantzer and Carl F. H. Henry, *Evangelical Affirmations* (Grand Rapids: Zondervan, 1990), 38.

Chapter 6 Evangelicals Are Not All Rich Americans

1. For an example of this scenario from the evangelical side, see Michael Spencer, "The Coming Evangelical Collapse," *Christian Science Monitor*, March 10, 2009.

2. The situation in South America is different from the other two continents in that it has been majority Christian since colonization. The religious shift here has been twofold. First, there is renewed vitality within Catholicism (the predominant form of Christianity in the area) as well as increasingly indigenous forms of worship and leadership. The second major shift is a rapid growth in Protestantism, particularly of the Pentecostal variety.

3. One example is the growth of Christianity in Africa. In 1900, Christians comprised 9 percent of the population. In 2000, they were estimated at 46 percent of the population of the continent. See David Barrett, ed., *World Christian Encyclopedia*, 2nd ed. (New York: Oxford University Press, 2001), 1:13. In raw numbers, that is a change from around 10 million in 1900 to more than 360 million a century later.

4. Ibid., 1:13–15.

5. David B. Barrett and Todd M. Wilson, eds., *World Christian Trends AD 30–AD 2200* (Pasadena, CA: William Carey Library, 2001), 320–33.

6. Barrett, *Encyclopedia*, 1:5.

7. Ibid., 1:13.

8. Stan Guthrie, *Missions in the Third Millennium* (Waynesboro, GA: Paternoster, 2000), 137.

9. Alister McGrath, *The Future of Christianity* (Malden, MA: Blackwell, 2002), x.

10. Barrett and Wilson, *Trends*, 321.

11. Barrett, *Encyclopedia*, 1:14.

12. Ibid.

13. An interesting article in *Atlantic Monthly* (March 2003): 26–27, written by David Brooks, who describes himself as a "recovering secularist," traces his journey away from a "secularist fundamentalism that assumed that the march of secularism was inevitable." He notes with irony that the same magazine had published an essay in 1942 titled "Will the Church Survive?" Sixty years later, he notes, there are two billion Christians in the world. See Lamin Sanneh, *Whose Religion Is Christianity? The Gospel Beyond the West* (Grand Rapids: Eerdmans, 2003), 7.

14. Perhaps nothing illustrates Western paternalism more clearly than the elevation of an openly gay bishop within the American Episcopal Church, Gene Robinson, in 2003. Among the mainline denominations, the Episcopalians would be the first to condemn imperialism. However, as a body of two million within a broader global community of eighty million, the American Episcopal Church actions went contrary to the desires of the vast majority of world Anglicans.

15. Donald E. Miller, "Emergent Patterns of Congregational Life and Leadership in the Developing World: Personal Reflections from a Research Odyssey," *Pulpit and Pew: Research on Pastoral Leadership* no. 3, Winter 2003, 2–31.

16. This is the primary reason it is difficult to get a clear count of missionaries sent from the Majority World. Also, it should be mentioned that this paradigm has been strategically useful for gaining entrance to countries where professional missionaries are barred.

17. One variant is the emergence of the so-called Prosperity Gospel, found in numerous segments of Majority World evangelicalism. The Prosperity Gospel promises that those who exhibit the proper beliefs or lifestyle will be rewarded by God, monetarily or in other ways,

such as physical healing. While this aspect of Southern Hemisphere Christianity is subject to frequent criticism from the North (although American evangelicalism has its share of "health and wealth" advocates), Jenkins offers an important reminder. He says: "For a Northern world that enjoys health and wealth to a degree scarcely imagined by any previous society, it is perilously easy to despise believers who associate divine favor with full stomachs or access to the most meager forms of schooling or health care; who seek miracles in order to flourish, or even survive. The Prosperity Gospel is an inevitable by-product of a church containing so many of the very poorest." See Philip Jenkins, *The New Faces of Christianity: Believing the Bible in the Global South* (New York: Oxford University Press, 2008), 97.

18. Jenkins sums this up nicely: "At the grassroots level, among the poor and poorly educated, the rise of Christianity has, in an amazingly short time, effected dramatic changes in gender attitudes. In the long run, the greatest change might be the new emphasis on faithful monogamous marriage and on new concepts of masculinity, the 'reformation of *machismo*' that is proceeding apace despite the vestiges of polygamy that remain in some independent churches." See Jenkins, 165.

19. Michael Pocock, Gailyn van Rheenen, and Douglas McConnell, *The Changing Face of World Missions: Engaging Contemporary Issues and Trends* (Grand Rapids: Baker, 2005), 149.

20. Jenkins, *New Faces*, 136.

Chapter 7 Evangelicals Are Not All Calvinists

1. David F. Wells, " 'No Offense: I Am an Evangelical': A Search for Self-Definition," in *A Time to Speak Out: The Evangelical-Jewish Encounter*, eds. A. James Rudin and Marvin R. Wilson (Grand Rapids: Eerdmans, 1987), 37; in *The Variety of American Evangelicalism*, eds. Donald W. Dayton and Robert K. Johnston (Downers Grove, IL: InterVarsity Press, 1991), 1.

2. Thomas A. Askew, "A Response to David F. Wells," in *A Time to Speak Out*, eds. Rudin and Wilson, 43; in *The Variety of American Evangelicalism*, ed. Dayton and Johnston, 1.

3. Robert K. Johnston and Donald W. Dayton, "Introduction," in *The Variety of American Evangelicalism*, eds. Dayton and Johnston, 4.

4. "The Cambridge Declaration," 1996, Alliance of Confessing Evangelicals, Inc. Homepage, 2009 <http://www.alliancenet.org/partner/Article_Display_Page/0,,PTID307086_CHID615424_CIID1411364,00.html> accessed 24 March 2010.

5. "The Cambridge Declaration," "Introduction" and "A Call to Repentance & Reformation."

6. Roger E. Olson, "Don't Hate Me Because I'm Arminian," *Christianity Today*, September 6, 1999, 87–94; cf. *Christianity Today* Home Page, Archives http://www.christianitytoday.com/ct/1999/september6/9ta087.html (accessed August 4, 2009).

7. Robert E. Webber, *Common Roots: A Call to Evangelical Maturity* (Grand Rapids: Zondervan, 1977), 32.

8. John Feinberg, "God Ordains All Things," in *Predestination and Free Will: Four Views of Divine Sovereignty and Human Freedom*, eds. David Basinger and Randall Bansinger (Downers Grove, IL: InterVarsity, 1986), 37.

9. Norman Geisler, "God Knows All Things," in *Predestination and Free Will*, eds. David Basinger and Randall Bansinger, 79.

10. Bruce Reichenbach, "God Limits His Power," in *Predestination and Free Will*, eds. David Basinger and Randall Bansinger, 54–55. This statement was made in response to Feinberg, but it also applies to Geisler; see 89–94.

11. The chart comes from Don Thorsen, *An Exploration of Christian Theology* (Peabody, MA: Hendrickson, 2008), 256, and the definitions come from Millard J. Erickson, *Concise Dictionary of Christian Theology* (Grand Rapids: Baker, 1986).

12. I am tempted to designate this category of Arminianism as "All have sinned" (a la Rom. 3:23). Then the acronym for Arminianism would spell ACURA, which also stands for a brand

of cars. However, I am not familiar with meanings of the Japanese word *Akyura* from which the name is apparently derived. Be that as it may, the acronym ACURA would make a catchy contrast with TULIP. It would be better than DAISY, which critics of Arminianism caricature by the children's game that involves picking off daisy petals and saying, "God loves me; God loves me not; God loves me; God loves me not," and so on.

13. Ironically, the words "penal" and "substitution" are not explicitly mentioned in Scripture. They represent historical formulations thought to be representative of Scripture, but the focus of the theory was on a legal (penal) perspective of the atonement—a view that appealed to Calvin, who had been trained as a lawyer and who emphasized the apostle Paul's legal (law-oriented) discussion of the topic.

14. See *The Fundamentals: A Testimony to the Truth*, eds. R. A. Torrey and A. C. Dixon (Grand Rapids: Baker, 1994).

Chapter 8 Evangelicals Are Not All Republicans

1. Craig Payne, *What Believers Don't Have to Believe* (Lanham, MD: University Press of America, 2006), 99–100.

2. Ted Olsen, "The Evangelical Electoral Map," *Christianity Today Politics Blog*, November 5, 2008. Olsen's numbers came from CNN exit polls.

3. Some polls identify evangelicals according to denominational affiliation. However, this probably skews the numbers even more. First, traditionally African American denominations are put in a separate category from other evangelicals (usually something like "Black Protestant"). Also, African Americans who belong to a denomination in the "evangelical" category often are moved to the "Black Protestant" category. Finally, many Christians who consider themselves evangelicals are placed in the "Mainline Protestant" category because they belong to denominations that match this category. For an example of this sort of categorization, see Appendix A of Clem Brooks and Jeff Manza, "A Great Divide? Religion and Political Change in U.S. National Elections, 1972–2000," *Sociological Quarterly* 45, Part 3 (2004): 421–50.

4. Frank Newport and Joseph Carroll, "Another Look at Evangelicals in America Today," *Gallup Survey*, December 2, 2005.

5. *An Evangelical Manifesto: A Declaration of Evangelical Identity and Public Commitment* (Washington DC: Evangelical Manifesto Steering Committee, 2008), 4.

6. Amy Black, *Beyond Left and Right: Helping Christians Make Sense of American Politics* (Grand Rapids: Baker, 2008), 79. See also Susan Page, "Churchgoing Closely Tied to Voting Patterns," *USA Today*, June 2, 2004; Rodney Stark, *What Americans Really Believe* (Waco: Baylor University Press, 2008), 19; and "Election Polls—Vote by Groups, 2008," *Gallup Survey*.

7. The more frequently one attends worship, the more likely one is to use the term "conservative" as a political self-description.

8. The chart below is adapted from Table 30 (Defining the Religious Landscape: Measures of Religion) in "The American Religious Landscape and Politics, 2004," The Pew Forum on Religion and Public Life.

	Worship Attendance:			View of Tradition:		
	Regular	Often	Rarely	Preserve	Adapt	Adopt
ENTIRE SAMPLE	43%	32	25	45%	40	15
Evangelical Protestant:						
Traditionalist Evangelical	87%	11	2	78%	18	2
Centrist Evangelical	36%	41	23	48%	43	9
Modernist Evangelical	23%	46	31	30%	42	28
Mainline Protestant:						
Traditionalist Mainline	59%	33	8	61%	35	4
Centrist Mainline	33%	45	22	33%	53	14

Modernist Mainline	19%	46	35	3%	62	35
Latino Protestants	63%	31	6	57%	29	14
Black Protestants	57%	33	10	43%	38	19
Catholic:						
Traditionalist Catholic	87%	11	2	65%	32	3
Centrist Catholic	45%	36	20	29%	55	16
Modernist Catholic	21%	49	30	3%	66	31
Latino Catholic	47%	41	12	44%	31	25

Worship attendance: "Regular"=weekly or more; "Often"=1–2 a month, few times a year; "Rarely"=seldom or never.

View of Tradition: "Preserve"=strive to preserve beliefs/practices; "Adapt"=strive to adapt beliefs/practices to new times; "Adopt"=strive to adopt new beliefs/practices.

9. Ron Sider, *The Scandal of Evangelical Politics* (Grand Rapids: Baker, 2008), 89.

10. Stephen F. Hayward, *The Real Jimmy Carter* (New York: Regnery, 2004), 68.

11. Mark Noll, *American Evangelical Christianity* (Malden, MA: Blackwell, 2001), 23.

12. While our focus is on evangelicals, the party alignments of other Christian segments have experienced swings toward the Democratic Party. For example, in 1992, evangelical and mainline Protestants were almost equally split in political affiliation. Some 48 percent of evangelicals were Republican (vs. 32 percent Democratic), compared with 50 percent of mainline Protestants being Republican (vs. 32 percent Democratic). By 2004, evangelicals were increasingly Republican (56 percent vs. 27 percent Democratic), while mainline Protestants edged toward the Democrats (44 percent vs. 39 percent). See "The American Religious Landscape and Politics, 2004," *The Pew Forum on Religion and Public Life.*

13. As D. Michael Lindsay puts it, "In a [Clinton] White House where reactions to evangelical faith ranged from general indifference to blatant animosity, evangelicals did not feel welcome." See D. Michael Lindsay, *Faith in the Halls of Power* (Oxford: Oxford University Press, 2007), 22.

14. Ibid., 16–29.

15. Frank Newport, "Democrats View Religious Groups Less Positively than Republicans," *Gallup Survey,* September 7, 2006. Individuals from both parties were asked their opinions on ten groups—Jews, Catholics, Methodists, Baptists, LDS/Mormons, Muslims, Evangelical Christians, Fundamentalist Christians, atheists, and scientologists. With a couple of exceptions, Republicans had more favorable views toward all religious groups. Republicans and Democrats both registered the same favorability rankings for Muslims. Democrats were slightly more favorable toward scientologists than Republicans, and 11 points more favorable in their views of atheists.

16. "The American Religious Landscape and Politics, 2004," *The Pew Forum on Religion and Public Life.*

17. Ibid. The same 20 percent spread could be seen in favoring traditional marriage (75 percent evangelicals vs. 55 percent U.S. average).

18. *Evangelical Manifesto*, 13–14.

19. Amy E. Black, *Beyond Left and Right: Helping Christians Make Sense of American Politics* (Grand Rapids: Baker, 2008), 27.

Chapter 9 Evangelicals Are Not All Racist, Sexist, and Homophobic

1. Mitra Toossi, "A Century of Change: The U. S. Labor Force, 1950–2050," *Monthly Labor Review* (May 2002): 22.

2. A Christian student of mine from Lebanon made it clear to me when he said that Mideasterners do not usually make a distinction between Western culture and Christianity. When Mideasterners watch movies, they may think that characters such as "Dirty Harry" and "Rambo" are Christians, representative of Christian as well as Western values. When he moved to the United States, the Lebanese student was surprised to discover that not everyone carries guns!

3. For a fascinating survey of the Oberlin movement, see Donald W. Dayton, *Discovering an Evangelical Heritage* (Peabody, MA: Hendrickson, 1976), chapter 4.

4. While it is not the case for all egalitarians, some argue that while gender equality is not found at all points in Scripture, the trajectory of Scripture points in this direction. Just as some Christians consider divine revelation to be progressive (e.g., old covenant → new covenant), biblical teachings about gender issues are also progressing.

5. Margaret Fell, "Women's Speaking Justified," letter from the "Women's Yearly Meeting at York, 1688," the Augustan Reprint Society (n.p.: William Andrews Clark Memorial Library, 1979).

6. Douglas A. Sweeney, *The American Evangelical Story: A History of the Movement* (Grand Rapids: Baker, 2005), 94.

7. David Kinnaman, *unChristian: What a New Generation Really Thinks about Christianity . . . And Why It Matters* (Grand Rapids: Baker, 2007), 34.

8. Don Thorsen, "Revelation and Homosexual Experience," *Christianity Today*, November 11, 1996, 34, 36, 38.

9. Wolfhart Pannenberg, "Revelation and Homosexual Experience," trans. Markus Bockmuehl for publication in the *Church Times*, in *Christianity Today*, November 11, 1996, 35, 37.

10. Sometimes the Q refers to "questioning," rather than "queer." However, both terms convey the idea that people are increasingly asking questions about age-old views regarding homosexuality.

11. Until 1973, homosexuality was included as a psychological disorder in the *Diagnostic and Statistical Manual of Mental Disorders*, the diagnostic manual of the American Psychiatric Association.

12. David Kinnaman and Gabe Lyons, *unChristian: What a New Generation Really Thinks about Christianity . . . and Why It Matters* (Grand Rapids: Baker, 2007), 108–9.

13. Peter Meiderlin, also known as Rupertus Meldenius, said, "*in necessariis unitas, indubiis libertas, in omnibus caritas*," which is also translated as "unity in necessary things; liberty in doubtful things; charity in all things." See Philip Schaff, *History of the Christian Church*, 8 vols. (1870; repr., Grand Rapids: Eerdmans, 1965), 7:650–53.

14. Merriam-Webster Online, "Bigot," http://www.merriam-webster.com/dictionary/bigot (accessed May 2, 2009).

Chapter 10 Conclusion

1. Socrates, in Plato, *The Last Days of Socrates: Euthyphro, The Apology, Crito, and Phaedo*, trans. Hugh Tredennick, ed. Harold Tarrant (New York: Penguin Classic, 2003), 63.

2. Robert M. Calhoon, *Evangelicals and Conservatives in the Early South, 1740–1861* (Columbia, SC: University of South Carolina Press, 1988), 1.

3. Ibid.

4. David W. Bebbington, *Evangelicalism in Modern Britain: A History from the 1730s to the 1980s* (London: Unwin Hyman, 1989), 2f.

5. Ibid., 3.

6. Kenneth J. Collins, *The Evangelical Moment: The Promise of an American Religion* (Grand Rapids: Baker Academic, 2005), 21.

7. Roger E. Olson, *Reformed and Always Reforming: The Postconservative Approach to Evangelical Theology* (Grand Rapids: Baker Academic, 2007), 43.

8. *Evangelicalism and the Orthodox Church*, in *A Report by the Evangelical Alliance Commission on Unity and Truth among Evangelicals* (London: Acute for Paternoster, 2001), 7–13.

9. Ronald H. Nash, *Evangelical Renewal in the Mainline Churches* (Wheaton: Crossway, 1987), xii–xiii.

10. World Evangelical Alliance, quoted by the World Evangelical Fellowship, Home Page, Introduction, http://www.worldevangelicals.org/aboutwea/statementoffaith.htm (accessed December 8, 2008).

11. National Association of Evangelicals, Home Website, Statement of Faith, http://www.nae.net/about-us/statement-of-faith (accessed December 8, 2008).

12. National Association of Evangelicals, Home Website, Mission Statement, http://www.nae.net/about-us/mission-statement (accessed December 8, 2008).

13. Billy Graham, Introduction, in John D. Allan, *The Evangelicals: An Illustrated History* (Grand Rapids: Baker, 1989).

14. To these categories, one could add "orthosocietas" (right society or community) or other "orthos." For example, see Brian Cooper, "Orthosocietas: A Wesleyan Ecclesiology for the 21st Century Church," paper, Wesleyan Theological Society, Azusa Pacific University, Azusa, California, March 6, 2010.

Select Bibliography

Abraham, William J. *The Coming Great Revival: Recovering the Full Evangelical Tradition*. San Francisco: Harper & Row, 1984.

Ball, William Bentley, ed. *In Search of a National Morality: A Manifesto for Evangelicals and Catholics*. Grand Rapids: Baker, 1992.

Balmer, Randall Herbert. *Encyclopedia of Evangelicalism: Revised and Expanded Edition*. 2nd ed. Waco: Baylor University Press, 2004.

_____. *The Making of Evangelicalism: From Revivalism to Politics and Beyond*. Waco: Baylor University Press, 2010.

Bartholomew, Craig, Robin Parry, and Andrew West, eds. *The Futures of Evangelicalism: Issues and Prospects*. Grand Rapids: Kregel Academic & Professional, 2004.

Bebbington, David W. *The Dominance of Evangelicalism: The Age of Spurgeon and Moody*. History of Evangelicalism. Downers Grove, IL: InterVarsity, 2005.

_____. *Evangelicalism in Modern Britain: A History from the 1730s to the 1980s*. New York: Routledge, 1989.

Bloesch, Donald G. *The Evangelical Renaissance*. Grand Rapids: Eerdmans, 1973.

_____. *The Future of Evangelical Christianity*. Garden City, NY: Doubleday, 1983.

Bolich, Gregory G. *Karl Barth and Evangelicalism*. Downers Grove, IL: InterVarsity, 1980.

Carson, D. A. *Evangelicalism: What Is It and Is It Worth Keeping?* Wheaton: Crossway, 2010.

Collins, Kenneth J. *The Evangelical Moment: The Promise of an American Religion*. Grand Rapids: Baker Academic, 2005.

Colson, Charles, and Richard John Neuhaus, eds. *Evangelicals and Catholics Together: Working Toward a Common Mission.* Dallas: Word, 1995.

Dayton, Donald W. *Discovering an Evangelical Heritage.* New York: Harper & Row, 1978.

Dayton, Donald W., and Robert K. Johnston, eds. *The Variety of American Evangelicalism.* Downers Grove, IL: InterVarsity, 1991.

Ditchfield, G. M. *The Evangelical Revival.* London: Taylor & Francis, 2007.

Dorrien, Gary J. *The Remaking of Evangelical Theology.* Louisville: Westminster John Knox, 1998.

Eddy, Paul, and Gregory Boyd. *Across the Spectrum: Understanding Issues in Evangelical Theology,* 2nd ed. Grand Rapids: Baker Academic, 2009.

Edwards, David L., and John Stott. *Essentials: A Liberal-Evangelical Dialogue.* Downers Grove, IL: InterVarsity, 1988.

Ellingsen, Mark. *The Evangelical Movement: Growth, Impact, Controversy, Dialog.* Minneapolis: Augsburg, 1988.

Emerson, Michael O., and Christian Smith. *Divided by Faith: Evangelical Religion and the Problem of Race in America.* Oxford: Oxford University Press, 2001.

Evangelical Action! A Report of the Organization of the National Association of Evangelicals for United Action. Boston: United Action Press, 1942.

Fackre, Gabriel. *Ecumenical Faith in Evangelical Perspective.* Grand Rapids: Eerdmans, 1993.

Fournier, Keith A. *Evangelical Catholics: A Call for Christian Cooperation to Penetrate the Darkness with the Light of the Gospel.* Nashville: Thomas Nelson, 1990.

Fournier, Keith A., and William D. Watkins. *A House United? Evangelicals and Catholics Together: A Winning Alliance for the 21st Century.* Colorado Springs: Navpress, 1994.

Frank, Douglas W. *Less than Conquerors: How Evangelicalism Entered the Twentieth Century.* Grand Rapids: Eerdmans, 1986.

Gallagher, Sally K. *Evangelical Identity and Gendered Family Life.* New Brunswick, NJ: Rutgers University Press, 2003.

Geisler, Norman L., and Ralph MacKenzie. *Roman Catholics and Evangelicals: Agreements and Differences.* Grand Rapids: Baker, 1995.

Gier, Nicholas F. *God, Reason, and the Evangelicals.* Lanham, MD: University Press of America, 1987.

Grenz, Stanley J. *Revisioning Evangelical Theology: A Fresh Agenda for the 21st Century.* Downers Grove, IL: InterVarsity, 1993.

Gundry, Robert Horton. *Jesus the Word according to John the Sectarian: A Paleofundamentalist Manifesto for Contemporary Evangelicalism, Especially Its Elites, in North America.* Grand Rapids: Eerdmans, 2001.

Harrell, David E., Jr., ed. *Varieties of Southern Evangelicalism*. Macon, GA: Mercer University Press, 1981.

Harris, Harriet A. *Fundamentalism and Evangelicals*. Oxford Theological Monographs. New York: Oxford University Press, 2008.

Hart, D. G. *Deconstructing Evangelicalism: Conservative Protestantism in the Age of Billy Graham*. Grand Rapids: Baker, 2005.

Haykin, Michael A. G., and Kenneth J. Stewart. *The Advent of Evangelicalism: Exploring Historical Continuities*. Nashville: B&H Academic, 2008.

———, eds. *The Emergence of Evangelicalism*. Downers Grove, IL: InterVarsity, 2008.

Henry, Carl F. H. *Evangelical Responsibility in Contemporary Theology*. Grand Rapids: Eerdmans, 1957.

———. *Evangelicals at the Brink of Crisis*. Waco: Word, 1967.

———. *Evangelicals in Search of Identity*. Waco: Word, 1976.

———. *A Plea for Evangelical Demonstration*. Grand Rapids: Baker, 1971.

Horton, Michael Scott. *Made in America: The Shaping of Modern American Evangelicalism*. Grand Rapids: Baker, 1991.

Howard, David M. *The Dream That Would Not Die: The Birth and Growth of the World Evangelical Fellowship, 1846–1986*. Exeter: Paternoster Press, 1986.

Hunter, James Davison. *American Evangelicalism: Conservative Religion and the Quandary of Modernity*. New Brunswick, NJ: Rutgers University Press, 1983.

———. *Evangelicalism: The Coming Generation*. Chicago: University of Chicago Press, 1987.

Inch, Morris A. *The Evangelical Challenge*. Philadelphia: Westminster, 1978.

Johnston, Robert K. *Evangelicals at an Impasse*. Atlanta: John Knox, 1979.

Jorstad, Erling. *Evangelicals in the White House: The Cultural Maturation of Born Again Christianity 1960–1981*. New York: Edwin Mellen Press, 1981.

———. *Popular Religion in America: The Evangelical Voice*. Westport, CT: Greenwood Press, 1993.

Kantzer, Kenneth S., and Carl F. H. Henry, eds. *Evangelical Affirmations*. Grand Rapids: Zondervan, 1990.

Kidd, Thomas S. *The Great Awakening: The Roots of Evangelical Christianity in Colonial America*. New Haven: Yale University Press, 2009.

Kik, J. Marcellus. *Ecumenism and the Evangelical*. Grand Rapids: Baker, 1958.

Kilpatrick, Joel. *A Field Guide to Evangelicals and Their Habitat*. New York: HarperOne, 2006.

Klauber, Martin, and Scott M. Manetsch, eds. *The Great Commission: Evangelicals and the History of World Missions*. Nashville: B&H Books, 2008.

Kostenberger, Andreas J. *Quo Vadis, Evangelicalism? Nine Presidential Addresses from the First Fifty Years of the Journal of the Evangelical Theological Society*. Wheaton: Good News and Crossway, 2008.

Kyle, Richard. *Evangelicalism: An Americanized Christianity*. Piscataway, NJ: Transaction Publishers, 2006.

Labanow, Cory E. *Evangelicalism and the Emerging Church*. Farnham, Surrey, UK: Ashgate, 2009.

Lahr, Angela M. *Millennial Dreams and Apocalyptic Nightmares: The Cold War Origins of Political Evangelicalism*. New York: Oxford University Press, 2007.

Lanham, Robert. *Sinner's Guide to the Evangelical Right*. New York: NAL Trade for Penguin, 2006.

Larsen, Timothy, and Daniel J. Treier, eds. *The Cambridge Companion to Evangelical Theology*. Cambridge: Cambridge University Press, 2007.

Lee, Timothy S. *Born Again: Evangelicalism in Korea*. Honolulu: University of Hawaii Press, 2010.

Lightner, Robert P. *Neo-evangelicalism*. Findlay, OH: Dunham, 1962.

Lindsay, D. Michael. *Faith in the Halls of Power: How Evangelicals Joined the American Elite*. New York: Oxford University Press, 2007.

Livingstone, David N., D. G. Hart, and Mark A. Noll, eds. *Evangelicals and Science in Historical Perspective*. Religion in America Series. New York: Oxford University Press, 1999.

Marsden, George M., ed. *Evangelicalism and Modern America*. Grand Rapids: Eerdmans, 1984.

————. *Reforming Fundamentalism: Fuller Seminary and the New Evangelicalism*. Grand Rapids: Eerdmans, 1987.

————. *Understanding Fundamentalism and Evangelicalism*. Grand Rapids: Eerdmans, 1991.

McCune, Rolland. *Promise Unfulfilled: The Failed Strategy of Modern Evangelicalism*. Greenville, SC: Ambassador-Emerald International, 2004.

McGrath, Alister. *Evangelicalism and the Future of Christianity*. Downers Grove, IL: InterVarsity, 1995.

McLoughlin, William G., ed. *The American Evangelicals: 1800–1900*. New York: Harper Torchbooks, 1968.

Meeking, Basil, and John Stott, eds. *The Evangelical-Roman Catholic Dialogue on Mission, 1977–1984*. Grand Rapids: Eerdmans, 1986.

Millet, Robert L., and Gerald R. McDermott. *Claiming Christ: A Mormon-Evangelical Debate*. Grand Rapids: Brazos, 2007.

Mulder, Philip N. *A Controversial Spirit: Evangelical Awakenings in the South*. New York: Oxford University Press, 2002.

Murch, James DeForest. *Cooperation without Compromise: A History of the National Association of Evangelicals*. Grand Rapids: Eerdmans, 1956.

Murray, Iain H. *Evangelicalism Divided: A Record of Crucial Change in the Years 1950–2000*. Carlisle, PA: Banner of Truth, 2000.

————. *Old Evangelicalism: Old Truths for a New Awakening*. Carlisle, PA: Banner of Truth, 2005.

Nash, Ronald, ed. *Evangelical Renewal in the Mainline Churches*. Westchester, IL: Crossway, 1987.

————. *Evangelicals in America: Who They Are, What They Believe*. Nashville: Abingdon, 1987.

Nassif, Brad, Michael S. Horton, Vladimir Berzonsky, and George Hancock-Stefan. *The New Evangelicalism*. Grand Rapids: Zondervan, 1963.

————. *Three Views on Eastern Orthodoxy and Evangelicalism (Counterpoints)*. Grand Rapids: Zondervan, 2004.

Nelson, Rudolph. *The Making and Unmaking of an Evangelical Mind: The Case of Edward Carnell*. New York: Cambridge University Press, 1987.

Noll, Mark A. *The Rise of Evangelicalism: The Age of Edwards, Whitefield, and the Wesleys*. History of Evangelicalism. Downers Grove, IL: InterVarsity Press, 2004.

————. *The Scandal of the Evangelical Mind*. Grand Rapids: Eerdmans, 1995.

Noll, Mark A., David W. Bebbington, and George A. Rawlyk, eds. *Evangelicalism: Comparative Studies of Popular Protestantism in North America, the British Isles, and Beyond, 1700–1990*. New York: Oxford University Press, 1994.

Olson, Roger E. *How to Be Evangelical without Being Conservative*. Grand Rapids: Zondervan, 2008.

————. *Pocket History of Evangelica Theology*. Downers Grove, IL: InterVarsity, 2007.

————. *Reformed and Always Reforming: The Postconservative Approach to Evangelical Theology*. Grand Rapids: Baker Academic, 2007.

Packer, J. I., and Thomas C. Oden, eds. *One Faith: The Evangelical Consensus*. Downers Grove, IL: InterVarsity, 2004.

Padilla, C. René, ed. *The New Face of Evangelicalism: An International Symposium on the Lausanne Covenant*. Downers Grove, IL: InterVarsity, 1976.

Phillips, Timothy R., and Dennis L. Okholom. *The Nature of Confession: Evangelicals and Postliberals in Conversation*. Downers Grove, IL: InterVarsity, 1996.

Pierard, Richard V. *The Unequal Yoke: Evangelical Christianity and Political Conservatism*. Philadelphia: J. B. Lippincott, 1970.

Pinnock, Clark H., and Delwin Brown. *Theological Crossfire: An Evangelical-Liberal Dialogue*. Grand Rapids: Zondervan, 1990.

Quebedeaux, Richard. *The Worldly Evangelicals*. San Francisco: Harper & Row, 1978.

_____. *The Young Evangelicals*. New York: Harper & Row, 1974.

Radosh, Daniel. *Rapture Ready! Adventures in the Parallel Universe of Christian Pop Culture*. New York: Scribner, 2008.

Rah, Soong-Chan. *The Next Evangelicalism: Freeing the Church from Western Cultural Captivity*. Downers Grove, IL: InterVarsity Press, 2009.

Ramm, Bernard. *The Evangelical Heritage*. Reprint, Grand Rapids: Baker, 1981.

Ranger, Terence O. *Evangelical Christianity and Democracy in Africa (Evangelical Christianity and Democracy in the Global South)*. New York: Oxford University Press, 2008.

Rausch, Thomas P., ed. *Catholics and Evangelicals: Do They Share a Common Future?* New York: Paulist Press, 2000.

Rawlyk, George A., and Mark A. Noll, eds. *Amazing Grace: Evangelicalism in Australia, Britain, Canada, and the United States*. Grand Rapids: Baker, 1993.

Rosell, Garth M. *The Evangelical Landscape*. Grand Rapids: Baker, 1997.

_____. *The Surprising Work of God: Harold John Ockenga, Billy Graham, and the Rebirth of Evangelicalism*. Grand Rapids: Baker, 2008.

Rudin, A. James, and Marvin R. Wilson, eds. *A Time to Speak: The Evangelical-Jewish Encounter*. Grand Rapids: Eerdmans, 1987.

Schaeffer, Francis A. *The Great Evangelical Disaster*. Westchester, IL: Crossway Books, 1984.

Shelley, Bruce L. *Evangelicalism in America*. Grand Rapids: Eerdmans, 1967.

Shibley, Mark A. *Resurgent Evangelicalism in the United States*. Columbia, SC: University of South Carolina Press, 1996.

Sider, Ronald J. *The Scandal of the Evangelical Conscience: Why Are Christians Living Just Like the Rest of the World?* Grand Rapids: Baker, 2005.

_____. *The Scandal of Evangelical Politics: Why Are Christians Missing the Chance to Really Change the World?* Grand Rapids: Baker, 2008.

Sider, Ronald J., and Diane Knippers. *Toward an Evangelical Public Policy: Political Strategies for the Health of the Nation*. Grand Rapids: Baker, 2005.

Smidt, Corwin E., ed. *Contemporary Evangelical Political Involvement*. Lanham, MD: University Press of America, 1989.

Smith, Christian. *American Evangelicalism: Embattled and Thriving*. Chicago: University of Chicago Press, 1998.

Smith, Timothy L. *Revivalism and Social Reform: American Protestantism on the Eve of the Civil War.* New York: Harper Torchbooks, 1957.

Smith, Warren Cole. *A Lover's Quarrel with the Evangelical Church.* Colorado Springs: Authentic Publishing, 2009.

Stoll, David. *Is Latin America Turning Protestant? The Politics of Evangelical Growth.* Berkeley: University of California Press, 1991.

Stone, Jon R. *On the Boundaries of American Evangelicalism: The Postwar Evangelical Coalition.* New York: St. Martin's Press, 1997.

Sweeney, Douglas A. *The American Evangelical Story: A History of the Movement.* Grand Rapids: Baker, 2005.

Tanenbaum, Marc H., Marvin R. Wilson, and A. James Rudin, eds. *Evangelicals and Jews in Conversation on Scripture, Theology, and History.* Grand Rapids: Baker, 1978.

Thorsen, Don. *The Wesleyan Quadrilateral: Scripture, Tradition, Reason and Experience as a Model of Evangelical Theology.* 1990; Lexington, KY: Emeth Press, 2005.

Turner, John G. *Bill Bright and Campus Crusade for Christ: The Renewal of Evangelicalism in Postwar America.* Chapel Hill, NC: University of North Carolina Press, 2008.

United . . . We Stand: A Report of the Constitutional Convention of the National Association of Evangelicals. Boston: National Association of Evangelicals, 1943.

Van Til, Cornelius. *Karl Barth and Evangelicalism.* Philadelphia: Presbyterian and Reformed, 1964.

Ward, W. R. *Early Evangelicalism: A Global Intellectual History, 1670–1789.* Cambridge: Cambridge University Press, 2007.

Warner, Rob. *Reinventing English Evangelicalism, 1966–2001.* Studies in Evangelical History and Thought. Carlisle, UK: Paternoster, 2007.

Watt, David Harrington. *A Transforming Faith: Explorations of Twentieth-Century American Evangelicalism.* New Brunswick, NJ: Rutgers University Press, 1991.

Webber, Robert E. *Common Roots: A Call to Evangelical Maturity.* Grand Rapids: Zondervan, 1978.

———. *The Younger Evangelicals: Facing the Challenges of the New World.* Grand Rapids: Baker, 2002.

Wells, David F. *No Place for Truth; or What Happened to Evangelical Theology?* Grand Rapids: Eerdmans, 1993.

Wells, David F., and John D. Woodbridge, eds. *The Evangelicals.* Grand Rapids: Baker, 1977.

Wicker, Christine. *The Fall of the Evangelical Nation: The Surprising Crisis Inside the Church.* New York: HarperOne, 2008.

Williams, Daniel H. *Evangelicals and Tradition: The Formative Influence of the Early Church*. Grand Rapids: Baker, 2005.

————. *Retrieving the Tradition and Renewing Evangelicalism: A Primer for Suspicious Protestants*. Grand Rapids: Eerdmans, 1999.

Witherington, Ben, III. *The Problem with Evangelical Theology: Testing the Exegetical Foundations of Calvinism, Dispensationalism, and Wesleyanism*. Waco: Baylor University Press, 2005.

Wolffe, John. *The Expansion of Evangelicalism: The Age of Wilberforce, More, Chalmers and Finney*. History of Evangelicalism. Downers Grove, IL: InterVarsity, 2007.

Woodridge, Charles. *The New Evangelicalism*. Greenville, SC: Bob Jones University Press, 1969.

Wuthnow, Robert. *The Struggle for America's Soul: Evangelicals, Liberals, and Secularism*. Grand Rapids: Eerdmans, 1989.

Zoba, Wendy Murray. *The Beliefnet Guide to Evangelical Christianity*. New York: Three Leaves, 2007.